HIS DARK MATERIALS
ILLUMINATED

Critical Essays on
Philip Pullman's Trilogy

Edited by Millicent Lenz with Carole Scott

Wayne State University Press Detroit

Library of Congress Cataloging-in-Publication Data

His dark materials illuminated : critical essays on Philip Pullman's trilogy /
edited by Millicent Lenz with Carole Scott.
p. cm. — (Landscapes of childhood)
Includes bibliographical references and index.
ISBN 0-8143-3207-2 (pbk. : alk. paper)
I. Pullman, Philip, 1946– His dark materials. 2. Young adult fiction, English—History and
criticism. 3. Fantasy fiction, English—History and criticism. I. Lenz, Millicent.
II. Scott, Carole. III. Series.
PR6066.U44H554 2005
823'.914—dc22
2004029438

∞The paper used in this publication meets the minimum requirements of the American
National Standard for Information Sciences—Permanence of Paper for Printed Library
Materials, ANSI Z39.48-1984.

ISBN-13: 978-0-8143-3207-8
ISBN-10: 0-8143-3207-2

To my own "Don," Robert Gilson—

husband, lifetime love, and forever friend.

MLG

CONTENTS

ACKNOWLEDGMENTS

Thank you to Wayne State University Press; the anonymous readers, who, despite sometimes posing hard questions, have contributed to the quality of the essays; Philip Pullman, without whom none of this would have come to pass; all the contributors, who have shown keen intellect and sensitivity and expressed themselves with clarity and grace; and, not least, my husband, who has seen me through the rough spots.

—*Millicent Lenz*

Due to Millicent Lenz's untimely death, she was unable to finish her work on this book. I have been proud to bring her vision to completion.

—*Carole Scott*

EDITOR'S NOTE

Given the many editions of the trilogy of *His Dark Materials* and the different titles of the first volume in the United Kingdom (*Northern Lights*) and the United States (*The Golden Compass*), page references to the trilogy are to the specific edition noted by the author in the bibliography following a given essay.

In addition, the *His Dark Materials* books referred to in this text are frequently abbreviated in parenthetical references as follows:

GC   *The Golden Compass: His Dark Materials, Book One*
NL   *Northern Lights: His Dark Materials, Book One*
SK   *The Subtle Knife: His Dark Materials, Book Two*
AS   *The Amber Spyglass: His Dark Materials, Book Three*

Introduction

Awakening to the Twenty-first Century: The Evolution of Human Consciousness in Pullman's *His Dark Materials*

MILLICENT LENZ

It is only through a change in human consciousness that the
world will be transformed.
New Dimensions Radio

I'm just trying to wake up—I'm so afraid of sleeping all my life
and then dying—I want to wake up first! I wouldn't care if it
was just for an hour, as long as I was properly alive and awake.
Lyra to Roger's ghost, *The Amber Spyglass* (56)

At the threshold of the twenty-first century, Philip Pullman's trilogy offers readers of all ages an adventure-packed story that speaks to some
of the most urgent dilemmas of our time and suggests, for the thoughtful
reader, not *answers* to the ills that presently beset us but rather ways of meeting them with courage and surviving them with grace. Pullman has created
a cross-age classic trilogy with the power to move people at the deepest levels, the potential to change their consciousness, and even (admitting the
boldness of my claim) the possibility to transform themselves and the
world they inhabit. The singularity of Pullman's accomplishment shows in
the award of the 2002 Whitbread Prize for the third novel in the series, *The
Amber Spyglass*, in both the adult and juvenile categories. If the mark of a
classic is its ability to "appeal to readers of all ages, backgrounds, and levels of education" (Bobby),[1] then this same feat shows the trilogy's classic
power as well.

Though there exists already a generous body of literature about Pullman's works (including many insights from Pullman himself in interviews
and articles), this gathering of scholarly interpretations undertakes something not yet accomplished: submitting the three novels to sustained literary criticism by a variety of scholars representing a range of perspectives.[2]

The Familiar and the Uncommon:
Myth Reinterpreted for Our Time

One reviewer notes elements in Pullman's trilogy that are familiar in juvenile fantasy and adventure novels: "juvenile heroes who undergo life-threatening and character-forming trials; an epic struggle between good and evil; love and hatred; and a cliffhanging narrative." What is not common about the trilogy is also remarkable: Pullman's impassioned grappling with serious metaphysical issues, reflecting his conviction that "children's literature should be about grown-up things: Where did we come from? Where do we go? What is our purpose as human beings, and how should we conduct our lives?" (McCrum). These are, of course, the kinds of questions asked by children and philosophers. Pullman can be credited, as Bernard Schweizer points out in his essay, with being an inveterate novelist of ideas, encompassing such concepts as "Goodness, and the related theme of tolerance" (McCrum) and ultimately implying a myth to live by—his "Republic of Heaven"—a place of joy, delight, and "the promise of connection with something beyond ourselves." Pullman has declared: "We all need some sort of myth, some sort of over-arching narrative to live by. For hundreds of years in the West, this need was fulfilled by the Christian story, but that is now either dead or dying" (qtd. in McCrum).

The mythic qualities of Pullman's narrative are enhanced by his expressive gifts, what Shirley Hughes calls an "extraordinary descriptive power" placing him alongside those whose "work will surely live for ever like all the finest children's writing. . . . He draws on the tradition of grand narrative and simply nothing can match the power of his imagination" (qtd. in McCrum). His remarkable metaphor-making ability shows in his creation of daemons, visible manifestations in some universes of people's souls (Maughan 25), an oft-remarked feature of the trilogy and one that most surely captivates readers regardless of age. As Susan Bobby notes, "His invention of daemons is the hook that pulls us into Lyra's world."

To Be Awake and Alive

In the above epigraph from *The Amber Spyglass,* the captive, drug-deadened Lyra, who is being held in a cave in the Himalayas by her benighted mother, pleads to be allowed to awake to full consciousness. Mrs. Coulter believes she can forestall Lyra's prophesied fate as the second Eve by keeping her in a comatose state. (Contrast Lyra's forced sleep, meant to deprive her of knowledge, with the sleep of Blake's "Lyca," meant to protect her from danger, differences elaborated in Susan Matthews's essay.) The idea that one must be in an awakened state to be truly alive has a long tradition in literature. Henry David Thoreau wrote in his essay "Where I Lived and What I Lived For": "Millions are awake enough for physical labor; but only one in a million is awake enough for effective intellectual exertion, only one in a hundred million to a poetic or divine life. To be awake is to be alive." He longed for the sort of awakening possible with what he called a Realometer (cf. "alethiometer"), which could cut through sham and appearances into "the secret of things" (*Walden* 117, 128). The metaphor of awakening in the world goes back at least as far as the Anglo-Saxons, who spoke of being born as "in worold wöcun"—to wake in the world (*Beowulf* 5, l.60).

At this crossroads in history, what the philosopher Jean Houston has called "jump time," the need to be fully "awake" takes on special urgency. As I have noted elsewhere, the trilogy may be seen as giving "a new map to define our place in the universe" (Hunt and Lenz 123) and a perspective that might help us survive contemporary crises, through its portrayal of young people who overcome disasters both personal and universal, such as widespread despair and soul loss, chaos in social and political realms, ecological ruin, massive wars, and catastrophes of apocalyptic dimensions. Pullman's ultimate metaphor for a changed consciousness is represented by the toppling of the "Kingdom" of Heaven, making way for the "Republic" of Heaven to be built in its stead. No construct of bricks and mortar, Pullman's Republic is rather a state of consciousness.[3] If we are to achieve such a state, we need twenty-first-century literature with potent mythic and metaphorical dimensions to shape our imaginations and strengthen our belief in the possibility that we might "repair the world" (*tikkun olam* in the Hebraic phrase,[4] expressing an idea shared by many religions; more will be said below of the relevance of the concept of *tikkun olam* to Pullman's Republic).

Myth, Music, and Consciousness Transformation

Pullman insists that fantasy must have a "psychological" connection with actual lives, remarking:

> If the republic [of Heaven] doesn't include fantasy, it won't be worth living in. It won't be Heaven of any sort. But inclusiveness is the whole point: the fantasy and the realism must connect. . . . Part of the connection which a republican story has to have with our lives—a very important part—is psychological. That's why Wagner's Ring is a

republican work of art, and Tolkien's [*The Lord of the Rings*] isn't. Wagner's gods and heroes are exactly like human beings, on a grand scale: every human virtue and every human temptation is there. ("Republic of Heaven," 661–62)

The mention of Wagner's Ring struck a chord in me, for by a fateful synchronicity, I had just finished reading M. Owen Lee's *Wagner's Ring: Turning the Sky Round.* Although *His Dark Materials* is in another genre and differs in many ways from Wagner's operatic epic, there are resonances that transcend genre, time, and national boundaries. The more I pondered the idea of the psychologically "republican" aspect of Wagner's *Ring* and its presentation "on a grand scale" of "every human virtue and every human temptation," the more it seemed Pullman was describing not just the *Ring* but also his own trilogy. I believe that Pullman, in a way analogous to Wagner, has given readers a myth about a transformation of consciousness (what Lauren Shohet calls "the evolutionary biology of consciousness") that reaches backward and forward in time, vivifies our experience of the "here and now," and ultimately shapes readers' perceptions of the world. Lee points out that Wagner drew upon the Old Norse Ragnarök, the myth of the twilight of the gods, thus incorporating into the Siegfried myths "a doomsday myth in which gods and heroes battle with the powers of evil, and all the combatants on both sides are destroyed, along with mankind, in a stupendous apocalyptic fire and flood" (26). Pullman modifies the apocalyptic elements, and rather than portraying "doomsday" for all, emphasizes how a "breakdown" can smooth the way for a "breakthrough," ushering in a day of awakening.

Another mythic element used by both Wagner and Pullman is that of the "Fall," or more accurately in their shared view, the birth of consciousness. Lee's observation gives the traditional mythic context:

At one stupendous evolutionary moment in pre-history, one of nature's creatures separated himself from the unconscious flowing and burgeoning of nature and became conscious of himself. Prometheus stole fire. Adam ate the apple. Man sundered his bond with nature and set himself on a course of conscious individuation. In his mythologies, man has forever after felt guilt about that sundering. For when he became conscious of himself, man was able to choose between good and evil, and he realized that he was flawed, striving for good but prone to evil. He had taken a momentous step forward, but something in him, and in his myths, still longed for the half-remembered union with unconscious nature, that innocence lost long ago. (40)

These "original sinners of myth," in Lee's words, are ambivalent figures, whose "primal offenses" open the gateway for ills of every kind to enter into the world. Ultimately, nonetheless, the "sin" has positive effects. Prometheus, who stole forbidden fire from heaven, enabled humankind to think and to learn through suffering. Adam (and Eve, though Lee does not name her) ate the forbidden fruit of the tree of the knowledge of good and evil, yet "the Church in her liturgy calls [this act] a *felix culpa*, a 'happy fault,' because it brought so wonderful a redeeming" (41). Wresting of consciousness from nature results in guilt, because it breaks the "bond" with earth (metaphorically the "mother"), but only by sundering the bond ("the bond that kept [the original parents] unaware, unthinking, merely intuitive like the animals") could humanity reach intellectual and moral maturity. As Lee says, "The race thereafter could think, and know, and do good or evil. It was, for the first time, fully human" (41). In terms of the present discussion, only then could our kind become fully awake, fully conscious.

In addition to a mythic resonance with Wagner's *Ring*, further evidence of the influence of music on Pullman's creative imagination occurs as a gloss by Pullman himself on a passage in *The Golden Compass* (GC). Lord Asriel opens a window into another world, and behold:

> The sight filled the northern sky; the immensity of it was scarcely conceivable. As from Heaven itself, great curtains of delicate light hung and trembled. Pale green and rose-pink, and as transparent as the most fragile fabric, and at the bottom edge a profound and fiery crimson like the fires of Hell, they swung and shimmered loosely with more grace than the most skilled dancer. (184)

The beauty of the Aurora in all its power and glory is almost "holy," and Lyra responds to the sublime sight by slipping into "the same kind of trance as when she consulted the alethiometer" (184). It is a stunningly Faustian scene, replete with musical and poetic allusions. Lord Asriel proclaims that piercing the vault of Heaven means "The end of all those centuries of darkness! Look at that light up there: that's the sun of another world! Feel the warmth of it on your skin, now!" (394). A moment later, seeing the palm trees waving on a shore in the new world, he asks, "Can you feel that wind? A wind from another world! Feel it on your hair, your face" (394). As Pullman wrote in a posting to child_lit LISTSERV (July 27, 2000), this passage echoes the German poet Stefan George, in his poem "Entrueckung" (Transcendence): "*Ich fühle luft von anderem planeten*" (I feel an air from other planets blowing). Pullman gives a musical analogy: "Schoenberg's String Quartet No. 2 in F Sharp Minor . . . incorporates a setting of

the poem for soprano. It's the point at which the composer finally leaves
tonality altogether and launches into the new world of no fixed keys: a profoundly dramatic moment." Asriel has opened new worlds of unimaginable
wonders and—though yet undefined—equally unimaginable terrors such as
those of the specters that devour consciousness (Hunt and Lenz 128–29).
The vistas opened up by Asriel's act are worlds of "no fixed keys"; instead,
they present the multiple and shifting "realities" of the postmodern consciousness.

In a new century beset by the terror-spawning forces of fear, increasing
repression of thought, and spiraling materialism, selfishness, and cynicism,
His Dark Materials dramatizes the struggle between these destructive forces
(metaphorically expressed in the subtle knife and the Specters) and human
aspirations toward greater awareness, aliveness, expanded consciousness, and
self-transcending love. Elsewhere I stated my belief that "the subject of *His
Dark Materials* is nothing less than the story of how "human beings . . .
might evolve towards a higher level of consciousness" (Hunt and Lenz, *Alternative Worlds in Fantasy Fiction* 123), and given the present course of events
in the world, "might" should be changed to "must."

Pullman calls his readers not only to sharpened consciousness, awareness of the present moment, but also to a keener *memory*, without which our
experience lacks feeling, meaning, cohesiveness, and applicability. When Dr.
Mary Malone hears from Atal the story of how the *mulefa* came to consciousness when they gained the knowledge of *sraf* (the word for Dust in
Atal's universe), she realizes how the story, including the snake and the attainment of knowledge, with its attendant gift of language, was the *dawn*
of "memory and wakefulness" (*Amber Spyglass* [*AS*] 224) as well as being a
parallel world version of the story of Adam and Eve in the Garden of
Eden. Memory, wakefulness (and one might add history) began with the
so-called but misnamed Fall. This theme of evolving consciousness weaves
in and out of the narrative and knits the whole together.

Levels of Consciousness and Their Functions in the Novels

What are the hallmarks of a fully awake mode of consciousness? Repeatedly, readers are made aware of the receptive mode of consciousness (a
"negative capability" in the poet John Keats's term[5]), which seems more like
a dream state than a fully awakened one. This mode of negative capability
is the state of mind that Dr. Malone has to maintain to see "shadow particles"—particles of "consciousness"—whether on the computer screen,
through the Spyglass, or in the semimystical state induced by I Ching (*Sub-*

tle Knife [*SK*] 88). Lyra must also be in this state of mind to read the alethiometer (92, 94–95). It is also the state of mind wherein people from "our" world (such as Will and Mary Malone) can see their own daemons (*AS* 458). Serafina teaches Mary

> to hold on to her normal way of looking while simultaneously slipping into the trancelike open dreaming in which she could see the Shadows. But now she had to hold both ways together, the everyday and the trance, just as you have to look in two directions at once to see the 3-D pictures among the dots. (*AS* 506)

Pullman implies that humans need multiple states of consciousness to see multiple realities.

The knowledge gained in this semimystical mode of consciousness (much like the "alpha" mode in brain-wave terminology), as desirable as it may be for certain functions, is balanced by another more active mode required for disciplined artistic creation. As Lyra progresses through the world of the dead, she grows toward this "maker's" fully awake state of consciousness, learning from the harpy No-Name the necessity of evolving a *true* and creative imagination, as distinct from a fanciful one. This wide-awake mode, capable of shaping meaningful stories out of the chaos of the "dark materials" of unmediated experience, appears to have much in common with what the poet Percy Bysshe Shelley meant by the imagination as "the great instrument of moral good."[6] M. H. Abrams has remarked on the concept of the "sympathetic imagination," central to Shelley's thought:

> [It is] . . . the faculty by which an individual is enabled to overleap the limits of his own nervous system and identify himself with the thoughts and feelings of other men. Shelley claims that [this faculty that] . . . enables us to share the joys and sufferings of invented characters is also the basis of all morality, for it compels us to feel for our neighbors as we feel for ourselves, hence to do unto others, as we would have them do unto us. (qtd. in *Norton* 478–79n)

Ultimately, Lyra, along with Will, shows this sympathetic imaginative faculty, as when mutually they commit to the heart-wrenching decision to dedicate the single opening between the worlds for the ghosts to exit from the world of the dead. The "good" of countless others takes precedence over personal desires. Lyra becomes the novel's major exemplar of the power of the creative imagination to shape the aforementioned dark materials into meaningful stories, thereby making more "dust"—expanding consciousness.

Daemons, whether external or internal, may represent yet another characteristic of awakened consciousness: its "dialogic" nature. It has been said that all sensitive and thinking people carry on a sort of ongoing internal "conversation" with themselves, and certainly this occurs frequently in the novels, when characters argue with their "best" or "worst" impulses. In a sense, consciousness of this kind might be equated with "conscience." The outstanding example of this kind of dialogue takes place when, after Serafina tells Pantalaimon and Kirjava (Will's now-manifested daemon) they "have to tell them what you know" (474): the terrible reality that the subtle knife creates Specters ("children of the abyss" as Kirjava calls them, 486), and why all windows must be closed (485, except as mentioned, the one left open as an exit for the ghosts from the underworld). This seals the separate destinies of Will and Lyra, for they know (as the daemons do not yet realize) how their daemons cannot survive long in a non-native world. Life without the conscious "discourse" with one's daemon would be unbearable.

These states of mind may be contrasted with the highly focused, predatory, obsessive mentality depicted in Lord Asriel and his counterpart, Marisa Coulter. Throughout most of the narrative, both are possessed by a self-serving "intention" that closes their minds to larger realities though their goals are—until the last moment, when they join in mutual sacrifice to save the world for Lyra (*AS* 406ff.)—diametrically opposed. Asriel's single-minded mission is to defeat the Authority and establish the Republic of Heaven; Marisa Coulter devoutly pursues a "victory" over the "evil" (as she mistakenly sees it) of Dust.

The Specters are another matter altogether, for they covet what they do not have. Specters devour human consciousness and creativity, aspects of the soul or daemon, leaving in their wake zombies who have no minds of their own. Pullman may be suggesting several things: "complete attention," a hallmark of the mature psyche, becomes increasingly difficult to achieve and maintain in a world of distractions, where "specters" of unreality feed upon the human intellect and soul. Creativity and untrammeled expression, a maximizing of human experience in the here and now, are rendered impossible when the Specters eat consciousness, leaving in their wake a terrible loss of memory and concentration, an emptiness like a kind of cosmic Alzheimers. In this state, the person's ghost is deprived of true stories to tell to the harpies and, unable to arise from the world of the dead, is doomed to an eternal emptiness.

Windows left unclosed, the product of technology run amok, cause the seeping away of consciousness to other universes. Pullman is showing us that escapism is fatal to consciousness, for it means neglecting to deal with the world at hand, the "here and now" of everyday life, and it also means missing out on the joys of being in the present moment. Another interpretation of windows might offer itself as well—namely, the opening of awareness to multiplicity and "otherness"—but the close of *The Amber Spyglass* favors the first reading; moreover, our daemons (at least at our present state of evolution) cannot survive long outside their native universes. Thus, fantasies of escape to an alternate world are foreclosed: we must live in this one and make it as much like "heaven" as humanly possible. As Andrew Leet observes, drawing upon Erica Wagner, "our duty should be to the present time and those around us, not to an image of a potentially rewarding afterlife"—what Pullman would regard as an illusory "elsewhere."

Theme of Creativity in *His Dark Materials*

> We can think of a work of art as a statement about the "evolution" of intelligence. It touches us if it challenges and animates at the edge of who we are as creative entities.
> Charles M. Johnston, *The Creative Imperative* (47)

The antithesis of drugged or deadened consciousness is represented metaphorically by the creativity and wholeness of mind realized in the "Republic of Heaven," an open and joyful awareness of the splendors of life. Fullness of consciousness manifests in creativity, with a mind like that described by Xaphania: "Open and free and curious" (*AS* 492), having an "imagination," which is a "form of seeing" (494), not a game of "let's pretend." It might be described as "complete attention" married to "flow." It may also link to the creative imagination that plays in the "phase space."[7] This openness of imagination manifests in what Shelley King calls the "naïve understanding" exemplified by Lyra's speculations on Dust (*GC* 398), which transcend the "flawed scholarship" of the Consistorial Court of Discipline (whose closed minds have concluded they already possess the whole "truth").

The scene of the disintegration of the Authority (*AS* 410), read metaphorically, dramatizes the passing of an old and no longer viable mode of consciousness to make way for a new, creative way of being in the world. As Mary Harris Russell says of the passing of the Authority, "This is not murder but a transition." M. Owen Lee, writing about Richard Wagner's *Ring of the Nibelung*, observes that "The rising of new myths, or the re-appearance of old ones, even in children's books, reflects important changes in society" (20). He points to depictions of the death of gods in literature: in *Agamemnon,* by Aeschylus, the central chorus tells how before Zeus, "two previous dynasties of gods, two father gods, had arisen, ruled, and passed away": Uranos, father sky, was overthrown by his violent son, Kronos, and Kronos similarly was overthrown by Zeus, his son, not a nature god but "a god of consciousness." Lee continues, "The question in all of this then becomes: Does god die, or is it rather that evolving man emerges into new levels of awareness and so, feeling the changes in himself, changes his god?" (88). According to Lee, at the time of the composition of the *Ring* cycle, with its dramatization of the death of Wotan and his attendant deities, this question was answered by Ludwig Feuerbach, who emphatically said, "What we call God is actually man's projection of his inner self" (Lee 89). In this reading, the Authority is "the sum of our present awareness," as Wagner said of Wotan (Lee 96). Thus viewed, "The great deaths in myths are symbols of inner transformations in man, who makes the myths" (94), and the "old" awareness must disintegrate to make way for the new. Only through such a metaphorical Götterdämerung may the world be transformed and the way be made clear for evolving creativity.[8]

Creativity and Responsibility of the Storyteller

Pullman's Arbuthnot lecture explores the social and artistic responsibilities that accrue to the storyteller. The lecture needs to be read in full, as no summary can do it justice. However, several points illuminate the present discussion of creativity. One is the necessity of "finding" good stories from many cultures, for the imagination "stagnates" and becomes "rotten" without "fresh streams of story" (38) from all over the world.[9] Consciousness needs refreshment and variety to remain porous to aliveness. The storyteller also has an artistic responsibility to language, as Pullman affirms, and his own craftsmanship shows in his love of the evocative nature of words and in his subtle wordplay. A further artistic responsibility, truthfully to convey "values" and "the world view and even the temperament" of the author, means for Pullman revealing a personal "mental universe" called the "Republic of Heaven." He describes an "attitude" underlying everything he does, and writes:

> I suppose I could describe it as coming to terms with an absence— the absence of God—because I cannot believe in the God who is described by churches and in holy books. So I'm conscious of God only as an absence, but an absence which is full of echoes, troubling echoes

and unhappy ones, consoling ones and kindly ones, chastening ones and wise ones. These echoes fill my mental universe just as the background radiation which apparently fills the cosmos is an echo of the original Big Bang. Echoes in the space where God has been. (2002 Arbuthnot Lecture 39)

Creative consciousness thrives, perhaps, on such echoes in empty spaces. (Cf. Anne-Marie Bird's comment that Pullman's "system" leaves room for "the free play of meaning"—which implies an empty space opening to creativity.) This personal testament, one of his most all-encompassing statements about the "making" of art, underscores how he values "what people do more highly than what they say they believe or they feel." Both passionate feeling and burning conviction are highly prized in our culture, but he takes exception to this emphasis on mere *feeling:* "The people I most value— and consequently the people my stories esteem most highly—are those who do good things; no matter what they believe or don't believe, no matter what they feel. It's better to have hatred in your heart, and yet do something good, than to have a heart overflowing with love, and do nothing." Literature, he reminds us, shows the complexity of and contradictory elements in human nature (Arbuthnot Lecture 39). Mrs. Coulter's complexity serves as a good example—a mix of selfishness and intellectual brilliance, the femme fatale, the cold-heartedness of an executioner, tantalizingly unpredictable—which helps to explain why she saves Lyra first from the silver guillotine in *The Golden Compass* and then together with Lord Asriel sacrifices herself to preserve the world for their daughter. She is ultimately more admirable than those who "have a heart overflowing with love" yet *do* nothing.

In this emphasis on doing rather than feeling (or indulging in ivory tower philosophizing about what *should* be done), Pullman's perspective fits well with the previously mentioned Hebraic concept of *tikkun olam* elaborated by Luria, who believed it describes "the true role of humanity . . . in the ongoing evolution of the cosmos," to restore a now-broken world to wholeness (see note 4). It is important to note, however, that in contrast to Luria, Pullman has repudiated the other-worldliness of Gnosticism in no uncertain terms, saying in an interview: "My myth does owe something to Gnosticism, but it differs in one essential characteristic. The Gnostic worldview is Platonic in that it rejects the physical created universe and expresses a longing for an unknowable God who is far off. My myth is almost the reverse. It takes this physical universe as our true home. We must welcome and love and live our lives in this world to the full" (qtd. in Cooper 355). Pullman's expressed atheism (or agnosticism, as he has differently described his stance at various times) consistently places responsibility for betterment of the human condition with human beings themselves, for just as there is no "elsewhere," there are no legitimate "authorities" to do the "saving" for us. Maude Hines expresses it well: the close of *The Amber Spyglass* places on the young shoulders of Lyra and Will the enormous task of constructing the "Republic" from materials at hand, which hardly seem sufficient. Burton Hatlen notes, in a similar vein, that the last novel depicts how "'God' and 'Satan' [that is, Metatron and, in the scene he is referencing, Lord Asriel] perish together, leaving us with the human, Lyra and Will."

Does Pullman convince us that humans are equal to what is required of them? "Individuality of response," in Margaret Mackey's phrase, will create various interpretations from various readers. Those who can make the "affect link" to Lyra's and Will's situation (or perhaps more generically, optimists) may reply "yes"; others may remain unpersuaded. Yet is there something about *His Dark Materials* that may captivate even those who find the concept of the Republic of Heaven not totally engaging? Many will be drawn to his sensitive depiction of the erotic innocence of first love. The philosophically inclined may delight in the notion that, as Lisa Hopkins says, "Pullman tells his readers that they *are* a trinity," in lieu of admonishing them to believe in a trinity. Those who read from a feminist theological stance may find in Pullman a "kindred spirit" despite his emphasis on "debunking" religion, for reasons admirably expounded by Pat Pinsent. Those fascinated by the influence of quantum physics on Pullman's construction of fantasy worlds will find the process of creation powerfully expressed as "a world dreaming of other worlds." Those who enjoy seeing Pullman's trilogy as simultaneously drawing upon traditions and carving out new territory will find satisfaction in his "casting new enchantments upon old conventions" (Karen Patricia Smith), and, as Carole Scott aptly puts it, see in his artistic innovations "a replay of Temptation, Fall, and Redemption" culminating in a different perspective on "old systems of belief."

In closing, I will offer a few observations on *His Dark Materials* as reading for young people. In her presidential address to the Children's Literature Association in 2003, "Utopia, Ltd.: or ChLA as Imaginary Kingdom," Judith Plotz critiques the "utopians of both the right and the left," who in their own ways and for their own ends encourage the production of contemporary texts that foolishly and tragically assume the "utter isolation" and "malleability" of children. She alludes to Randall Jarrell quoting E. M. Forster, who long ago noted, "the only thing we learn from spoon-feeding is the shape of the spoon,"[10] and continues, "the only thing the children of America will ever take from their enforced diet of subliterary utopian texts

is contempt for the whole propagandistic and servile process of reading"
(Plotz 28). *His Dark Materials*, because it respects and excites the intelligence
and imagination, counters this "subliterary" current. Pullman's artistic mas-
tery, the universality of his ultimate concerns, his melding of intertextuality
and originality, and the timeliness of his call for intellectual honesty, emotional moderation, and awakened consciousness have inspired the present
book. In keeping with his openness to divergent views, the essays present
differing and sometimes-contradictory interpretations, and they have been
so arranged that the critical "dialogue" that informs them will stimulate further discussion and research, and thereby, substantially enrich the quotient
of Dust in our literary universe.

Notes

1. Susan Bobby also quotes from Julie Boehning: "It takes a remarkable book to
   cross over from the juvenile to the adult division of a major publisher. Philip
   Pullman's *The Golden Compass*, an ambitious fantasy inspired by John Milton's
   Paradise Lost . . . is such a book." See Boehning, "Philip Pullman's Paradise," *Library Journal* February 15, 1996: 175.
2. Two recent books on Pullman deserve note: *Philip Pullman's "His Dark Materials"
   Trilogy: A Reader's Guide*, by Claire Squires (London: Continuum, 2003), and
   Darkness Visible: Inside the World of Philip Pullman, by Nicholas Tucker (Cambridge:
   Wizard, 2003). Both have appeared too late to allow more than brief mention
   in this collection. See the Further Reading section for more listings of secondary sources on Pullman's works.
3. See Pullman's "The Republic of Heaven" for a full elaboration of the meaning
   of the phrase.
4. "Isaac Luria, the renowned sixteenth-century Kabbalist, used the phrase 'tikkun
   olam,' usually translated as 'repairing the world,' to describe the true role of humanity in the ongoing evolution of the cosmos. In his view, God created the
   world by forming vessels of light to hold the Divine Light. But as God poured
   the Light into the vessels, they catastrophically shattered, tumbling down toward
   the realm of matter. Thus our world consists of countless shards of the original
   vessels entrapping sparks of the Divine Light. Humanity's great task involves
   helping God by freeing and reuniting the scattered Light, raising the sparks back
   to Divinity and restoring the broken world" (Inner Frontier, "Tikkun Olam:
   Perfecting the World," http://www.innerfrontier.org/Practices/Tikkun-
   Olam.htm). Related concepts in other religions include Christ's promise of a
   coming Kingdom of Heaven and his exhortation that people prepare for it
   "through love, wakefulness, and charity." The Bodhisattva of Buddhist belief for-
   goes liberation until all beings can be freed from suffering. Gnostics believe that
   "a spark of Divinity resides entrapped within the soul of humans."
5. Negative capability is thus explained by Keats: "when man is capable of being in

uncertainties, Mysteries, doubts, without any irritable reaching after fact & reason," an ability that enables a person to live creatively with uncertainty and contradiction. Keats used the phrase in a letter to George and Thomas Keats dated December 21, 1817. See *The Selected Letters of John Keats,* ed. Lionel Trilling (Garden City, NY: Doubleday, 1956), 103–04.

6. See Shelley's "Defense of Poetry" (1840, posthumously), 478 in *Norton Anthology*.

7. Pullman has spoken of the "phase space" as "the untrackable complexity of changing systems . . . to serve as a metaphor for . . . the notional space which contains not just the actual consequences of the present moment, but all the possible consequences." See his "Let's Write It in Red: The Patrick Hardy Lecture" (47), as well as Margaret Mackey's "Playing in the Phase Space," which comments on Pullman's use of the concept and explores the textual "play" that crosses media boundaries (17).

8. It is clear that the *Ring* was on Pullman's mind as he was writing *The Amber Spyglass.* Consider the (tongue-in-cheek) title of his article "*Götterdämmerung* or Bust," *Horn Book* January/February 1999: 31.

9. This is surely a conscious echo of Salman Rushdie, who wrote *Haroun and the Sea of Stories* (London: Granta/Penguin, 1990; New York: Viking Penguin, 1991) for his own son.

10. Randall Jarrell quotes Forster in "The Taste of the Age," *A Sad Heart at the Supermarket: Essays and Fables* (New York: Atheneum, 1962), 16–42.

Works Cited

Beowulf, a New Verse Translation. Trans. Seamus Heaney. New York: Farrar, Straus and Giroux, 1999.

Bobby, Susan R. "What Makes a Classic? Daemons and Dual Audience in Philip Pullman's *His Dark Materials.*" *The Looking Glass* 8.1 (2004). http://www.the-looking-glass.net/rabbit/v8i1/academy1.html.

Cooper, Ilene. "Pullman on the Theology of 'His Dark Materials.'" *Booklist* 97.3 (2000): 355.

Houston, Jean. *Jump Time: Shaping Your Future in a World of Radical Change.* New York: Jeremy Tarcher/Putnam, 2000.

Hunt, Peter, and Millicent Lenz. *Alternative Worlds in Fantasy Fiction: Ursula [K.] Le Guin, Terry Pratchett, Philip Pullman and Others.* London: Continuum, 2001.

Johnston, Charles M., M.D. *The Creative Imperative: A Four-Dimensional Theory of Human Growth and Planetary Evolution.* Berkeley, CA: Celestial Arts, 1986.

Lee, M. Owen. *Wagner's Ring: Turning the Sky Round: An Introduction to* The Ring of the Nibelung. New York: Summit, 1990. New York: Proscenium, 1994.

Luria, Isaac. "Tikkun Olam: Perfecting the World." http://www.innerfrontier.org/Practices/TikkunOlam.htm.

Mackey, Margaret. "Playing in the Phase Space: Contemporary Forms of Fictional Pleasure." *Signal* 88 (1999): 16–33.

Maughan, Shannon. "Whose Dark Materials?: The Culmination of Philip Pullman's *His Dark Materials* Trilogy Raises Theological Questions." *Publishers Weekly* December 18, 2000: 25.

McCrum, Robert. "The Observer Profile: Philip Pullman, Daemon Geezer." *Guardian* January 27, 2002. http://observer.guardian.co.uk/comment/story/0,6903,-640003,00.html.

New Dimensions Radio. "Quote of the Day." February 3, 2004. http://www.newdimensions.org.

Plotz, Judith. "Utopia, Ltd.: or ChLA as Imaginary Kingdom." Presidential Address to the Children's Literature Association, El Paso, TX (June 7, 2003). http://ebbs.-english.vt.edu/chla/address.html.

Pullman, Philip. "The 2002 May Hill Arbuthnot Lecture, 'So She Went into the Garden.'" *Journal of Youth Services in Libraries (JOYS)* 15.4 (2002): 35–41.

———. *The Amber Spyglass.* New York: Knopf, 2000.

———. *The Golden Compass.* New York: Knopf, 1996.

———. "Let's Write It in Red: The Patrick Hardy Lecture." *Signal* 85 (January 1998): 44–62.

———. "The Republic of Heaven." *Horn Book* 77.6 (2001): 655–67.

———. *The Subtle Knife.* New York: Knopf, 1997.

Shelley, Percy Bysshe. "A Defense of Poetry." *The Norton Anthology of English Literature.* Vol. 2. New York: Norton, 1962. 473–86.

Thoreau, Henry David. *Walden.* With an Introduction by Joseph Wood Krutch. 1854. New York: Harper, 1950.

I
READING FANTASY, FIGURING HUMAN NATURE

The essays in this section range widely in their emphases, from the sophisticated literary analyses of the modes of reading represented in *His Dark Materials*, the illumination of the rich intertextuality of Pullman's narratives, exploration of the ideological roots of his portrayal of human nature (including the place of daemons), and how a reader-response approach to the first volume in the trilogy, *Northern Lights/The Golden Compass*, can contribute to an understanding of its connection to readers' lives on a personal, emotional level. Despite their differing emphases, the essays connect at many levels to the theme of the human activity of meaning-making through literature.

In the opening essay of this section, "Reading Dark Materials," Lauren Shohet, using the framework of Renaissance allegory, discusses Pullman's reworkings of C. S. Lewis, William Blake, and John Milton to illuminate the centrality of concepts of reading and consciousness to the entire trilogy. Lyra's "new mode of reading" following her fall into experience ("joyous, Blakean, infinitely preferable" to innocence), "the modes of reading" represented throughout, and "the stakes of good reading" are seen as set forth in the trilogy's "interrelated models of art, identity, and ethics." Lyra's reference to her innocent mode of reading as "like a monkey in the trees, it was so quick" evokes not only "the trilogy's interest in the evolutionary biology of consciousness" but also (given the prominence of *Paradise Lost* in Pullman's novelistic framework) the Miltonic emphasis on work as a key feature distinguishing humans from animals. Shohet demonstrates how Pullman's trilogy engages the imaginations of his broad readership, from children to adults, from nonspecialists to scholars, particularly through the central figure of the alethiometer, which represents not only the process of reading and writing but also the trilogy's relationship to canonicity. Similarly, the amber spyglass, with its "double lens of perception," can be understood as a metaphor for the "layering" of textured narratives and their resulting enrichment. A close intertextual reading of the ending of *The Amber Spyglass* brings out the significant contrast between the "human separation from the divine as the price of the fall" in the Miltonic tradition and the separation of Lyra and Will (figuratively, "art and desire") at the close of *His Dark Materials*. In Shohet's interpretation, Pullman's ending underlines how the "imperfect coincidence of art and will enables—indeed, demands—the perpetual production of new narrative."

Maude Hines, in "Second Nature: Daemons and Ideology in *The Golden Compass*," begins with a look at "ideology" as natural and invisible from the "inside," and obvious only to those who can see it from an out-sider's perspective. Her synthesis of sociological, psychological, philosoph-ical, and literary approaches to the ideologies in *His Dark Materials* illumi-nates how daemons and their relationships to humans represent a troubled and troubling perspective on the meanings of "natural" and artificial, "nat-ural" and unnatural/uncanny. Drawing upon ideas drawn from philosophy (Althusser), psychology (Bettelheim), sociology (Bourdieu, Halttunen, Mechling), semantics (Péchaux), and literature (Baum and Twain), Hines makes clear the difficult and demanding situation of Lyra at the close of the trilogy, when she faces the necessity of returning to the "frustrating and un-avoidable reality" of her *habitus,* where she must try to construct "the Re-public of Heaven" with the only materials she has available there. Hines shows how Lyra as a young teenager faces fundamental existential choices in defining the "natural" for herself and at the same time resisting the ruling ideologies of her culture.

"Dyads or Triads? *His Dark Materials* and the Structure of the Human," by Lisa Hopkins, addresses two related issues: What actually is a daemon? What is the structure of the human being? She notes the link between Lyra's and Lewis Carroll's Oxford plus the shared interest of these two au-thors in evolution and the "structure" of the human, though Carroll's dif-ferentiation between the human and the nonhuman differs significantly from Pullman's: where Carroll thinks in primarily "binary" terms, Pullman ultimately seems to eschew dyads and concentrate instead on triadic or other multiple patterns. At the outset, a binary, dyadic structure seems to underlie such polar opposites, as for example the "two kinds of beardom" in Iorek and Iofur, and Pullman's "doubling" technique. The most obvious example of "doubling" is the dual entity of human/daemon. Hints of the "triadic," however, are inherent in the trilogy structure, plus other subtle tex-tual elements. Tripling begins in earnest in *The Subtle Knife,* and with *The Amber Spyglass* it becomes increasingly evident that "a whole in Pullman's world typically *is* made up of three separate parts." This is illustrated by the "threefold roles" of many characters and, most explicitly, by the conversa-tion between Will and Lyra that establishes the triadic structure of human beings—body, daemon (soul), and a mysterious third, later explained by Mary Malone as "spirit" in her explication of St. Paul. As Hopkins demon-strates, however, Pullman's "ultimate message," though superficially in line with Christian orthodoxy (the trinity of Father, Son, and Holy Ghost), ac-tually undercuts it in asserting the trinity of *human* nature in the absence of an Authority and an "elsewhere."

It has been said that the poet is one upon whom nothing is lost, one who lives with "complete attention" to the moment. The opening of Margaret Mackey's "*Northern Lights* and Northern Readers: Background Knowledge, Affect Linking, and Literary Understanding" exudes this kind of attention as she recounts her personal experience of driving through a majestic northern prairie winter landscape illuminated by a "magical airborne stream of golden flecks," her mind "swarming with magical creatures and majestic themes" derived from reading *The Amber Spyglass.* "[B]ook met life," as she says, "and each was enlarged by the encounter." Though we may have had such privileged moments, how many of us have reflected upon these "recognition" scenes with an awareness of "affect linking" (an idea drawn from David Gelernter), and gone on, as Mackey does, to show how this concept can enlighten our understanding of the links (or sometimes the absence or failure of links) between literature and life? The phenomenon of book meeting life underlies and enriches the discussion of "the experiential North" and "the fictional North" and the ways they may enhance or contradict each other. Insights into the importance of winter and "the North" in *His Dark Materials*—and especially in *Northern Lights/The Golden Compass,* as the British title emphasizes—lead to a realization of the gap between Mackey's own "experiential repertoire of winter," "too tangible and quotidian" in its *feeling* aspect to match Pullman's literary North. Therefore, she questions, what sort of "repertoire" does work? How does the repertoire that readers bring to fictional texts engage or distract them from the kind of effect the author is intent upon creating? Gelernter's concept of "affect linking," the process by which the mind associates ideas through "the precise connection of a shared emotion," illuminates the nature of reader response, with evidence drawn from Mackey's work with teenagers reading Gillian Cross's *Wolf* and Mackey's own reading of Pullman's *His Dark Materials.* It becomes evident that "the individuality of response" is never predictable nor orderly, but when affective links do connect, consciously or not, "[t]he story leaps into emotional life." This fusion of personal emotions with those of another renders "the profoundly personal satisfaction of recognition and delight."

I

Reading Dark Materials

Lauren Shohet

"Imagine having to carry a pile of books everywhere," exclaims Philip Pullman's protagonist Lyra, as she comes to understand that the Fall has taken away her ability to read by intuition the alethiometer—the "truth-measure"—that has given her guidance throughout her journey (*Amber Spyglass* [*AS*] 517). Innocent, Lyra read the golden compass "like climbing down a ladder at night" (*Golden Compass* [*GC*] 151), "without even having to think about it . . . [feeling] her mind settle into the right meanings" (204). "Fallen" into experience (joyous, Blakean, infinitely preferable), Lyra must relearn to read the alethiometer as adults do, by painstakingly cross-referencing the instrument's thirty-six multivalent symbols with "the books . . . in Bodley's Library," where "the scholarship to study them is alive and well" (*AS* 513). As the angel Xaphania tells her, "You [once] read it by grace . . . you can regain it by work" (491). In accordance with the trilogy's thorough-going preference for experience over innocence, reading "by work"—that is, "carrying a pile of books everywhere"—"will be even better . . . deeper and fuller than grace that comes freely" (491).

I am interested in how that pile of books is to be carried: in the modes of reading the trilogy figures, and the stakes of good reading for the trilogy's interrelated models of art, identity, and ethics. When Xaphania explains that Lyra's new mode of reading by "thought and effort [and] . . . conscious understanding" (*AS* 491) will supplant what Lyra calls reading "like a monkey in the trees, it was so quick" (513), the prelapsarian monkey image evokes ontogeny recapitulating phylogeny, drawing on the trilogy's interest in the evolutionary biology of consciousness. It also evokes John Milton's notion in *Paradise Lost* (the text most prominent among the trilogy's intertextual conversation partners, and the source of the trilogy's epigraph) that work is what distinguishes humans from animals:

Man hath his daily work of body or mind
Appointed, which declares his Dignity,
And the regard of Heav'n on all his ways;
While other Animals unactive range
And of their doings God takes no account.
    (IV: 618–22)

In its emphasis on a rich labor of reading, Pullman's trilogy speaks to readers invested in literary traditions. The trilogy's figures for reading come together with its models of identity and ethics in the tradition of Milton, Edmund Spenser, and other Renaissance writers whose texts create readable worlds where ethics and art are inseparable.

Like Renaissance allegory, *His Dark Materials* creates a legible world that demands adequate reading for more than cognitive reasons. Indeed, the trilogy accommodates reading along the four levels of Renaissance allegory: narrative (recounting the story of Will and Lyra); symbolic (exploring Lyra's and Will's relationship as the relations between art/storytelling ["the Lyric"] and desire/action ["Will"]); moral (plumbing the nature of persons and communities in the different worlds the novels depict); and "anagogical" or apocalyptic (the battle between opposing supernatural forces that includes resolving the problem of death).[1] Unlike some later models, Renaissance allegory is anything but reductive. Rather, its multiple levels intertwine and develop in ways that demand deep readerly attention and flexibility. Hence, many medieval and Renaissance allegories offer various figures of readers and reading inside the text, to train the attentive receiver in approaching the work's interpretive complexity. *His Dark Materials* recapitulates this trait. The trilogy signals how we might read the alethiometer, for example, as a figure for the novels' project of engaging Renaissance traditions when the witch consul, Dr. Lanselius, tells Lyra that alethiometers were invented "in the seventeenth century. Symbols and emblems were everywhere. Buildings and pictures were designed to be read like books. Everything stood for something else; if you had the right dictionary, you could read Nature itself. . . . But, you know, they haven't been used seriously for two centuries or so" (*GC* 173).[2]

Not "used seriously for two centuries or so," the trilogy's rich mode of signification is above all a way of "carrying books around," of examining what makes "the books in Bodley's Library" "alive and well." The trilogy suggests that good books depend upon their sophisticated awareness of their relationship to past texts: on flexible, nuanced, and self-conscious (i.e., "fallen") relationships between individual artwork and literary history. Good reading, which comprises effective agency and ethics as well as artistic sensitivity, likewise requires a sophisticated awareness (similarly flexible, nuanced, and self-conscious) of relationships between individual identity and communal consciousness.[3]

The trilogy's opening scene shows Lyra placing herself within a tradition of narrative exegesis (and specifically of exegesis narrated as juvenile fantasy), ducking into a wardrobe like Lucy at the beginning of C. S. Lewis's Narnia adventures. But this wardrobe is more capacious than Lewis's: Lyra finds that "the wardrobe was bigger than she'd thought" (*GC* 8). Following as it does upon the trilogy's epigraph—a particularly complex "what if" passage from *Paradise Lost*—the wardrobe passage introduces an implicit critique of the oversimplifying directness with which Lewis deploys canonicity, in both the literary and dogmatic senses of that word. The Narnia chronicles reproduce canonical moments, adorned by openings created when they suspend the original texts' momentum sufficiently to insert new material, but Lewis's narratives always rejoin the canonical text after these excursions in a way that leaves the tradition intact. *The Magician's Nephew*, for example, rewrites Adam's temptation from *Paradise Lost* such that Digory resists taking the apple (this novel's "obviously private" Eden [157] excludes Polly's Eve entirely), enabling Narnia to repel evil for a bounded amount of time ("The Witch whom you have brought into this world will come back to Narnia again [although] . . . [the] tree will protect Narnia from her for many years" [142]). Thereafter, the narrative of fall and redemption resumes unchanged.

By contrast, Lyra takes Lucy's place in the wardrobe in a way that shifts the terms of intertextual engagement from reproduction to transformation. *His Dark Materials* takes the tradition as a starting point: "Lyra shifted around to find a more comfortable position for herself. With enormous care she took one of the robes—a full-length fur—off its hanger and laid it on the floor of the wardrobe" (*GC* 18). But even though Lyra here "carefully" uses a literary antecedent as her basis ("on the floor"), her daemon (used in the Platonic sense, as something like the soul) cautions her against becoming complacent in it: "If you get too comfortable you'll go to sleep" (18). Accordingly, the first book of Pullman's trilogy takes the reader through a bracing series of identifications and revelations that magnifies the readerly process of Books I and II of *Paradise Lost. Paradise Lost* entices the reader to identify with Satan, then attempts to retract that possibility and bring the reader face to face with how she has fallen through her misdirected sympathies—that is, through listening to Satan's arguments, like Eve in the garden. The passages Satan narrates famously depict Hell as the dwelling of

"free choice" (*Paradise Lost* [*PL*] II: 19), of those with "courage never to sub-
mit or yield" (*PL* I: 108), of the nobly resolute mind that "in itself / Can
make a Heav'n of Hell, a Hell of Heav'n" (I: 254–55). By contrast, the
fallen angels depict Heaven as the realm of "thralls" (I: 149), "warbl'd
Hymns" and "Forc't Halleluiahs" (II: 242–43), "upheld by old repute" (I:
639). *Paradise Lost* then retreats from such "error," cautioning, for example,
that when a fallen angel speaks,

> . . . all was false and hollow; though his Tongue
> Dropt Manna, and could make the worse appear
> The better reason
>   (II: 112–14)[4]

The *Golden Compass* recapitulates *Paradise Lost*'s process of enticing initial readerly assent to a character's errant desires (here, Lord Asriel's), followed by the reader's shocked recognition of the path she has pursued. But
The Golden Compass extends the Miltonic agon; the reader ends the book in
genuine moral confusion about the position of the text itself, not merely, as
in *Paradise Lost*, about the potential separation between the characters' and
the narrator's positions. (Could Lord Asriel's revolt be admirable if it requires the sacrifice of a *child*? Will the trilogy *really* continue along the path
of advocating full-scale rebellion against God?) The novel firmly refuses to
recant: "'We thought Dust must be bad too, because they were grown up
and they said so. But what if it isn't? . . .' [What] if it were to be sought and
welcomed and cherished . . .'" (*GC* 398). As the trilogy continues, it extends
its amplification of what remains latent in *Paradise Lost*, producing a whole-
hearted challenge to the orthodoxy that *Paradise Lost*'s narrator articulates.
The trilogy's model of literary history thus makes the evolution of new
texts analogous to the evolution of new organisms in the trilogy's paleontology: evolutionarily, conscious beings focus and amplify the resonance of
"Dust," or preexisting universal material consciousness ("thirty [or] forty
thousand years ago . . . the human brain became the idea vehicle for this amplification process [and] suddenly we became conscious" [*Subtle Knife* [*SK*]
238]); literarily, new texts focus and amplify the resonance of old texts.

The radical (and ultimately successful) challenge to what the trilogy calls
"Authority" depends upon Pullman's two protagonists, Lyra Silvertongue
and Will Parry. As I have suggested, in the trilogy's symbolic dimension,
Lyra figures something like lyric/narrative/art; Will, something like human
will/desire/agency.[5] Unlike Lewis's novels, which obediently parrot—however charmingly—their canonical sources, Pullman's narrative art lies, steals,

and transforms. Lyra inveterately spins tall tales ("by the end of the fourth repetition of the story Lyra was perfectly convinced she did remember it" [*GC* 132]) and gleefully appropriates what she needs without paying ("What you doing?" she amazedly asks Will when he leaves coins to pay for goods he takes from deserted Cittàgazze establishments [*SK* 63]). As she deliberately eavesdrops from the wardrobe, Lyra's transgressions of gender-based prohibitions, of respect for property and hierarchy, of historical accuracy (all embraced by Lewis's protagonists) position her in the trilogy's first chapter to avert a murder. The figure she saves from poisoning is Lord Asriel, eventual leader of the rebellion against heaven, and, unbeknownst to Lyra, her father. Understood in terms of the trilogy's allegory of narrative art, this suggests that breaking rules enables Lyric to keep alive the emancipating rebellion against tradition—its unrecognized progenitor.

Lyra's storytelling is complemented by her reading, specifically of the alethiometer. Offering one of the trilogy's central figures for writing and reading, the alethiometer's operations help us further understand *His Dark Materials'* relationship to canonicity. To use the alethiometer, the inquirer must determine what combination of three symbols should orient the instrument's three short hands;[6] the user enters into the appropriate mental state to compose a question; then, the fourth hand swings "where it want[s] to," on a "never-ceasing errant way" (*GC* 79) in which an adept perceives hesitations that index each symbol's many meanings. Pointing to preexisting but deeply multivalent symbols, the three short hands function rather like orientations to apposite points in literary tradition. The reader/writer must choose them well, hold a related but distinct question in a separate register (the individual mind), then learn to interpret the operations of the errant hand. Like new, true art, the response is produced by the relationship between the text's multiple orientations to preexisting work and the writer's original cogitation. As the irreducible multivalence of the symbols and the errancy of the fourth hand suggest, reading this rare and precious instrument is never simple, and the directions it indicates are never predictable.

For its part, "Will" is similar to art in its negotiations between individual self-determination and the complex web of agency that enables it to act. Like the nuances of the alethiometer, Will's surname, "Parry," suggests the way the will must flexibly deflect and engage the challenges it meets.[7] Indeed, a primary quality associated with Will is "subtlety": in the "subtle knife" he bears and in the coat of his cat-daemon, Kirjava ("to see the meaning of the word *subtlety*, you had only to look at her fur" [*AS* 498]). The same quality, we might note, defines Satan's choice in *Paradise Lost* of the form that will allow *him* to act in the world: he

. . . found
The Serpent subtlest Beast of all the Field.
Him after long debate . . .
. . . his final sentence chose
Fit Vessel.
   (IX: 85–89)

Will is deeply effective in the trilogy, but he acts through an instrument—the subtle knife—that wounds its wielder. Every bearer of the knife has fought for its possession, and it cuts off two fingers from the left hand of every victor. "Will," thereafter, can execute action better than anyone in the trilogy, but is made incomplete and bleeds continually from his left hand.[8] Accepting the instrument through which the will can act in the world, that is, compromises the will's integrity. Both *The Subtle Knife* and *The Amber Spyglass* emphasize Will's fierce desire to be undetermined, as he refuses to follow the angels' instructions in the former, and declares to Xaphania in the latter that "Whatever I do, I will choose it, no one else" (*AS* 496).[9] Appropriating the weapon that enables Will's unique capacity to act, however, demands that he cede some autonomy. As the armored bear Iorek Byrnison explains to Will, instruments have their own histories, purposes, and drives: "The knife has intentions . . . sometimes a tool may have other uses that you don't know. Sometimes in doing what you intend, you also do what the knife intends" (181). Both desire and art can act in the world only by embracing tools (which include literary genres and intellectual traditions) that pursue their own trajectories, with consequences unintended by the user.[10]

The consequences of conjoined art and desire show themselves to be most powerful, if not fully intended, when Will and Lyra renegotiate the terms of death. It is Lyra's notion to go to the world of the dead (not, initially, for the grand purpose that emerges while she is there); it is Will who cuts open an exit from the underworld. Each individual's ghost thereafter can earn its own release from death (in pointed distinction to Christian myth), and the coin for the passage is narrative. Lyra first enables this redemption when she exchanges her innocent, facile storytelling (in which "*Lyra* and *liar* were one and the same thing" [*AS* 293]) for the art of experience ("the truth" [317], not "*making things up*" but "a form of seeing" that is "hard, but much truer" [494]). Subsequently, every ghost's "truth about what they've seen and touched and heard and loved and known in the world" will serve as payment for the harpies' guidance to the door that Will cuts to the Edenic world of the *mulefa* (317). Every individual's story—

rather than the Christian sacrifice of a single privileged individual—serves to release the soul from death. The joyous conclusion to the journey, more-over, disperses individual ghosts into the universe as the particles of mate-rial consciousness that Lyra's world calls "Dust." Only by producing specific narratives can individuals gain access to the ecstatic release into collective "Dust," "turning into the night, the starlight, the air . . . and then . . . gone, leaving behind . . . a vivid little burst of happiness" (364). The knowledge that art overcomes death produces art: "we've got to tell people that . . . the harpies want to hear [true stories] . . . if people live their whole lives and they've got nothing to tell about it when they've finished, then they'll never leave the world of the dead" (492–93). Conversely, the universe depends upon these individual narratives—upon the consciousness released back into the world when narrative earns a ghost the right to ascend from the un-derworld—to avoid a lethal deficit in the Dust that animates the cosmos.

The effective conjunction of Lyra and Will—of art and desire/agency—first opens the door from the world of the dead. Maintaining this passage, however, requires that they part. Since mature consciousness can generate enough energy to repair the inevitable cosmic damage inflicted by only one opening between worlds, keeping open a door between Lyra's world and Will's would necessitate sealing off the underworld. So, in a gar-den, Lyra and Will separate. In *Paradise Lost* Adam laments the loss of di-vine immanence, mourning that exile from the garden will prevent him from recounting to his sons that God "under *this* Tree / Stood visible, among *these* Pines his voice / I heard, here with him at *this* Fountain talk'd" (XI: 320–22, emphasis added). In closely parallel terms, Lyra and Will both mourn and mitigate their loss of immanence to each other. Lyra takes Will and "led him past a pool with a fountain under a wide-spreading tree, and then struck off . . . toward a huge many-trunked pine" (*AS* 507). At "a wooden seat under a spreading, low-branched tree," they agree that in their separate worlds, at the summer solstice, each will "sit on this exact same bench" (507) and "pretend we were close again—because we *would* be close, if you sat *here* and I sat just *here* in my world" (508). Lyra's and Will's exile from each other, by the Miltonic garden pool under the Miltonic pine, gains poignancy from these lovers being forced to forego precisely what Milton's Adam and Eve retain. Leaving paradise together, Adam and Eve take with them their shared paradise within: "with thee to go, / Is to stay here; with-out thee here to stay, / Is to go hence unwilling" (XII: 615–17), Eve tells Adam. Whereas *Paradise Lost* follows *Genesis* in imposing human separation from the divine as the price of the fall ("No more of talk where God or Angel Guest / With Man, as with his Friend, familiar us'd / To sit indulgent [IX: 1–3]), *His Dark Materials* requires the separation of art and de-sire—painful, partial, always seeking reconnection—in order to maintain every conscious being's passport into immortality.

This imperfect coincidence of art and will enables—indeed, de-mands—the perpetual production of new narrative. The requirement that Lyra and Will draw apart from each other in order for all other beings to have the opportunity to narrate their way out of death suggests that if Lyric and Desire could fully and perpetually inhabit the same world, no new art would arise. Art would be fully effectual—signification would be fully ade-quate—and this would compromise the vitality of both art and life.

Vitality—the striving for full being, for dynamic interrelation, for what the angels in Mary Malone's computer call "complexification" (*SK* 249; a word entailing both "complication" and "combination")—animates the en-tire cosmos of *His Dark Materials.* The trilogy does not separate metaphysics and physics, subjects and objects, but rather imagines the universe animated by the particles of material consciousness that different communities in the trilogy variously call "Dust," "angels," "Light," and "Shadows." These parti-cles are the medium of a monist and vitalist understanding of the cosmos: "the entire world [is] alive and conscious" (*AS* 448); "everything . . . throb-bing with purpose and meaning" (449); "matter loves matter. It seeks to know more about itself, and Dust is formed" (31–32).[11] Accruing to indi-viduals at puberty, accruing to species as they evolve into sentience, "Dust" figures something like a mature consciousness of self, "a conscious and in-formed interest in the world" (*SK* 280). The Calvinistic villains of Lyra's world abhor Dust (their original sin), because their notion of a disciplined community prefers to sidestep consciousness of self. Indeed, the Church un-dertakes to keep children uncorrupted by severing them from the part of their consciousness that resides in their daemons. Undertaking a project for the Church, Lyra's frightening mother, Mrs. Coulter, claims that "Dust is something bad, something wrong, something evil and wicked. Grownups and their daemons are infected with Dust. . . . But a quick operation on chil-dren means they're safe from it. Dust just won't stick to them ever again" (*GC* 282–83). When separated from their spirits, people are isolated from the mature consciousness streaming through all worlds, consciousness made by "thinking and feeling and reflecting, by gaining wisdom and passing it on" (*AS* 491).

Dust, then, both expresses and constitutes the interrelation of all be-ings, the participation of all mind and all matter in a cosmic ecology of consciousness. This produces a Blakean vision of integration, to be sure, but differs from Blake's model of the ecstatic oneness of being in its emphasis on the nuances, complexity (that angelic word), and self-difference interior to each individual consciousness. The subjectivities of various species in the trilogy consistently exhibit both division within the self and a related inter-dependence among beings. This is most evident, perhaps, in Lyra's world, where part of every person's consciousness resides in a separate, visible, an-imal-formed "daemon," "the [self's] other part" (*AS* 285). Part of the per-son's consciousness but not identical to it, daemons can keep secrets from the rest of the self (517), provide a co-investigator of the self ("without Pantalaimon, [Lyra] couldn't ask herself what [the feeling] meant" [303–04]), and offer a potentially dissenting view from within the self. In Lyra's world, the two-part nature of the psyche produces conversations within the self; in the world of the *mulefa*, corporeal morphology relatedly induces collective labor and culture. Since *mulefa* have no opposing digits, they labor in pairs ("they worked . . . two by two, working their trunks to-gether to tie a knot . . . [Mary] could tie knots on her own . . . she realized how it cut her off from others" [128]). Interdependence is the condition of all people; humans from our own world also have daemons, although we cannot see them. When the witch Serafina Pekkala instructs the human physicist Mary Malone how to see her daemon, she tells her to "hold on to her normal way of looking while simultaneously slipping into the trance-like open dreaming in which she could see the Shadows" (506). Perceiving consciousness requires double, separated, overlayered reading.

Such a linked, double lens of perception is of course precisely what the amber spyglass itself is designed to provide. Among the trilogy's communi-ties, only the *mulefa* perceive Dust with their naked eyes (indeed, it is they who call it "Light"). To replicate this vision, Mary creates an instrument by producing and layering lacquer made from the sap of a tree. The novel de-scribes this sheet of lacquer as being "about the size of a page from a pa-perback book" (*AS* 228), and the spyglass indeed offers another of the tril-ogy's central figures for reading. Mary's first, single lens yields "nothing in particular. It was perfectly clear, but it showed her a double image, the right one quite close to the left and about fifteen degrees upward" (228). Simple refraction of light, like simple fictional rearticulation of a preexisting text or reality, yields only reality at one remove. This describes, perhaps, texts like the Narnia chronicles. Doubling the lens does something more: "She moved the two pieces apart, watching how the appearance of things changed as she did so. When they were about a hand span apart, a curious thing happened: the amber coloring disappeared, and everything seemed its normal color, but brighter and more vivid" (229). Separation of the refracting lenses—like the gaps between a traditional text and a new text that engages it at a hand's remove—intensifies what it represents beyond mere quotidian reality. This describes texts more like *Paradise Lost* (in its relationship to Scripture) or Blake's *Milton* (in its relationship to *Paradise Lost*) than Lewis's Narnia novels. The "hand span" of separation evokes a *writerly* hand: writerly agency makes these less obedient texts brighter and more vivid. Finally, Mary finds that the lenses maintained a handsbreadth apart and coated with the oil from the *mulefa's* trees of knowledge enable her to see particulate consciousness, the beautiful "swarm of golden sparkles" surrounding conscious beings and the artifacts they have worked (*AS* 230). Its text and pre-texts separated by a writerly handsbreadth, anointed with the fruits of "fallen" self-consciousness, the amber spyglass works like the trilogy itself.

The *mulefa's* ability to see Dust without technology is one of many elements that make their world Edenic. Oriented by their trees of knowledge, the *mulefa's* world exhibits ideally adapted ecological synergies. Animals (*mulefa*), plants (seedpod trees), and technology (the *mulefa's* using seedpods as wheels, lubricated with the trees' oil) have evolved into mutual interdependence that both requires and produces Dust. The *mulefa's* origin myth holds that

> One day a creature with no name discovered a seedpod and began to play . . . a snake coiling itself through the hole in the seedpod . . . said . . . "What do you know? What do you remember? What do you see ahead?" And she said "Nothing, nothing, nothing." So the snake said, "Put your foot through the hole in the seedpod where I was playing, and you will become wise." So she put a foot in where the snake had been. And the oil entered her blood and helped her see more clearly than before, and the first thing she saw was the sraf [Dust]. (*AS* 224)

This story accounts for *mulefa* culture, in which individuals mature as they grow large enough for the seedpods produced by their trees of knowledge to fit them as prosthetic wheels. Upon maturity, the *mulefa* (like all sentient beings) produce Dust, which exposure to the oil enables them to see emanating from others as well. Using the seedpods for wheels, in turn, breaks down the pods sufficiently for them eventually to release their seeds. These grow into trees that flower and, when pollinated by Dust, produce more wheels.

Consciousness—"*sraf,*" "light," "Dust"—here streams from species to species, in interdependent ecology. *Mulefa* narrative art is oral, presumably for the same reason that *mulefa* mend nets in pairs: lacking opposable thumbs, they do not write. Rather, the *mulefa* keep their entire thirty-three-thousand-year history culturally accessible: "How can you know so exactly?

Do you have a history of all those years?" Mary asks; "'Oh yes,' said Atal. 'Ever since we have had the *sraf*, we have had memory and wakefulness'" (*AS* 224). Whereas people in Lyra's world and Mary's world alike labor throughout the novel to recover the history and nature of consciousness, the *mulefa's* collective narrative never forgets. Their well-trained memory enhances their stewardship of their world: "They knew the location of every herd of grazers, every stand of wheel trees, every clump of sweet grass, and they knew every individual within the herds, and every separate tree, and they discussed their well-being and their fate" (127).

The visibility of universal consciousness to the *mulefa*, combined with the collectivity of labor arising from their physiology and their economy, produces a world that is Edenic in the adequacy and elegance of its community, art, and technology. This ecology does not, however, develop in ways that can address catastrophic disruption. A *mulefa* elder tells Mary, "You can see things that we cannot, you can see connections and possibilities and alternatives that are invisible to us, just as sraf was invisible to you. And while we cannot see a way to survive, we hope that you may" (*AS* 234). Individual *mulefa* do not seem to have daemons; they visibly perceive universal *cosmic* consciousness in place of experiencing the overlayered, sometimes self-contradictory *individual* consciousness of other sentient beings. By contrast, Mary sees "connections and possibilities and alternatives": being forced to redress her perceptual deficiencies yields different interpretive tools. Mary can tie knots alone; humans can hold pencils, write, use computers, manipulate alethiometers. But both Mary's science and the trilogy's model of art take this human instrumental capacity for autonomy as simultaneously an inadequacy. Telling an isolated narrative, unlinked to literary history, would be as ineffective as mending a net with one trunk—just as a single lens of the amber spyglass cannot reveal Dust.

The imperative that realizing subjectivity requires both individual articulation and communal connection further elucidates the necessary union, and eventual separation, of Lyra and Will. In *Paradise Lost* Adam explains to God Adam's longing for a companion in terms that emphasize human incompleteness, even before the fall:

> Thou in thyself art perfet, and in thee
> Is no deficience found; not so is Man,
> . . . the cause of his desire
> By conversation with his like to help,
> Or solace his defects.
>   (VIII: 415–18)

Redress of human incompleteness comes, moreover, through "conversation": not through perfect unity but through dialogic ("two-worded") discourse. *Mulefa* must tie knots together; humans and daemons must negotiate; Will and Lyric must seek to reconnect across their separate worlds. Indeed, the trilogy depicts Will and Lyra realizing their love at a time when they have been painfully distanced from their daemons. Arguably, the deficiency this produces in each of their subjectivities enables them to conjoin. Conversely, it is when their daemons rejoin them—when all four beings sit together and pool the different knowledges humans and daemons have gained—that it becomes clear that Will and Lyra must part. In love, Will and Lyra wish that "the world could stop turning, and everyone else could fall into a sleep . . . and you and I could live here forever and just love each other" (*AS* 497). The full, saturated consciousness of Will and his daemon, Lyra and hers, cannot be sustained without fixing the world too rigidly: stopping time, excluding all other beings from wakeful consciousness.

Herein lie the stakes for ethics of the trilogy's conjoined ontology, hermeneutics, and aesthetics. Will and Lyra's ecstatic union transforms the universe. But its consequences for human society can be realized only if they separate. *Paradise Lost* locates the origins of society in the "mysterious Law" of "wedded Love": "by thee," rhapsodizes the narrator, "Relations dear, and all the Charities / Of Father, Son and Brother first were known" (IV: 750–57). What *Paradise Lost* here gives with one hand it takes away with the other: elevating mutual erotic love, the poem ambiguously uses it as either the origin, or the mere precursor, to the patriarchal society of "Father, Son and Brother." *His Dark Materials* portrays a related move from erotic love to ethics—from a pair of lovers to broad, charitable society—as Will and Lyra stumble toward the rest of their lives, in their separate worlds. Will leaves the garden not with his lover Lyra, but with his friend Mary, enacting the ethical extrapolation of "wedded Love" to profound friendship. While mourning the great sacrifice of erotic love, the trilogy also portrays friendship taking over many of its functions for the bereaved lover. Conversation, for instance, moves from love to friendship. Like *Paradise Lost*, *His Dark Materials* foregrounds "conversation with his like" as a primary pleasure of love; the angelic lovers Balthamos and Baruch confide that "talking is best" (*AS* 25). But with love between Will and Lyra acknowledged and realized, language escapes them: they enter a "trance of happiness[,] murmuring words whose sound was as confused as their sense" (481). Separated from Lyra, Will reclaims conversation through friendship: Mary promises that "if you'll let me, I'll be your friend for the rest of our lives . . . there isn't anyone else we can *talk* to about all this, except each other" (510).

For her part, the bereft Lyra is succored by the Masters of two Oxford colleges. At the beginning of the trilogy, it had actually been the Master of Jordan College whose attempt to poison Lord Asriel Lyra foiled from her wardrobe. At that time, ambivalently in service to the Church, this Scholar saw the leader of the revolt—the father of Lyra, the father of Lyric—as an untenable threat. It was, however, this same Master of Jordan who secretly gave Lyra the alethiometer, through which Dust spoke to her. In the world transformed, he becomes Lyra's protector, and his colleague offers Lyra tutelage in her new, fallen mode of rich reading. Art and knowledge—the lyric and the academy—come back together as they seek ways to move forward.

Moving forward resolutely into an unpredictable future—"like having the alethiometer but no idea how to read it" (*AS* 514)—is the first step toward building the "Republic of Heaven" (518). This phrase chiastically transforms the model of *Paradise Lost* in which *Hell* is a republic, *Heaven* a kingdom. Hereby *The Amber Spyglass* holds itself a writerly hand span away from *Paradise Lost,* effecting this transformative shift. Mary wryly tells Will that "we've both got to get used to living with our daemons" (510). Insofar as the combined, intimate, but never univocal consciousness of people and their daemons offers a figure for novels and their antecedents, Mary's emphasis must fall as much on "living" as "with our daemons." Like the bells that toll from all the Oxford steeples at the very end of the trilogy, "this one high, that one low, some close by, others farther off, one cracked and peevish, another grave and sonorous" (518), the sound of the trilogy—of any serious artwork—*lives* as part of a slightly discordant chorus of voices.

Notes

1. On Renaissance allegory, see, e.g., Hamilton.
2. The alethiometer itself operates like rich Spenserian allegory (but with more than four levels), with its range of related meanings arrayed under each of its symbols.
3. This is made difficult by the omission of intertextual epigraphs from some editions; the publisher apparently believes that many readers do not like to carry a pile of books around.
4. Generations of readers have questioned the sincerity or efficacy of the poem's recantations; other readers find them convincing. Consider the various possible readings of the way that three books after Satan's claim that "the mind is its own place, and in itself / Can make a Heav'n of Hell, a Hell of Heav'n" (*PL* I: 254–55), the narrator rebuts him: "within him Hell / [Satan] brings, and round about him, nor from Hell / One step no more than from himself can fly / By change of place" (IV: 20–23). Is this narrative demurral, or the long delay be-

tween Satan's stirring claim and the poem's retraction, more prominent? On foundational criticism exploring this question, see Fish and Empson.

5. The nuances of these figurations are entirely characteristic of rich Renaissance allegory. In Spenser's *Faerie Queene*, for instance, the figures for holiness, temperance, chastity, and so forth (together with their readers) need to journey through twelve cantos of adventure apiece in an effort to fully define themselves. Lyra's not being fully named as "Silvertongue" until the end of the first volume is similarly consistent with Renaissance practice.

6. For instance, Lyra explains that "I just put three pictures together because . . . I was thinking about Mr. de Ruyter, see. . . . And I put together the serpent and the crucible and the beehive, to ask how he's a getting on with his spying . . . because I thought the serpent was cunning, like a spy ought to be, an the crucible could mean like knowledge, what you kind of distill, and the beehive was hard work, like bees are always working hard; so out of the hard work and the cunning comes the knowledge, see, and that's the spy's job; and I pointed to them and I thought the question in my mind" (*GC* 143–44).

7. Will's father is a polar explorer and a shaman, connoting that physical and spiritual journeys engender the will.

8. This resonates with the "achievements of the left hand" that Milton uses to describe oratorical intervention in the world. We also might consider the way this displaces the stigmata of Christ, who is incapacitatingly wounded in the centers of his hands and fully cedes earthly action in the moment that enables redemption (opening a door between worlds). Will's wound is off-center and bleeds for days. It severs two digits but allows him to continue acting in the world (even as he also, like Christ, opens the door to another world).

9. Or, as he says to his father's ghost, "I can't choose my nature, but I can choose what I do. And I *will* choose, because now I'm free" (*AS* 418).

10. Iorek's comment about tools nicely describes Milton's conundrum when *Paradise Lost* adopts epic conventions that plug Satan into a heroic role; as Romantic readers of Milton demonstrate, the narrator's disavowals of Satan may not adequately deter the reader's admiration once powerful epic machinery gears up.

11. For an illuminating discussion of how the seventeenth century articulates this vitalist philosophy, and a thorough consideration of how this idea in natural philosophy affects politics and aesthetics as well as physics, see Rogers.

Works Cited

Empson, William. *Milton's God*. Norfolk, CT: New Directions, 1961.
Fish, Stanley. *Surprised by Sin: The Reader in "Paradise Lost."* 2nd ed. Cambridge: Harvard UP, 1998.
Hamilton, A. C. *The Structure of Allegory in the "Faerie Queene."* Oxford: Clarendon, 1961.
Lewis, C. S. *The Lion, the Witch, and the Wardrobe*. 1950. New York: Collier, 1972.
———. *The Magician's Nephew*. 1955. New York: Collier, 1972.
Milton, John. *Paradise Lost*. Ed. Merritt Y. Hughes. New York: Macmillan, 1962.

Pullman, Philip. *The Amber Spyglass.* New York: Knopf, 2000.
―――. *The Golden Compass.* New York: Knopf, 1996.
―――. *The Subtle Knife.* New York: Knopf, 1997.
Rogers, John. *The Matter of Revolution: Science, Poetry, and Politics in the Age of Milton.* Ithaca: Cornell UP, 1996.

2

Second Nature: Daemons and Ideology in *The Golden Compass*

Maude Hines

In *The Golden Compass*, Philip Pullman presents us with Lyra, a young girl in a grown man's world, a girl of "noble" birth who hangs out with urchins and servants, a girl who in essence doesn't belong where she is. Like and unlike our world, recognizable in some aspects and totally unfamiliar in others, Lyra's world presents an uncanny reality that is "natural" to her and yet unnatural to us. This layered distance—between Lyra and her world, and then between Lyra's perception and the reader's—presents an opportunity to examine from the outside (as ideologically constituted) what from the inside appears to be natural or obvious.

According to philosopher Louis Althusser, ideology works invisibly and insidiously, imposing "obviousnesses as obviousnesses, which we cannot *fail to recognize*" (172). Ideology, in fact, appears natural, experienced as if not operating at all: "those who are in ideology believe themselves by definition outside ideology"—in the realm of the natural, the simply true (175). On the other hand, it is possible to see that others are operating under a contradictory ideology: "the accusation of being in ideology only applies to others, never to oneself" (175). In *The Golden Compass*, Lyra is in the interesting position of being raised outside of the structures that constitute others like her as subjects, a kind of feral child raised by Scholars rather than wolves. The perfect "bad subject," Lyra acts against the apparatuses that attempt to constitute her, in the process revealing and reifying those apparatuses. Philosopher Michel Pêcheux, building on Althusser, argues that "bad subjects," through counter-identification, help to establish the very ideology they critique. For Althusser and Pêcheux, it is impossible to get outside of ideology.

The Golden Compass is divided into three sections: "Oxford," "Bolvangar," and "Svalbard." Each of these sections represents a different treatment of nature, a different relationship between Lyra and her parents, and a different view of ideology. As Lyra travels outside of the world of Jordan College to Bolvangar and Svalbard, she encounters the "unnatural" in various forms, unnatural events that serve to strengthen what she sees as natural in her world. Readers of *The Golden Compass*, drawn into Lyra's world but not raised in it, see and even experience this process, while recognizing as constructed what for Lyra seems natural. Lyra's encounter with our world in *The Subtle Knife*, accompanied by the experience of our ambassador, Will, calls the "natural" into question and exposes ideological process for readers in our own world.

One of the most remarkable aspects of Lyra's world is the presence of daemons, external human souls in animal form. Daemons must remain close to their humans as if attached by a sort of umbilical cord.[1] Separation of more than a few yards brings unbearable physical and psychic pain. Children's daemons change shapes according to mood or necessity, "settling" at puberty. As an old sailor tells Lyra,

> there's compensations for a settled form. . . . Knowing what kind of person you are. Take old Belisaria. She's a seagull, and that means I'm a kind of seagull too. I'm not grand and splendid nor beautiful, but I'm a tough old thing and I can survive anywhere and always find a bit of food and company. That's worth knowing, that is. And when your daemon settles, you'll know the sort of person you are. . . . There's plenty of folk as'd like to have a lion as a daemon and they end up with a poodle. And till they learn to be satisfied with what they are, they're going to be fretful about it. (*Golden Compass* [*GC*] 197)

In the old sailor's speech, we can see a familiar admonition to know—and be—oneself.

On the other hand, daemons make people legible to others as well as themselves. The "Master" of Jordan College's "impassive" face is belied by "the daemon on his shoulder . . . shuffling her feathers and moving restlessly from foot to foot" (*GC* 16). Lord Asriel's face "was a face to be dominated by, or to fight. . . . All his movements were large and perfectly balanced, like those of a wild animal, and when he appeared in a room like this, he seemed a wild animal held in a cage too small for it" (12). The reading of Lord Asriel's face, focalized through Lyra, is a device familiar to readers of nineteenth-century European and American novels, though in Lyra's world it is translated into similes that suggest his snow leopard daemon. The idea of the daemon is so natural that Lyra relies on it to imagine reading a person's face.

The form of the daemon is also an important key to character and even to class position. If the old sailor's speech separates the lions from the poodles of the world, the poodles of the world are often associated with servitude. While members of the aristocracy have diverse daemons, servants' daemons are invariably canine. At Jordan College, the Butler's daemon is "a dog, like all servants' daemons" (5), and the Steward's dog daemon is superior to the Butler's: "a superior servant, so a superior dog" (7). The natural place of servants (among themselves and as servants) is obvious, observable, through the dog shape of their daemons. Servant is not merely a profession, but ontology: the figure of the daemon naturalizes the rigidity of the class system in Lyra's world. While not all people with dog daemons are necessarily servants, the fact that all servants have dog daemons belies the infinite possibility the daemon represents before puberty.

The interpretive quality of daemons recalls earlier European and American responses to anxieties about "true" character that proliferated in the late nineteenth and early twentieth centuries. These anxieties, produced in the wake of growing industrialization and urbanization, were reflected in fears of confidence men in the city, the merit badges of the Boy Scouts, and pseudosciences like phrenology and physiognomy.[2] They found literary expression in stories like L. Frank Baum's *The Master Key* and Mark Twain's *The Prince and the Pauper*, the rags-to-riches stories of Horatio Alger, and of course in literary fairy tales.[3] Fantasies of reading the body as a key to the self persist today in a multiplicity of discriminatory practices against people with visible disabilities and racist, sexist, and ageist practices. In *The Golden Compass* these reading practices are directed at the shape of daemons, familiar and yet unfamiliar to us, natural to Lyra.

Lyra first encounters the unnatural separation of humans from their daemons when she finds coins etched with representations of daemons in skulls of Scholars interred in the catacombs beneath Jordan College. She switches the coins and is visited by a "night-ghast" in which three headless robed figures point the "bony" fingers of their "horny yellow-gray hands" at her. Convinced she has performed something unnatural, she rushes down the next day, restoring "the daemon-coins to their rightful places, and whisper[ing] 'Sorry! Sorry!' to the skulls" (45). Since the daemon inscriptions are "crudely engraved," and we learn later that daemons disappear (rather than turn into coins) when their humans die, the coins are likely metaphorical. As a representation of the importance of the connection between humans and daemons in the culture that devised the funeral rites, the connection between the coins and the skulls is constructed but nonetheless so real to Lyra that she's visited by the night-ghast.

Lyra's action, decried by both her daemon, Pantalaimon, and her companion Roger, is typical of her relation to authority. Lyra's character is one
that consistently pokes and prods at the edges of things, testing rules and
acting against her destiny. Jordan College, Lyra's world within a world, is
part of an Oxford University enshrouded in religious tradition, uncannily
similar to the Oxford of our world. For Lyra this world is natural, the only
world she knows, while for readers it is an uncanny world, familiar and yet
unfamiliar.[4] Born of noble parents, she's a "savage" (33), a street urchin in
the tradition of Dickens and Alger (36–38), and a dirty tomboy (56). She
resists the attempts of her mother, Mrs. Coulter, to feminize her and has an
irresistible urge to return to her savage life (75). Despite urging by Father
Heyst, the "Intercessor" who leads college services, that she should play
with other "nobly born children" or at least "other girls," Lyra prefers the
company of Roger the kitchen boy, a servant despite his daemon's still-dy-
namic form (46–47). Although she's a tomboy, she has a disdain for women
Scholars (59), echoing the ideology in which her upbringing is steeped.

This is a familiar fairy-tale narrative, where the nobly born princess is
found in rags or ashes. Unlike that narrative, in which the princess's beauty
or discernment serves as a visible sign that she is nobly born, this story presents a heroine whose difference is already known. Although her daemon
hasn't yet "settled," Lyra's noble birth is known to herself and the other
characters. Lyra is clearly an exceptional child, standing out among the gyptians with her blonde hair, gaining an audience with their king though only
a child, and being immune to Gobblers—unlike "children from the slums
[who] were easy enough to entice away" (40). One would expect a final re-
version to proper place, especially in a novel in which proper place is made
so visible by the conceit of the daemon, and yet that doesn't happen. Instead, Lyra is "destined to bring about the end of destiny. But she must do
so without knowing what she is doing, as if it were her nature and not her
destiny to do it" (271). Destiny works like ideology here; nature, like free
will.

The story follows the Freudian family romance, but Lyra's parents,
when found, turn out to be not at all what the typical fairy tale plot allows.[5]
Bruno Bettelheim has theorized that the good parent–bad stepparent dyad
is a way for the child to reconcile his ambivalent feelings about his own parents. In *The Golden Compass*, there is no stepparent, and the true parents are
monsters in their own ways. Lyra's journeys to Bolvangar and Svalbard are
also encounters with the true natures of her unnatural natural parents—
Mrs. Coulter in Bolvangar and Lord Asriel in Svalbard. Before her discovery of what her father is capable of in Svalbard, Lyra views him with awe.

Likewise, Mrs. Coulter initially appears beautiful, charismatic, and kind.

Mrs. Coulter is revealed to be a kind of wicked witch in Bolvangar, a place where the unnatural repeatedly supplants the natural. When Lyra arrives in Bolvangar, she assumes her familiar liminal position, this time as a spy disguising herself among the other children, donning a pseudonym, and sneaking about in crawl spaces. She is shown once more to be naturally superior to the others, setting her apart. Pantalaimon's victory in a staring match with another daemon establishes Lyra's dominance over another child, a process that appears to make her superiority natural by avoiding the contingencies and variables that might necessitate rematches in contests between humans: "It was quite common for struggles between children to be settled by their daemons in this way, with one accepting the dominance of the other. Their humans accepted the outcome without resentment, on the whole, so Lyra knew that Annie would do as she asked" (235). This exercise extends readers' knowledge of Lyra's superiority (earlier, the narrator describes Lyra as a "natural leader") to other characters (221).[6] Daemons thus can function to reflect natural human hierarchies even before they have settled.

The unnatural treatment of daemons at Bolvangar underscores their function as representations of nature and the natural.[7] On her journey to Bolvangar, Lyra discovers its mystery—the unnatural process of "intercision" that separates children from their daemons—when she encounters a severed child, described by her alethiometer as "uncanny and unnatural" (184). Pantalaimon is a meter for the unnaturalness of the scene. He refuses to speak, running about "uttering little frightened sounds" (186).[8] The narrator makes a connection, focalized through Lyra, with Pan's behavior when Lyra "and Roger in the crypt at Jordan had moved the daemon-coins into the wrong skulls" (186). When Lyra realizes that the child has no daemon, "her first impulse [is] to turn and run, or to be sick. A human being with no daemon was like someone without a face, or with their ribs laid open and their heart torn out: something unnatural and uncanny that belonged to the world of night-ghasts, not the waking world of sense" (188). The distance between our understanding of Lyra's world and Lyra's understanding exposes her physical reaction as dependent on her (world's) understanding of what constitutes a natural body; readers need to be shown that this is "unnatural" through analogy with images unnatural to us and through Lyra's physical reactions. The severing of humans and daemons is figured as monstrous. Lyra and the gyptians must struggle with their reactions to act compassionately toward the "half-child" (190). Another connection is made to the crypts beneath Jordan College when Lyra carves the name of the boy's daemon in a gold coin and places it in his mouth—she has come to understand the significance of the ritual.

When they discover the boy, Lyra knows that Pan's "impulse [is] to reach out and cuddle the little half-child, to lick him and gentle him and warm him as his own daemon would have done; but the great taboo prevented that, of course" (189). The word "taboo" suggests something created by human beings, something constructed rather than natural, in contrast to Pan's (animal) instinct. By the time Lyra discovers other worlds later in the trilogy, it becomes clear that touching another's daemon is a sexual act, producing "guilt and strange pleasure" for [two guys] in *The Subtle Knife* (293), and similar feelings for Lyra in *The Amber Spyglass* when she touches Will's daemon (409). By this time the strong word "taboo" disappears, and the act is "forbidden . . . by politeness" and "something deeper . . . like shame" (409).[9]

The sexualized descriptions of contact with another's daemon in the rest of the trilogy are useful for understanding the extent of Bolvangar's unnaturalness. When Lyra and Pan are discovered and threatened with intercision, an adult man touches Pan, and the interaction is figured as sexual molestation: "It was as if an alien had reached right inside where no hand had a right to be, and wrenched at something deep and precious. . . . She *felt* those hands. . . . It wasn't *allowed*. . . . Not *supposed* to touch. . . . Wrong." Lyra feels "faint, dizzy, sick, disgusted, limp with shock." Pan "was shaking, nearly out of his mind with horror and disgust" (241). Attention to the sexual connotations of touching daemons in the rest of the trilogy reveals that while "right inside where no hand had a right to be" refers literally to Lyra's daemon as her soul or spirit, it also refers metaphorically to her vagina.

Other adults at Bolvangar are complicit in this literal and metaphorical horror through their ability to calmly carry on a conversation with the perpetrator while he is committing his double violation. Their verbal intercourse functions to illustrate both how horribly unnatural the adults are (as sexual molesters) *and* how surprisingly unnatural the taboo is to them despite its physical impact on Lyra (the adults have been conditioned out of it). The real unnaturalness resides in Lyra's age (molestation) and unwillingness (rape); we learn later that the taboo against seeing consensual sexuality as natural resides with the unnatural Church.[10]

For the intercision itself they all gang up on her, including their daemons, and this is even more unnatural for Lyra, who cries, "Why? Why are *you* doing this? Help us! You shouldn't be helping them!" (243). Daemons shouldn't be capable of unnatural acts. Lord Asriel later connects intercision to castration (328). The men are "panting" (243). The double horror of uncanny intercision and metaphorical gang rape is prevented by Lyra's superior difference. Mrs. Coulter, the inventor of the blade, interrupts, recognizes her daughter, and is "horror-struck" (243). Mrs. Coulter gives a speech about the benefits of intercision as a way to avoid sexual feelings: "at the age we call puberty . . . daemons bring all sort of troublesome thoughts and feelings" (248). Daemons are connected with natural sexual animal/feelings, which should be eliminated—but only for the children of the poor, apparently. The chapter ends with Mrs. Coulter asking, "My dear, dear child. . . . However did you come to be here?" (244). Again, Lyra doesn't belong. Lack of broad applicability exposes unnatural thinking in the Church.

Bolvangar is also unnatural in its separation from nature. In the North, away from where European humans belong, the artificial dominates the natural. Bolvangar itself is out of place. The children are provided with coats made of "coal silk," but "the trouble was that coal silk wasn't as warm as proper fur, no matter how much it was padded out with hollow coal-silk fibers. Some of the children looked like walking puffballs, they were so bulky, but their gear had been made in factories and laboratories far away from the cold, and it couldn't really cope. Lyra's furs looked ragged and they stank, but they kept the warmth in" (257). This passage links Bolvangar with another kind of unnaturalness, one contrasted to a more natural animal world. Finally, Bolvangar is a site of one of the worst atrocities committed in the name of the Church. The Church, in turn, is revealed by the end of the trilogy to be an agency of a God who has unnaturally made himself king. Serafina prophecies that if Lyra doesn't fulfill her destiny to dethrone God by reenacting the *felix culpa*, "the universes will all become nothing more than interlocking machines, blind and empty of thought, feeling, life" (272).

Having discovered the horrible truth about her mother, Lyra journeys to Svalbard to rescue her imprisoned father. Since the Church, for whom her mother is working, is responsible for his imprisonment, Lord Asriel perhaps represents a way out for Lyra. Lyra sees her father as unjustly imprisoned and compares him to the bear Iorek Byrnison, who is the rightful king of Svalbard: "See, one reason I love Iorek, it's because of my father doing what *he* did and being punished. Seems to me they're like each other" (277). The bears have an order that confirms the class order reflected in daemons. As Iorek tells Lyra, "If your father is a prisoner of the Svalbard bears . . . he will not escape. . . . On the other hand, if he is a nobleman, he will be treated fairly. They will give him a house to live in and a servant to wait on him, and food and fuel" (197). The bears, outside of the human class system of East Anglia, still recognize Lord Asriel's noble status as natural, entitling him to certain privileges, including servants.

In Lord Asriel's privilege, and in Iorek Byrnison's rightful place on the throne of Svalbard, Pullman plays with the old fairy tale trope of the rightful heir. If Lord Asriel's place transcends the boundaries of the culture that created it, somehow residing with him, Iorek's place is even more ontological. The witch Serafina asks Lyra if Iorek has told her "who he is" and explains that "He is highborn. He is a prince" (277). That this is "who he is" makes high birth and rank (what might be properly considered an accident and a construction) ontology.

In Svalbard, where she is once again out of place as a human and a prisoner, Lyra discovers an unnatural state of affairs quite different from what she has encountered at Bolvangar. Iofur Raknison's daemon doll, and those of his court, represent his attempt to transcend his natural place, creating an artificial realm where bears are "unconscious semihumans conscious only of a torturing inferiority" (311). Bears, in trying to be human, discover themselves to be inferior. Raknison's daemon doll has a human face, in an inversion of the relationship between human beings and their animal daemons. In reversing the order of things, Raknison has created something unnatural, exposing himself to Lyra's trickery. Iorek has told her, "When bears act like people, perhaps they can be tricked. . . . When bears act like bears, perhaps they can't" (278). For bears, then, to be unnatural is to "act like people." This is precisely what's going on with Iofur Raknison and his daemon dolls. The unnatural here is figured again through animals and daemons, but this time they are not identical. The (animal) bears have uncanny (daemon) dolls. In turn, the dolls with blank faces resemble unnatural humans who have lost their daemons.

Raknison has also transcended his natural place by usurping the throne of Iorek Byrnison. The fight between them, which restores natural order to Svalbard, is described in similes that compare it to the processes of nature. The bears come together "like two great masses of rock balanced on adjoining peaks and shaken loose by an earthquake," and Iorek moves "like a wave that has been building its strength over a thousand miles of ocean" (307, 310).

The nature imagery of the fight reflects the ways that bears are, like daemons, naturally more natural—closer to nature—than are humans. Iorek is exiled for killing another bear who didn't surrender to Iorek's natural superiority; the bear must have been drugged, because "bears never fail to recognize superior force in another bear and surrender to it" (278). This rule recalls the way daemons stare each other down to establish hierarchies among their humans. Iorek's victory restores both nature and order to Svalbard, and the bears become "real bears" who aren't trying to be human (311).

The sociologist Pierre Bourdieu tells us that "the essential thing about historical realities is that one can always establish that things could have been otherwise, indeed, *are* otherwise in other places and other conditions" (*In Other Words* 15).[11] As Lyra leaves the world of Jordan College and encounters the unnatural in its various forms, she also comes to question what she has taken for granted. The naturalness of sexuality and identity is both represented by and tested by the daemon's animal-ness: sexuality as animal urges, class hierarchies as animal taxonomies. While daemons function as a conceit for playing out questions of the natural in Lyra's world, the second book of the trilogy complicates those questions by interrogating what the first book sets up as natural. When Lyra meets Will, the reader's ambassador in *The Subtle Knife*, he is surprised by Lyra's daemon—the most "natural" thing of all. By seeing familiar ideologies naturalized through different apparatuses, readers can see the constructed nature of our own ideologies. The class hierarchies naturalized by daemons are, after all, reflections of those in our own world.

Lyra asks Serafina why people have daemons, and she says, "Everyone asks that, and no one knows the answer. As long as there have been human beings, they have had daemons. It's what makes us different from animals" (276–77). This is, of course, a paradox—daemons *are* animals—one that illustrates the way daemons function, by relying on connections between animals and nature, and a concomitant separation of human beings from the natural world. It would be more appropriate, perhaps, to say that daemons are what connect us to animals, reminding us that we too are animals. At the same time, as Lyra develops a witchlike ability to separate herself from her daemon by great distances, perhaps she learns to distance her animal nature.

At the end of the trilogy, Lyra and Will must return to their own worlds and stay there. This frustrating and unavoidable reality is reminiscent of Bourdieu's notion that we can't escape our "habitus," that set of cultural structures that we as subjects internalize as subjects, and that in turn organize our thoughts, feelings, and actions, and find expression in social representations and practices. We experience the "habitus," which organizes our thought patterns, as natural.[12] The unnatural state of affairs in Lyra's world is largely the work of the Church, which strives to make the natural—sexuality, self-knowledge, and ultimately growing up—unnatural. The rebellion against the Church and God is also a rebellion against Lyra's parents, a separation that enables her maturity. By transferring the Republic of Heaven to the individual, it also places responsibility for her future directly upon her shoulders. The trilogy's ending seems to suggest that she can build the Republic of Heaven only with the materials she has available—what she comes to decide for herself is natural, whether or not she's acting within ideology—in her world.

Notes

Many thanks to Melissa Mullins, Elisabeth Ceppi, Jennifer Ruth, Marie Lo, Amy Greenstadt, Henry Mansfield, and Millicent Lenz for their helpful comments on early drafts of this essay. Thanks also to Juli Fiske, the student who ripped out Sykes's *Vanity Fair* article and handed it to me in class.

1. The term "umbilical cord" is Sykes's (178).
2. See Halttunen and Mechling.
3. In *The Master Key*, Baum invents the device of the "character marker," spectacles that, when worn, reveal the character of the person observed through the placement of a letter on the forehead: *G* for good, *E* for evil, *W* for wise, *F* for foolish, *K* for kind, *C* for cruel.
4. Pullman notes that Jordan is loosely modeled on the real-life Exeter College and "occupies the same physical space" (*Oxford Today*).
5. Freud's 1908 essay "Family Romances" describes the child's longing to be the child of a king as "an expression of the child's longing for the happy, vanished days when his father seemed to him the noblest and strongest of men and his mother the dearest and loveliest of women" (45).
6. Lyra herself is already aware of her special position. In the face of her fear at approaching a ghost who turns out to be a severed child, Lyra asks, "but who was she? Lord Asriel's daughter. And who was under her command? A mighty bear. How could she possibly show any fear?" (184).
7. Daemons seem to represent the natural primarily because they are animals, seen as closer to nature and somehow more authentic—free of the artifice that characterizes humans. This is similar to the way flowers work in nineteenth-century Anglo-American children's fiction, in which a "rose of a girl" might be contrasted to a mere "daisy." (While botanical metaphors proliferated in Victorian fiction for girls, the particular text I'm thinking of here is *The Wayside Flower* [1877].)
8. Pan's lack of voice connects him with animals and nature, and thus makes him a better gauge for reading the unnatural.
9. In *The Amber Spyglass* Lyra blushes, "because of course it was a gross violation of manners to touch something so private as someone else's daemon. It was forbidden not only by politeness, but by something deeper than that—something like shame."
10. And God's unnatural position as the king of Heaven—as the angel Balthamos tells it in *Amber Spyglass*, "the first angels condensed out of Dust, and the Author-

ity was the first of all. He told those who came after him that he had created them, but it was a lie" (28).

11. This follows Bourdieu's claim that "sociology's misfortune is that it discovers the arbitrary and the contingent where we like to see necessity or nature . . . and that it discovers necessity, social constraints, where we would like to see choice and free will" (14). I suggest that this "misfortune" is essential to understanding Lyra's relation to free will and destiny.

12. See *Logic,* Chapter 3, "Structure, Habitus, Practices."

Works Cited

Althusser, Louis. "Ideology and Ideological State Apparatuses (Notes towards an Investigation)." *Lenin and Philosophy and Other Essays.* New York: Monthly Review, 1972.

Baum, L. Frank. *The Master Key: An Electrical Fairy Tale.* 1901. New York: Books of Wonder, 1997.

Bettelheim, Bruno. *The Uses of Enchantment: The Meaning and Importance of Fairy Tales.* New York: Vintage, 1989.

Bourdieu, Pierre. *In Other Words: Essays Towards a Reflexive Sociology.* Trans. Matthew Adamson. Stanford, CA: Stanford UP, 1990.

———. *The Logic of Practice.* Trans. Richard Nice. Stanford, CA: Stanford UP, 1990.

Freud, Sigmund, *The Sexual Enlightenment of Children.* New York: Macmillan, 1963.

Halttunen, Karen. *Confidence Men and Painted Women: A Study of Middle-Class Culture in America, 1830–1879.* New Haven: Yale UP, 1982.

Harrison, Jennie. *The Wayside Flower.* New York: Dodd, Mead, 1877.

Mechling, Jay. "The Collecting Self and American Youth Movements." *Consuming Visions: Accumulation and Display of Goods in America, 1880–1920.* Ed. Simon Bronner. New York: Norton, 1989. 255–85.

Pêcheux, Michel. *Language, Semantics, and Ideology.* New York: St. Martin's, 1982.

Pullman, Philip. *The Amber Spyglass.* 2000. New York: Ballantine, 2001.

———. "From Exeter to Jordan." *Oxford Today* 14.3 (2002). http://www.oxfordtoday.ox.ac.uk/archive/0102/14_3/03.shtml.

———. *The Golden Compass.* 1996. New York: Ballantine, 1997.

———. *The Subtle Knife.* 1997. New York: Knopf, 1999.

Sykes, Christopher Simon. "Oxford's Rebel Angel." *Vanity Fair* October 2002: 174–80.

Twain, Mark. *The Prince and the Pauper.* New York: Penguin, 1997; London: Chatto and Windus, 1881.

3

Dyads or Triads?
His Dark Materials and the Structure of the Human

LISA HOPKINS

From the moment we become aware that *Northern Lights*, the opening volume of Philip Pullman's fantasy trilogy, *His Dark Materials*, is set in an Oxford that is subtly different from our own, we seem to be invited to consider this world as the Other of our own. In a classic Gothic doubling pattern, Lyra's Oxford seems an uncanny inversion of ours, almost a looking-glass world in the manner of Lewis Carroll—an impression that is strengthened when Lyra, escaping from Mrs. Coulter, tells the man who buys her a sandwich that her name is Alice (*Northern Lights* [*NL*] 101). Indeed the parallels with Carroll's Alice books run deep, for not only do both Carroll's works and Pullman's open in Oxford, but anyone who visits the Pitt-Rivers Museum there in quest of the skull that Sir Charles Latrom points out to Lyra (*Subtle Knife* [*SK*] 79–81) will find themselves walking past a model of a dodo and a caption about *Alice in Wonderland* on the way, since one cannot reach the Pitt-Rivers without passing through the Oxford University Museum of Natural History. Moreover, since both Carroll and Pullman evince a profound interest in evolution, we might feel further inclined to assume that Pullman shares with Carroll an urge to explore how the human is differentiated from the nonhuman, an investigation that is, in Carroll, conducted in essentially binary terms (humans on one side, nonhumans on the other).

A number of other features of *Northern Lights* seem calculated to underline this idea of a binary, dyadic structure. Lord Asriel and Mrs. Coulter appear to be set up as polar opposites, and this structure is later repeated in Iofur Raknison and Iorek Byrnison: "Iorek and Iofur were more than just two bears. There were two kinds of beardom opposed here, two futures, two destinies. Iofur had begun to take them in one direction, and Iorek would take them in another, and in the same moment, one future would close for ever as the other began to unfold" (*NL* 348–49). The name of the Barnard-

Stokes heresy provides another doubling that, initially, seems indeed to provide a clear clue to what we are to expect, since until the very last pages of the book we only ever hear of *one* other world, the city that can be glimpsed in the Aurora (which we later learn to be Cittàgazze), and Lord Asriel uses the inherently binary example of tossing a coin to illustrate the idea of parallel worlds (376–77). Moreover, we appear to be dealing with a patterning process involving not merely repetition but a consciously Gothicizing doubling technique, as for instance when the name of the man with whom Lyra is imprisoned on Svalbard, Jotham Santelia (328), recurs as the name of the city neighboring Cittàgazze, Sant'Elia (*SK* 61).

The most striking example of this binary pattern—and indeed arguably the most striking feature of Pullman's imaginary world—is his invention of the daemon. The nature of the human-daemon link is never defined and is sometimes expressed in mutually contradictory ways, but one thing seems clear: this looks like a reincarnation of the classic Gothic doubling motif expressed in texts from *Frankenstein* (of which Pullman wrote a 1990 theatrical version) to *Dr. Jekyll and Mr. Hyde* or *The Portrait of Dorian Gray*, with perhaps its closest analogue being George MacDonald's *Curdie and the Goblin*, where the true animal nature of a person is revealed in his or her handshake. Moreover, the vocabulary accruing to descriptions of the relationship is also heavy in echoes of another classic duality-based schema, the body/soul dichotomy. When Serafina Pekkala's daemon, Kaisa, arrives without her, the daemons of the other humans "affected the extreme politeness of keeping their eyes modestly away from this singular creature, here without his body" (*NL* 190), and Iorek Byrnison tells Lyra that "A bear's armour is his soul, just as your daemon is your soul" (196). It is true that this schema is not consistently maintained, and indeed it is not entirely clear that a daemon is incorporeal. It is suggested that they are so when Lyra releases the imprisoned daemons at Bolvangar, and "they clustered around her feet and even tried to pluck at her leggings, though the taboo held them back. She could tell why, poor things; they missed the heavy solid warmth of their humans' bodies; just as Pantalaimon would have done, they longed to press themselves against a heartbeat" (262). However, this idea is then apparently contradicted shortly after when "Pantalaimon pulled free of the monkey's solicitous paws . . . and . . . pressed his beating heart to hers" (279). Nevertheless, the entire thrust of the Bolvangar episodes is to make it quite clear that humans and daemons are in effect a dual entity, since any attempt to sever them is so disastrous and wrong.

However, there are also hints, even in the earliest stages of the narrative, of an emphasis on the triadic. In the first place, anyone reading *Northern*

Lights now is likely to know that it is the first volume of a trilogy, which will alert them to the possibility of a tripling pattern. Moreover, an insistence on the triple is already apparent from its opening sentences: "Lyra and her daemon moved through the darkening Hall, taking care to keep to one side, out of sight of the kitchen. The three great tables that ran the length of the Hall were laid already, the silver and the glass catching what little light there was, and the long benches were pulled out ready for the guests" (3). The detail of there being three tables cries out for our attention here, and indeed the very fact that we are never privy to any practical reason why there should be three of them underlines the sense that this must surely be symbolic (especially since, as I shall later discuss, three is a number often associated with symbolism). There are also three wheels on the alethiometer, all of which must be set before an answer can be produced.[1]

It is in *The Subtle Knife*, however, that the emphasis on tripling really begins. In the opening chapter we read that "Will waited till the man was framed in the open doorway, and then exploded up out of the dark and crashed into the intruder's belly. But neither of them saw the cat" (7). Each antagonist here thinks that they are locked in a dyadic conflict, but in fact there is a third combatant of whom both are unaware and whose intervention proves decisive in settling the outcome of the fight. This proves a powerful foreshadowing of the fact that although there is a strong temptation to see things in binary terms—Mrs. Coulter thinks that "This is at the heart of everything, this difference between children and adults!" (208), and John Parry tells Will that "[t]here are two great powers . . . and they've been fighting since time began" (335)—to do so is to ignore other salient possibilities. This is particularly clear when Will and Lyra are attacked by the children in Cittàgazze and Lyra urges Will to cut a window, but he refuses because he does not realize that he could cut through to anywhere other than his own Oxford, and he thinks they would be somewhere unsafe there (237). Clearly, Will needed to know at this point what Lord Boreal/Sir Charles tells Mrs. Coulter, that the world she is in "is one of millions" (208). Thus the appropriate model for apprehending "reality" is plural, as Mary Malone finds when she tries to reprogram the Cave (her computer) to use words: "the complexity of her task was about as baffling as getting three halves to make one whole" (258). Baffling such an enterprise may be, but it is, essentially, what not only Mary Malone herself but also the children are going to have to do, because a whole in Pullman's world typically *is* made up of three separate parts.

This becomes even clearer in *The Amber Spyglass*, where Pullman has the number three on the brain. Baruch has three things that he must tell Lord

Asriel before he dies (64); Iorek Byrnison has regard for only three humans (Lyra, Lee Scoresby, and Serafina Pekkala) (117); Will is three days' walk from the valley where Lyra is being kept (122); Mary thinks there are three criteria for "peoplehood" (language, fire, and society) (129); Mrs. Coulter has tried three times to save Lyra (148); the Gallivespians are three hours from Lyra (153); Tialys, Mrs. Coulter, and her daemon are locked in a three-pronged stalemate (166); three men block the path in front of Will (170); three men are burnt to cinders during the rescue of Lyra (183); the subtle knife is remade in three pieces (200); when Mrs. Coulter steals the intention craft, Lord Asriel does three things (231); the *mulefa* have existed for thirty-three thousand years (236); Atal and Mary catch three fish (238); it is three hundred years since the trees began to sicken (246); Mary's third arrow loops the tree (285); Mrs. Coulter has visited the College of St. Jerome three times before (339); it takes her three minutes to make her way through it (340); and Mrs. Coulter, Lord Asriel, and Metatron form a trinity in death. In short, virtually every significant action in the book is associated in one way or another with the number three.

Triples are of course characteristic of stories, which are, after all, essentially conditioned by the threefold structure of beginning, middle, and end, and that often present the number three as of special importance, and the nature and value of stories is a prominent and repeated concern of these books. However, Pullman's use of tripling is unusually emphatic, suggesting that the importance of the threefold patterning goes even further than its traditional value as a narrative device and concept. In particular, there is a crucial difference between traditional narrative uses of tripling motifs and the ends to which Pullman deploys them. In fairy tales, for instance, the salient feature of tripling motifs is generally repetition: it is the third of three brothers or three sisters who will be the hero or heroine, and there will be either a sequence of three tasks or the need for a threefold repetition of a task before the desired result is achieved. Fairy tales, of course, are typically providential; this structure can therefore be seen as echoing the triune structure of orthodox Christian belief—and that, I shall argue, is precisely what Pullman wants to challenge. Indeed, Pullman's work is at pains to put distance between itself and fairy tales in a number of respects, most notably in his willingness to kill off even likeable characters and in his portrayal of Mrs. Coulter and Lord Asriel, who, if this were a fairy tale, would be ideally suited to the roles of Lyra's wicked stepparents, but, because it is not, are instead all she will ever have in the way of parents.

Additionally—and unsurprisingly—Pullman's use of tripling motifs differs not only from fairy tales but also from the author he has most frequently and volubly criticized, C. S. Lewis (Ezard). In Lewis's Narnia books, the number three is sacred and reassuring: confronted with Peter's and Susan's doubts about Lucy's sanity, the Professor assures them that "There are only three possibilities" (Lewis 47) and that the preferable one is true; and throughout the book, three good children are pitted against one bad (the same pattern will also pertain later in the sequence, though it is finally Susan who is banished from Narnia and Edmund who is readmitted). For Lewis too then, it seems, the number three is associated with providence; but for Pullman, Lewis is engaged in nothing more than "propaganda in the cause of the religion he believed in" (Ezard), and providentialism is an aspect of traditional children's fiction that Pullman expressly eschews, since he subscribes instead to a quasi-existentialist view of responsibility and choice.

It is, therefore, an inevitable development of his aesthetic and moral outlook that Pullman's own use of threes centers not on patterns of repetition but on patterns of contrast. When his characters perform three tasks, they are, as I shall show below, distinctively different tasks rather than repetitions or variations of each other; when they are distinguished by three separate qualities, they are qualities that are stereotypically at odds with each other rather than ones that complement each other.

A primary factor contributing to the dominance of the tripartite in Pullman's work is the threefold role of many characters. Early in *Northern Lights,* the Master of Jordan makes a prediction that Lyra will be guilty of a great betrayal, which will hurt her terribly. The alert reader who keeps an eye open for this development will find that there are in fact three events that could be interpreted as constituting this betrayal. The first occurs when Lyra persuades Iofur Raknison to fight Iorek Byrnison as soon as he arrives at Iofur's palace. When Lyra sees how tired and poorly equipped Iorek is in comparison with Iofur, she fears that she has made a terrible mistake that will lead to the death of her friend; and the first-time reader may well expect that this will indeed be the case, especially when Iorek appears to be dangerously weakened and to be unable to use his left paw. Not until the battle is successfully concluded is the reader likely to realize that this cannot be the betrayal foretold by the Master, and scarcely has that occurred when we are hurried on to the disaster that befalls the next possible candidate for the victim of Lyra's great betrayal, Roger. Indeed one might well finish reading *Northern Lights* convinced that the betrayal that the Master prophesied has already occurred: Lyra, who thought that she was rescuing Roger and taking the alethiometer to Lord Asriel, has unwittingly led Roger to his death and is dreadfully grieved by it. Not until the final volume of the trilogy do we learn that Roger exonerates her from blame and that death is not as final as we had assumed. And not until the final volume of the trilogy do we learn, too, what the betrayal foretold by the Master was in fact going to be: Lyra's abandonment of Pantalaimon when she leaves for the world of the dead, and her subsequent agony. It is only this third occurrence that gives shape and meaning to the other two and allows us fully to understand their place in the scheme of things.

A similar pattern is discernible when it comes to the other prophecy about Lyra—that she is destined to achieve great things. This might well seem to have been achieved when her actions lead directly to the destruction of the hideous Bolvangar. Once again, however, this first achievement gives place to a second, in the light of which it must be retrospectively reinterpreted, for what feat could be more colossal than to break open forever the world of the dead? And yet this too proves to be a false trail: the act by which Lyra really changes the world proves to be first her realization and then her renunciation of her love for Will, who represents not only the temptation to which she must succumb but also another, and unexpected, temptation that she must reject, that of keeping open a door between the worlds so that their relationship may continue.

Other characters similarly prove to have threefold roles: Will finds his father, helps Lyra, and brings to an end the damage done by the subtle knife. Mary Malone wrecks the Cave and prevents its misuse by Sir Charles and whatever agencies he represents, discovers the true nature of Dust, and plays the serpent. Lord Asriel opens the way from his own world into Cittàgazze and the worlds beyond, initiates the war against the Authority and the attempt to build the Republic of Heaven, and ultimately sacrifices himself to destroy Metatron and so save Lyra. The Master of Jordan tries to poison Lord Asriel, gives Lyra the alethiometer, and introduces her to Dame Hannah at the end of *The Amber Spyglass,* thus deciding the future course of her life.

It is appropriate that the third defining action of each of these characters should occur close to the end of *The Amber Spyglass,* for that is, fittingly, not only itself the third book in the series, but also the one in which it is definitively revealed that humans have a triadic rather than a dyadic structure. We first begin to glimpse this new perspective on human makeup during a conversation between Will and Lyra:

> "What part of us does that? Because daemons fade away when we die—I've seen them—and our bodies, well, they just stay in the grave and decay, don't they?"
>
> "Then there must be a third part. A different part."

"You know," she said, full of excitement, "I think that must be true! Because I can think about my body and I can think about my daemon—so there *must* be another part, to do the thinking!" (175–76)

It is, presumably, this third part, this thinking, responsive part, on which the monstrous Specters prey, and the pitiful state of their victims makes it clear that this third part is quite as essential to human beings as the daemon is. Subsequently, it also becomes clear that Lyra's Death forms a third with herself and Pantalaimon when she says, "But Pantalaimon is my special and devoted friend! I don't know you, Death, I know Pan and I love Pan and if he ever—if we ever—" (282). And by the end of the book we are in no doubt that the tripartite structure of humans is a fact, as when we read that "it was the most searching examination Marisa Coulter had ever undergone. Every scrap of shelter and deceit was stripped away, and she stood naked, body and ghost and daemon together, under the ferocity of Metatron's gaze" (418). Indeed Mary Malone remarks that we should not even be surprised at this development: "As they neared the village, Will was telling Mary what he and Lyra had come to realize about the three-part nature of human beings. 'You know,' Mary said, 'the church—the Catholic Church that I used to belong to—wouldn't use the word *daemon,* but St. Paul talks about spirit *and* soul *and* body. So the idea of three parts in human nature isn't so strange'" (462–63). What might well surprise anyone reading these words as they approach the end of *His Dark Materials,* however, is to find Philip Pullman agreeing with any religious figure about anything at all. Why then does he concur with St. Paul about this?

This emphasis on the tripartite is, I think, partly a result of Pullman's profoundly inventive and complex characterization. In the passage about Mrs. Coulter that I quoted above, Metatron sums her up as evil through and through. Yet his examination of her takes place in the context of her firm decision to sacrifice herself to safeguard Lyra, an act we might well regard as entirely unselfish—were it not for the fact that Pullman, with typical lack of sentimentality, has already shown us that love for one's own child is entirely compatible with the most extreme forms of selfishness and ruthlessness. And yet even though we may realize this, it is still perfectly possible, as Will finds to his cost, to admire the audacity of Mrs. Coulter even as one loathes her. She is, in short, a creation of great complexity, a world away from the schematized division into good mother/bad mother that is the staple fare of children's fiction. So too is Lord Asriel—heroic, inspirational, and murderous—and so too are many less prominent characters, such as Balthamos, who is cowardly and pompous but a faithful lover and the ultimate savior of Will and Lyra.

The importance that Pullman attaches to the tripartite does not, however, stop at its usefulness for his peculiarly bravura and surprising brand of fiction. A stress on tripling is, I think, valuable not only to the style but also to the ultimate message of Pullman's project, and its value can, I would suggest, be traced to the fact that while Pullman's project of portraying humans as three-sided may be in line with Christian orthodoxy in the relatively minor respect cited by Mary Malone, it fundamentally cuts against it in a much more major one. Christianity has asked its followers to believe in a trinity, of Father, Son, and Holy Ghost. Pullman tells his readers that they *are* a trinity.

In a way, this is the single biggest revelation of the whole trilogy. *His Dark Materials* may appear to be primarily interested in fantasy, in the evocation of the otherworldly landscapes of the frozen North and indeed of literal other worlds. In fact, however, it shows its hand in these areas too early for us to have any sense that the unfolding of any secret about multiple worlds is going to provide its ultimate narrative telos. Instead, its real energies are focused more and more on personal relationships, both for their own sake and also, and I think primarily, for what they reveal about the nature and structure of the human. As the trilogy progresses, key elements of Pullman's vision of human identity are one by one revealed. In the first book, we discover the existence and importance of the element he expresses by the idea of the daemon. In the second, the emphasis is primarily on the weakness of humans—their tendency to behave badly, as demonstrated by the children of Cittàgazze and the persecutors of Will and his mother; their vulnerability to mental illness and to the hideous Specters; and their mortality, suggested by the fact that Sir Charles Latrom's surname is "mortal" backward, and emblematized in the deaths of John Parry and Lee Scoresby. In the third book, however, it is their strength that is finally revealed: death is seen not to be a threat at all, and we discover humans' ability to grow and mature, to assist each other, and to act nobly. Above all, we discover the full complexity of their tripartite nature. Humans are internally complete; they have no need to look outside themselves for a deity. The triune nature of the human is thus a fundamental part of Pullman's argument that the only worthwhile enterprise is to build the Republic of Heaven where we are.

Notes

1. For an explanation of how this works, see "The Alethiometer" at http://www.randomhouse.com/features/pullman/alethiometer/index.html.

Lisa Hopkins

Works Cited

Ezard, John. "Narnia Books Attacked as Racist and Sexist." *The Guardian* June 3, 2002. http://books.guardian.co.uk/guardianhayfestival2002/story/0,11873, 726-818,00.html.

Lewis, C[live] S[taples]. *The Lion, the Witch and the Wardrobe.* Harmondsworth: Puffin, 1959.

Pullman, Philip. "The Alethiometer." http://www.randomhouse.com/features/pullman/alethiometer/index.html.

———. *The Amber Spyglass.* London: Scholastic, 2000.

———. *Northern Lights.* London: Scholastic, 1995.

———. *The Subtle Knife.* London: Scholastic, 1997.

4

Northern Lights and Northern Readers: Background Knowledge, Affect Linking, and Literary Understanding

MARGARET MACKEY

In October 2000, *The Amber Spyglass* was published in Canada. A week after its appearance, Philip Pullman spoke to a children's literature conference held near my home. Eager to have read the final installment of the trilogy before hearing his keynote address, I galloped through the book. A day later I was on the road to Calgary, a drive of about three hours from where I live. My mind was still swarming with magical creatures and majestic moral themes.

I drove southward through the empty October prairie. The sun was shining, but there was no trace of color in the landscape; the leaves had fallen, but it was too early for snow. As far as I could see in all directions, the wide prairie was dun-colored and possessed of that stillness that marks the brief interlude between the end of harvest and the beginning of winter.

Two large trucks carrying enormous hay rolls pulled onto the highway. We took turns passing one another. Little bits of straw blew off the backs of these trucks and streamed around my car, glinting bright gold in the sun. They weren't Dust, but in terms of representing a captivated attention, they provided a startling substitute for someone whose mind was full of *His Dark Materials.*

I looked around the tranquil, monochrome prairie, illuminated by this magical airborne stream of golden flecks. No setting in those books could be more magnificent than this vast expanse of quiet land. A day later I was pleased but not surprised when Pullman told us that some of the prairie scenes in *The Amber Spyglass* were traceable to a visit he had made to this very landscape during the course of the writing.

What did I feel on that drive? Was it simple recognition? My first reading of *The Amber Spyglass* was so urgent and swift that I would have been hard-pressed, even a few days later, to locate a precise referent for my enhanced awareness of this setting. It was not a case of thinking, *Oh, Philip Pullman must really have seen something like this.* It was more a case of acknowledging a kind of goodness of fit: this vast, empty landscape had the right kind of moral power to be recognizable as something that could be in that book. Indeed, although I cannot believe I would have been indifferent to such a majestic scene under any circumstances, that book inspired me to look at this sight in new and different ways. For one exhilarating moment, book met life, and each was enlarged by the encounter.

This fleeting experience led me to reflect on how our experiences and our reading may enhance or may contradict each other. In this chapter I propose to explore issues of the reader's repertoire through an exploration of the role of the North in Pullman's trilogy and in my own reading experiences with these books. I will contrast two different elements of the North: the experiential North, a real territory on whose margins I happen to live, and the fictional North, a working construct of the author and also of the reader.

Because there are serious limitations to the singularity of autobiographical interpretation, my investigation will also include references to other readers of a different book: *Wolf* by Gillian Cross. Like *His Dark Materials, Wolf* is a young adult novel, winner of the Carnegie Medal for 1990 (*Northern Lights* was the 1995 winner). I worked intensively with ten adolescent readers of *Wolf*, and their observations about the processes involved in understanding this complex story stretched my understanding of many elements of reading that usually remain private and unarticulated, and certainly informed my reflections on my own reading of the Pullman trilogy. Later in this discussion, I will consider what these readings have to say about David Gelernter's concept of *affect linking*, an idea with much to contribute to our understanding of reading processes. First, however, I want to return to my own experience of *His Dark Materials.*

Winter and the North

Having experienced that moment of epiphany on the October prairie, I anticipated rereading the books with a newly opened eye for such embedded recognition of the profoundly familiar. The second time I read *The Amber Spyglass*, I read the whole trilogy straight through. It was Easter weekend of 2002, which happened to be brutally cold and snowy in Edmonton, even for an early Easter. I looked up from descriptions of the bleak North in *The Golden Compass* to see the snow swirling outside my own window. The roads were dangerous and the temperature was falling—surely a fit match for the challenging environment of Lyra's Arctic.

Yet, even as the icy winds beat at my front door, I was surprised to find that Lyra's North and my own quintessentially northern environment did not fuse in any truly vivifying way in my reading. There was nothing of that epiphanic recognition on the autumn prairie. Puzzled, I began to think about how our personal experience enlivens our reading of fiction. Why was that bleak fury of winter at my window not infusing my reading with greater depth of recognition? What was missing in the interaction between book and reader? I was enjoying the story enormously, but the fictional North was not being imbued by the reality of the North all around me. Surprised into curiosity, I began to explore how we draw on our own experience to bring fiction to life—not a new question for me, but one that struck me with particular force in this context.

Valentine Cunningham talks about "the utterly main function of literature as a shaper of the realities we perceive" (43). Certainly the recent experience of *The Amber Spyglass* definitely shaped my perception of the golden straw flying in the sunshine. Yet such a perfect match-up between book and life is fairly unusual.

The laments of colonized readers about how they never see their own realities in this shaping are commonplace enough nowadays, and I will represent them by a single quotation from my local newspaper that same snowy Easter week of 2002. Talking about the radiant spring background featuring in the television reports about the death of the Queen Mother in England, local journalist Paula Simons observed: "It was the perfect English storybook spring, like a scene out of *The Secret Garden* or *Watership Down.* It was the literary spring I always dreamed of, as a colonial prairie girl poring over the imperial children's classics. No wonder an Edmonton spring, with its brown grass, its mud puddles, its potholes, and its melting dog poop, always seemed like such a bleak disappointment. No wonder it never seemed 'real'—when all our books and movies and TV screens told us 'spring' should look quite another way" (B1).

In *His Dark Materials,* winter and the North play many roles. *The Golden Compass* in particular is a winter book; its British title, *Northern Lights,* emphasizes this connection even more strongly. The North functions as setting, in its dark remoteness and frigidity. It functions as plot ingredient, being far enough away from civilization to hide the evildoings at Bolvangar. It functions as an element of character development, particularly in the case

of the armored bears. It functions thematically as well: the relationship between the Northern Lights and Dust is resonant throughout the three
books.

And Pullman fully recognizes the glamour of this frozen world. His
descriptions are lavish with sensory detail and compelling in their clarity:

> The smell was of fish, but mixed with it came land smells too: pine
> resin and earth and something animal and musky, and something else
> that was cold and blank and wild: it might have been snow. It was the
> smell of the North. (*Golden Compass* [*GC*]147)

Under a sky peopled with millions of stars and a glaring moon, the sledges
bumped and clattered over the ruts and stones until they reached clear snow
at the edge of town. Then the sound changed to a quiet crunch of snow and
creak of timber, and the dogs began to step out eagerly, and the motion became swift and smooth. (177)

> As the lights behind them threw long shadows on the snow, Lyra
> found her heart moving out toward the deep dark of the arctic night
> and the clean coldness, leaping forward to love it as Pantalaimon was
> doing, a hare now delighting in his own propulsion. (255)

Awe-inspiring terrain to be sure; Pullman successfully conveys the
splendor of the Arctic. I have often experienced the majesty and clarity of
such icy winter nights, and I love them. But *my* winter is more than a glam-
orous and already achieved state of scenery. It happens over time; its challenges are sometimes sordid rather than magnificent. In Pullman's North, I
found little in the way of melting or frozen dog poop, so to speak. Its aus-
terity and hardship is larger than life, which is exactly what the story demands but that provides a particular challenge to a reader with a mismatched
repertoire.

Clive James, in his autobiography, describes his arrival in England from
Australia and his first experience of snow. "The snow was falling thickly
enough to replenish a half-inch layer on the footpath, so that my black
Julius Marlowe shoes could sink in slightly and, I was interested to notice,
be fairly rapidly made wet. It hadn't occurred to me that snow would have
this effect. I had always assumed snow to be some form of solid" (19). Pullman's northern setting, in all its magnificence and bleakness, existed in my
reading as "some form of solid," which is a roundabout way of describing
it as artificial, a magnificent stage setting, a stylized theatre for the perform-

ance of dreadful events. My own experiential repertoire of winter was too tangible and quotidian to serve my reading at any level of automaticity, a discovery that surprised me. I recognized Pullman's beautiful scenery at a sensory level, but it did not *feel* like my winter experience.

Arctic dwellers would not recognize me as a northerner, but I live in sufficiently wintry conditions that I intend to use my own reading experience as a starting point for a more abstract discussion. Where I live, in Edmonton, Alberta, winter often starts before the end of October and continues well into April. Temperatures can fall to -40 degrees, which is the point at which the Fahrenheit and Celsius scales converge, and which is also considerably colder than the -20 degrees that Lee Scoresby registered at an altitude of ten thousand feet (*GC* 273). Death from hypothermia is a genuine risk here if you are caught outdoors for too long without preparation. We see the Northern Lights every year, and the association of North and cold with power expresses itself literally in our homes by the buildup of static electricity in cold, dry weather. Many of our long winter nights are just as breathtakingly beautiful as the ones Pullman describes so evocatively.

All of this experience should equip me with a profoundly resonant repertoire for reading a book called *Northern Lights.* Certainly I supply a lavish sensorium of physical detail. I hear the squeak of the snow as Lyra and her companions lurk around Bolvangar; I feel the moistness of her breath chill into ice crystals on her hood (although in fact Lyra's hood is lined with wolverine fur that sheds the ice of your breath [*GC* 156], so my sensory response is inaccurately based on my own childhood experience of wool scarves). When I look carefully at the explicit details of the text, I discover Pullman's North is redolent with nuances that I recognize. Yet my responses somehow interpolate a kind of domestic familiarity that confounds his literary North, his stage setting for grand events. I am overloading his description with extra sensory and kinesthetic responses, which may engage me more deeply or may actually distract me from the kind of effect he is intent on creating.

If my own extensive repertoire of experience with winter, cold, and the North is excessive for the purposes of reading *His Dark Materials,* what kind of repertoire actually works successfully? My hypothesis is that it is a question of feeling rather than of visual or other sensory detail. To explore this question, I will investigate two diversions: I will explain David Gelernter's concept of affect linking; and I will draw on the responses of adolescent readers to Gillian Cross's young adult novel, *Wolf,* as examples of affect linking in action.

Affect Linking

Why and how does background experience matter to a reader? How does personal experience connect to the interpretation of a text that describes experience outside of the self? Is it possible that a saturated and excessive response can arise out of too much familiarity? Is it possible that a good-enough response is sometimes more effective for a reading than one redolent with multiple layers of embedded bodily history and experience?

One possible answer to such questions has important implications for how we think about both readers and texts. It is supplied by Gelernter in his account of the role of creative thinking in the development of artificial intelligence. He discusses how the mind associates ideas through the precise connection of a shared emotion, a phenomenon he calls *affect linking*. This concept of affect linking can usefully illuminate our understanding of the activity of fiction reading.

Gelernter presents a description of the mind at work that seems to lie somewhere between a theory and an extended metaphor. Human thought, he suggests, works on a continuum: "Every human mind is a spectrum; every human mind possesses a broad continuous range of different ways in which to think" (4). A person thinking at high focus is concentrating on methodical connections between facts, extracting the common factors for rational and useful grouping. At a lower focus, thought is less analytical and more concrete. Something resembling free association becomes more important. It is at this stage that metaphors and creative connections are engendered. The lowest stage of mental focus involves dreams and hallucinations where linkages are almost completely emotional.

The kinds of mental leaps that make a person associate two memories that appear to have nothing in common, Gelernter claims, "come about exactly when *two recollections engender the same emotion,* and they only happen towards the low-focus end of the spectrum" (6). He calls this phenomenon affect linking.

At high focus, Gelernter argues, we want answers to our questions and our problems. We search our memories for the *relevant* ingredient that certain incidents have in common; we are looking for solutions and explanations. We take a stack of memories and examine one aspect of all of them. At low focus, we are much more apt to recall broadly and inclusively; rather than combining and comparing one aspect of many memories, we draw up many aspects of one memory. Our thinking becomes more diffuse but also more concrete, less abstract.

In low-focus thinking, we recall the emotional ambience that surrounds a particular memory, and, according to Gelernter's argument, our mind can make a leap to a different memory that is swathed in the same emotion. Emotions, he says, are subtle, complicated, and idiosyncratic, but they create real links between experiences with nothing else in common. "[F]or affect linking to happen, remembered feeling must be *felt*, not just dispassionately examined. . . . For the affect link to work, the thinker must 're-experience,' *feel* his memories" (28). The connection between two disparate memories comes involuntarily, says Gelernter, if the two events share precisely the same emotional shading. The mind makes the leap and the affective power of one suffuses the second. "[A]s focus widens," he says, "you come to feel your thoughts" (30).

Some Examples of Affect Linking at Work

It is easy to be seduced by your own personal and private reading idiosyncrasies into thinking that everyone must naturally read in the same way as you do, but that comfortable assumption is a fallacy. Some aspects of reading may be universal, but the particular is more often plural in nature. Accounts of readers other than the critic writing the analysis date back at least to the work of I. A. Richards (1929), but work on reader responses really came to life in the 1970s (e.g., Norman Holland, 1975). Marisa Bortolussi and Peter Dixon (2003) provide a useful overview of the history of reader response work in their opening chapter; Richard Beach (1993) offers an analysis of the different disciplines that feed into reader response with a particular skew toward teaching.

I have often worked extensively with readers other than myself, but here I wish to allude only briefly to one such study. In an earlier project I worked with a group of young readers aged thirteen and sixteen, all reading *Wolf* by Gillian Cross. In their detailed responses to particular incidents, they demonstrated numerous examples of such affect linking, where their own emotional memories charged their readings of quite different scenes.

Eighth-grader Candace, for example, reading about Cassy's dream of running to the cottage, was reminded of her grandparents' farm. "They have a very long driveway and there's bears. . . . So you have to run, like, like, I always get scared and I run the last way but I never knew how many more bends there were till I got to the cabin. Um, yeah, and then where it says, 'Or the next, or the next,' and that's how I always feel" (Mackey 174).

Ed, an eleventh grader, also supplied his own affective connection to a dream sequence in *Wolf*, a nightmare in which Cassy screamed and screamed. He remembered being in the back seat of a car, as a child, with a bulldozer backing toward him. "It wasn't slowing down and I was sort of shouting because, you know, this thing would have crumpled our car with me in it, right, I didn't have enough room to get out, so, um, that reminded me of, sort of . . . panic" (179).

Ed and Candace both drew on memories that would supply an appropriately nuanced *emotional vivification* to their reading. Because they were talking about their reading experience to me, they made the affect linking explicit. In general, however, there is little reason to think that we necessarily articulate to ourselves the exact detail of the earlier experience from whose affective charge we draw to make stories come alive in our heads. Clearly Candace and Ed felt their personal experiences powerfully, but they were able to make a brief connection and then let them go as they proceeded with the story.

These simple examples represent a kind of generic affect linking whereby a reading experience is flooded with a suitable form of emotional life drawn from a reader's personal history. The infusion of affect is brief and temporary; the reader rapidly moves along to the next incident, not stopping to ponder the connections (unless asked to do so by an inquisitive researcher). In Gelernter's phrase, these readers are feeling their thinking, an under-acknowledged element of much fiction reading. It is a commonplace case of bringing life experiences to bear on a text in order to give emotional life to the fiction on the page.

The Fictional North

I hope this diversion into the description of affect linking and the readings of *Wolf* will prove helpful in terms of supplying useful vocabulary and a set of examples as I now move on to discuss the role of what I am labeling the fictional North in *His Dark Materials.* This "North" is cocreated by Pullman and his readers, and it seems to me that the more fleeting kind of affect linking that I described in Candace and Ed's readings of *Wolf* is sufficient for most readers to enliven this North and provide it with the requisite emotional charge. Pullman has made it amply clear in all his writings about *His Dark Materials* that his deepest commitment in these books is to tell the story in the clearest and most engaging way possible: "Now if the story is a path, then to follow it you have to ignore quite ruthlessly all the things that tempt you away from it. Your business as a storyteller is with the path, not the wood" ("Let's Write" 56). The North features as a *story* element. The thrust of the narrative is forward; as readers we are not really encouraged to linger in the detailed vivification of the northern experience. The implied reader is expected to supply a "good-enough North" and move on.

A different kind of writing would not only invite but also sustain a much more detailed enlivenment of a particular setting. Pullman's backgrounds are magnificent and powerfully evocative, but what they evoke is a grand story setting, not something as intimate and familiar as my own awareness of winter and the North. In a way, I had to set aside some of the daily detail and cadence of my own experiences in order to become the implied reader of *His Dark Materials.*

So What?

Why does this account of a particular reading matter to anyone but me? I have teased out my own responses in such detail because I am intrigued by the very personal nature of reading processes. Someone whose reading style is more visual and less affectively oriented than my own might well respond differently, and it is important to keep the significance of individual variations in mind. Nevertheless, the concept of affect linking offers a useful label for some of the ways readers bring words to life with the emotional nuances of their own personal experiences. But it is not a simplistic one-to-one match. It is the transfer of an emotional understanding—"feeling your thinking"—that matters, rather than the precise and actual details of an experience. As I drove through the golden stream of hay on the Alberta plain, the scenery looked right for the prairie scenes of *The Amber Spyglass,* but what was really striking was the precision of the affect link: it *felt* right. Lyra meets the North as a visitor, and many of my affective connections to the descriptions of that North are skewed by my own experience, which is as an in-dweller. In the end, I had to step back from my own lived experience in order to read *The Golden Compass* with a more useful reading repertoire. I had to supply the backdrop of Lyra's North with only those details that facilitated my progress through the book, and to stop looking for the full texture of daily winter life in a place where it was not reasonable to expect it.

Is this transfer of feeling too nebulous to be helpful in understanding how we read fiction and vivify someone else's story with our own emotional life? In fact, Gelernter emphasizes how precisely shaded our emotional nuances may be. "They are subtle. No grand passions need apply. They are *idiosyncratic,* blended to order for a particular occasion. They may contain recognizable traces of 'primary emotion' (a touch of sadness, a trace of anxiety), but these are nuanced, complicated mixtures. *They have no names*" (28). I suggest that part of the attraction of reading fiction is to recognize our own idiosyncratic and subtle brews of unnamed emotion when they are clad in the different clothing of someone else's experiences. As fiction readers, we are thinking with somebody else's words, and we are feeling those words with our own grasp of particular feelings. No wonder Harold Brodkey says, "Reading is an intimate act, perhaps more intimate than any other human act. I say that because of the prolonged (or intense) exposure of one mind to another" (qtd. in Booth 168).

My own "felt" winter sensations were not commensurate with Pullman's demands. In some cases, such a mismatch would cause me to abandon a book. In this case, my admiration for the achievement of the story prompted me to abandon, or at least downplay, the emotional repertoire I had initially expected to tap. I am an experienced reader, able, and in this case willing, to be flexible in the service of a story. But I do not find it difficult to imagine myself as a schoolteacher in Edmonton thinking, "We'll read *The Golden Compass;* that's a good northern story and the children will be able to identify with it." My own experience of the book is a chastening reminder that the individuality of response cannot be reduced to such a predictable and orderly process. Readers may make extremely precise affective connections to a particular story or scene, but such swift and deeply personal examples of bringing the narrative to life are not neat, manageable, nor predictable. When affective links successfully make a connection, however, whether consciously registered or otherwise, we experience the profoundly personal satisfaction of recognition and delight. The story leaps into emotional life. We think with someone else's words; we feel with a fusion of our own emotions and those of another. In this union lies much of the powerful human charm of storytelling.

Works Cited

Beach, Richard. *A Teacher's Introduction to Reader-Response Theories.* Urbana, IL: National Council of Teachers of English, 1993.
Booth, Wayne C. *The Company We Keep: An Ethics of Fiction.* Berkeley: U of California P, 1988.
Bortolussi, Marisa, and Peter Dixon. *Psychonarratology: Foundations for the Empirical Study of Literary Response.* Cambridge: Cambridge UP, 2003.
Cunningham, Valentine. *Reading after Theory.* Oxford: Blackwell, 2002.
Holland, Norman N. *Five Readers Reading.* New Haven: Yale UP, 1975.
James, Clive. *Falling towards England: Unreliable Memoirs II.* 1985. London: Picador, 1986.
Mackey, Margaret. *Imagining with Words: The Temporal Processes of Reading Fiction.* Diss. Edmonton: U of Alberta P, 1995.
Pullman, Philip. *The Amber Spyglass.* New York: Knopf, 2000.
———. *The Golden Compass.* 1996. New York: Ballantine, 1997.

———. "Let's Write It in Red: The Patrick Hardy Lecture." *Signal: Approaches to Children's Books* 85 (1998): 44–62.

Richards, I. A. *Practical Criticism: A Study of Literary Judgment.* New York: Harcourt, Brace & World/Harvest, 1929.

Simons, Paula. "After Shovelling Snow on Easter, Now We Look Forward to Brown Grass, Mud Puddles, Potholes, Melting Dog Poop." Edmonton, AB: *Edmonton Journal* April 2, 2002: BI.

II
INTERTEXTUALITY
AND REVAMPING TRADITIONS

When asked what sort of daemon he would have (assuming of course that people might have visible daemons in this universe), Pullman has replied, "a magpie or a jackdaw," "one of those birds that steal bright things" (qtd. in Susan Lyall, "Staging the Next Fantasy Blockbuster," *New York Times* [January 25, 2004], sec. 2: 5). It comes as no surprise that an author who likes to "steal bright things" weaves into his works so many riches from other literature, nor that all of the essays in this section treat some aspect of the intertextuality of *His Dark Materials.*

The opening essay by Burton Hatlen, "Pullman's *His Dark Materials,* a Challenge to the Fantasies of J. R. R. Tolkien and C. S. Lewis, with an Epilogue on Pullman's Neo-Romantic Reading of *Paradise Lost,*" explores the complex relationships between Pullman and two of his literary forebears, J. R. R. Tolkien and C. S. Lewis, members of "The Inklings," a group of Oxford-based Christian writers. The works of all three reflect their knowledge of English literary tradition, thus creating shared resonances, but Pullman's trilogy "challenges" his predecessors on several levels. Pullman's "secular humanist fantasy" is set against the orthodox Christianity of both Tolkien (a devout Roman Catholic) and Lewis (a liturgical Anglican). Pullman's reading of *Paradise Lost* is at odds with that of Lewis, who believed Milton expressed an orthodox Christian worldview, whereas Pullman aligns himself with the "neo-Romantic or 'subversive' reading" as exemplified later by William Blake. Pullman also differs with Tolkien, implicitly critiquing his vaguely medieval and hierarchical fantasy world and explicitly rejecting his metaphysical dualism. For Pullman, "good" and "evil" are potentials in every human heart. Pullman has spoken harshly of Lewis's Narnia series (e.g., his essay "The Dark Side of Narnia"), taking issue with the "life-hating ideology" evinced by some of his characters as well as his fear of adult sexuality. Paradoxically, *His Dark Materials* can nonetheless be seen as "a kind of inverted homage" to Lewis. The final portion of the essay takes up the related topic of the centuries-old quarrel between Christians and anti-Christians over the corpse of Milton, elucidating how the "Romantic" reading of Milton was challenged in the twentieth century by those who saw Milton as a perfectly orthodox Christian. The 1950s brought a revival of the "Romantic" reading, which was countered in the 1960s by a sophisticated version of the neo-Christian reading, and in the last decade this view in turn has been challenged by some equally sophisticated reaffirmations of the Blake/Shelley/Empson view. Pullman's trilogy offers a Blakean redaction of the Miltonic mythos. In contrast to the Romantic reading of Satan as the "true hero" of *Paradise Lost*, Hatlen affirms (and suggests Pullman would agree) that the "true hero" is Eve, with Adam in a key ancillary role. Similarly, Lyra and Will are "avatars" of the original pair, with responsibility for "moral choice" and "the future of the cosmos."

Carole Scott illuminates Pullman's use of three major literary sources— Milton, Blake, and the Bible—in "Pullman's Enigmatic Ontology: Revamping Old Traditions in *His Dark Materials*." Pullman redefines the human quest for meaningful purpose and the individual's responsibility in defining good and evil, at the same time interweaving "intricate threads of relationship" to create a "many-layered intertextuality": Scott likens the way in which his narrative technique incorporates text quoting text, and image quoting image, to "a metaphorical hall of mirrors." The moral complexities of Pullman's characters (with a few exceptions such as the Specters and the cliff-ghasts, who are obviously evil) challenge his readers to ascertain "the good and evil powers, people, and actions," and to try to decipher the "tantalizing accretions of information regarding the ontology that drives the trilogy." Sometimes there is a direct line of descent in the literary heritage, as for instance in Pullman's affirmation of love—both eros and agape, which "echoes the biblical story as well as Milton's and Blake's interpretations of it." Milton's influence is evident also in the "architecture" of Pullman's universe, the grand-scale vision, presenting a dramatic mythical/religious "backdrop" against which life is played out. As a writer of his time, however, Pullman conflates contemporary science (e.g., Heisenberg's principle) with religious ways of knowing (e.g., the story of the "fall" in several versions). Besides using biblical and classical traditions, Pullman weaves in other kinds of lore, such as that of shamans and witches, plus his own imaginative inventions (armored bears, Gallivespians, the *mulefa*). Blake's Jerusalem lends something to Pullman's Republic of Heaven, and Blake's legacy is even more fundamental to "the rebellious socio-politico-religious stance and the perception of innocence and experience in Pullman's trilogy." Scott shows how Pullman "melds religious, classical, and folk traditions" into a contemporary idiom to shape his "vision of the diligent creation of a harmonious universe."

Shelley King uses what may be a coincidence of names to place *His Dark Materials* in the exegetical tradition in her essay "'Without Lyra we would understand neither the New nor the Old Testament': Exegesis, Allegory, and Reading *The Golden Compass*." Opening with the fourfold structures of medieval biblical textual exegesis, central to Nicholas of Lyra's works, she explores the notion of the text of *The Golden Compass* as alethiometer, as self-reflexive reader's guide to its own interpretation. The novel is in this context "about . . . the process of textual interpretation," and moreover about how textual interpretation helps to frame metaphysical questions within a culture. As the alethiometer is marked by thirty-six symbols that signify multiple levels of meaning, the process of reading it is "a subtle art," as Farder Coram tells Lyra in the *Golden Compass* (144). Initially able to have "direct intuitive access" to the mysteries of the alethiometer, she eventually loses "the way of youth and innocence" and must reach meaning "through consciousness and cognitive effort." These two ways of understanding the mysteries of the alethiometer suggest Pullman's dual implied reader—"the child and the scholar"—and hence his oft-noted dual audience as well. King draws upon George MacDonald's conviction that youth is not necessarily a barrier to engagement with a complex text, given the power of "language clothed in mystery" to speak to all ages. Going beyond the first, literal level, Lyra may be interpreted on the second, moral level (what she *must do*) and the third, typological level (as second Eve). But the fourth, anagogical, level can hardly apply, as Pullman takes pains to posit no "future blessed state" for human beings. King explores a link between the metaphor of Pullman's "Dust" as original sin and the same metaphor in John Bunyan's *Pilgrim's Progress*, but with a significant difference: Christian sees the dust as a simple allegory of sin, whereas in Pullman's presentation, Dust becomes rather a challenge to received readings—and even to the notion of original sin itself. Against the background of Heinrich von Kleist's "On the Marionette Theatre," which affirms the importance of "acquired grace," Lyra's eventual "fall into scholarship" makes her, like her namesake Nicholas of Lyra, ready "to embrace the full complexity of signification to the adult mind."

Susan Matthews concentrates on the ways in which Pullman's trilogy works in "dialogue" with Blake in "Rouzing the Faculties to Act: Pullman's Blake for Children." She examines some of Pullman's many allusions to Blake's writings, exploring how the changing culture within which Pullman writes forces him to reread Blake's mythic imagination: for example, Pullman reuses Blakean images of splitting and wrenching apart from *The Book of Urizen* and reexamines his fascination with sexuality and the power of the female will. Matthews traces how the image of the cave, and of "cavern'd man" becomes a key image in *The Subtle Knife*. Finally she discusses how Pullman's narrative authority shifts through the three novels and closes with a comparison of the generic assumptions of the novel form to the shifting narratives of Blake's idiosyncratic poems.

In the concluding essay of this section, "Tradition, Transformation, and the Bold Emergence: Fantastic Legacy and Pullman's *His Dark Materials*," Karen Patricia Smith brings her abundant background in myth and British fantasy for young readers to an analysis of five key conventions of high fantasy as they are manifested (and also transformed) in Pullman's trilogy. The five key elements are: troubled young people invested with an important life mission; excursions into "invented worlds"; perilous journeys; the assistance of guides (adult and other); and the return to the primary world with new information, insights, and abilities. Revealing comparisons and contrasts are drawn between protagonists of George MacDonald's *The Princess and the Goblin* and *The Princess and Curdie*, C. S. Lewis's *Chronicles of Narnia*, Susan Cooper's *The Dark Is Rising* series, and Pullman's leading characters, Lyra and Will. Smith shows how Pullman works within and draws upon a tradition of high fantasy but creates his own individual variations upon the established patterns to give readers new connections to their contemporary lives.

Pullman's *His Dark Materials,*
a Challenge to the Fantasies of J. R. R. Tolkien
and C. S. Lewis, with an Epilogue on Pullman's
Neo-Romantic Reading of *Paradise Lost*

BURTON HATLEN

The power and charm of Philip Pullman's *His Dark Materials* trilogy lies in its astonishing inventiveness. I live with a large neutered tomcat, Gorby by name, who regularly leaps onto my bed at 4:00 A.M. with a series of small cries, as if he wants to tell me something urgent, and then settles in beside my shoulder, purring loudly. But if I lived in Lyra's world, Gorby *would* really talk to me. So too, whenever I talk to other readers of the trilogy, it turns out that almost all of us are bemused by the idea of our pets becoming our daemons and sharing our every thought. Thus it is that a great writer can change the way we see the world. Pullman also opens up familiar landscapes in new ways: ice cliffs of northern Norway and Svalbard; the raffishly decadent, vaguely Mediterranean or Caribbean city of Cittàgazze, inhabited now only by children and Specters; the land of the *mulefa,* which bears a vague resemblance to California before the coming of Europeans. But for me, Pullman's most distinctive contribution to the fantasy genre is his blurring of the line that separates the "real" from the fantasy worlds. At the start of *The Golden Compass,* we find ourselves immediately in an Oxford that is both "ours" (I've never been there, but I've read enough English novels and seen enough English movies about university life to recognize the place) and wonderfully different: no cars, zeppelins rather than airplanes, a history in which the Reformation never occurred, and so forth. How many variations can Pullman play on the relationship between our world and Lyra's world? This question alone can keep us turning the pages.

Like all good fantasy, however, Pullman's trilogy offers not only dazzling imaginative conceits and a suspenseful plot but also a coherent and intelligible worldview, and in this essay I want to try to elucidate that world-

view. I will do so initially by reading *His Dark Materials* against the background of two other important works of modern fantasy—J. R. R.
Tolkien's *The Lord of the Rings* and C. S. Lewis's Narnia series. Tolkien and
Lewis both composed their classic fantasies while teaching at Oxford University, and Pullman, as a graduate of that university and still a resident of
Oxford, is inevitably writing in the long shadow of his two redoubtable
predecessors. It is also important to remember that Lewis and Tolkien were
not only writers of fantasy but also scholars and teachers of English literature, and that Pullman too spent many years as a teacher of literature. The
knowledge of the English literary tradition that all three bring to their fantasy writings gives these writings an unusual resonance, while conversely
their fantasy writings also offer a tacit argument about how we should read
the English literary tradition itself. Despite these apparent similarities, however, Pullman has on several occasions assertively, even aggressively posi-
tioned himself in opposition to Tolkien and Lewis, and I will here argue
that Pullman's trilogy challenges the works of his predecessors on at least
two levels. First, Tolkien and Lewis were both orthodox Christians (Tolkien
a Roman Catholic, and Lewis an ecumenical Anglican),[1] whereas Pullman
rejects their Christian worldview as essentially life-denying. Accordingly, he
has set out to create a new kind of fantasy, a secular humanist fantasy.[2] On
the literary level, Pullman has tacitly challenged Lewis's reading of the English literary tradition, and in particular his reading of Milton's *Paradise Lost*
as an exposition of an orthodox Christian view of the world. Thus my exploration of the relationship between Pullman and Lewis will carry me into
the second part of my argument, as I attempt to show that in *His Dark Materials* Pullman has aligned himself with the neo-Romantic or "subversive"
reading of Milton's poem as exemplified by, for example, William Blake.

Pullman's public comments on Tolkien have been somewhat less negative than his comments on Lewis, so I will begin with Tolkien. Tolkien's
achievements as a literary scholar were relatively modest, and except for his
generalized nostalgia for the Middle Ages, his reading of the English literary tradition is, unlike Lewis's, of no particular interest to Pullman. But *The
Lord of the Rings* seems, with each passing year, increasingly central to the literature of the twentieth century, establishing a new paradigm for fantasy
that has haunted every later writer who has presumed to work in this genre.

I suspect that relatively few readers of Tolkien or viewers of the enormously popular movies based on his books suspect that they are being subjected to Christian propaganda, but Tolkien was a devout believer, and his
trilogy has solid theological underpinnings. Tolkien does not offer us a direct representative of God, and there is almost no talk about God in the

trilogy. But in Tolkien's universe the Good is embodied in a hierarchical structure of interrelationships among created beings. Each order of being (men, elves, dwarves, hobbits, even trees and their guardian Ents) has its own domain, and ideally all of them should work together for the good of the whole. In Tolkien's world, this harmonious hierarchical order *is* God. But Evil enters this world as a will to absolute power that becomes, in practice, a will to nothingness—thus the Ringwraiths have no physical substance, Sauron manifests himself as a kind of magnetic black hole that seeks to suck everything into itself, and the orcs seem to be manufactured rather than born. Theologically, this is all perfectly orthodox Christianity, out of Augustine. In rejecting Manichaeism, Augustine declared that God is Being itself, so that the "opposite" of God cannot be some sort of Satanic anti-God, but nothingness, a total deprivation of Being. Nevertheless, a will to rebel against God's order is inherent in every human heart and threatens always to undermine or destroy His order. Ultimately, only a pure redeemer can save us from the consequences of our inherent egoism, and Tolkien offers us, in Frodo, a Christ figure who frees the earth of evil by carrying the rings of power back to Mordor, where they can be uncreated. Furthermore, not only the theology but the narrative design of *The Lord of the Rings* is shaped by Christian assumptions, for Tolkien has suggested that his goal in the trilogy was to give us, vicariously, the experience of what he calls the "eucatastrophe," the "happy ending" that attests to the intervention of divine grace within the world ("Of Fairy-Stories" 68ff.).

We know that Pullman feels a significant admiration for Tolkien, because he says so: "What I remember from Tolkien was that here was a book full of the most tremendous excitement, with a narrative skill that left me breathless, and which continues to teach, I think, three very interesting things about the quest story, which is the basis of *The Lord of the Rings*" (Lexicon interview). Pullman doesn't go on to tell us what those "three very interesting things about the quest story" might be, but the comment allows us to speculate on some possible Tolkienian influences on *His Dark Materials.* Here I would point, first, to the trilogy form itself. The Victorian "three-decker" has not been a notably popular literary form in the twentieth and twenty-first centuries, but Tolkien memorably revived the form. I can still remember my sense of acute anxiety the first time when (the year was 1966) I came to the end of *The Fellowship of the Ring*, with Boromir dead, and Merry and Pippin in the hands of the orcs, and Frodo preparing to set off alone toward Mordor—I wanted *more*, and I wanted it *now*. And when I saw the film version of *The Fellowship of the Ring*, the audience reacted just as I had done while reading the book, with audible gasps and moans of mixed

pleasure and anxiety. The end of *The Golden Compass* doesn't leave us hanging in the same way, but it is clear that Pullman—like many other contemporary writers, notably Stephen King—learned a great deal about narrative
pace from Tolkien, and about how the multivolume form can generate
"tremendous excitement." Like Tolkien, furthermore, Pullman is writing a
quest story in which talismanic objects—Tolkien's ring, the compass and
the knife and the spyglass of Pullman's trilogy—play a central role. In both
trilogies the future of the universe hinges on the fate of children: the Eng-
lish-schoolboys-with-hairy-feet of Tolkien, and Lyra and Will in Pullman's
trilogy. Both trilogies build to a climactic battle in volume three, and in
these battles we are rooting for an alliance that brings together various kinds
of beings: in Pullman's world, humans-with-daemons and humans-without-
daemons, angels (some of them gay), witches, bears, tiny spies that ride on
dragonflies, and a legion of the dead, versus the more traditional elves,
dwarves, and so forth, of Tolkien's world—although at a climactic moment
in *The Return of the King* Aragorn too marshals an army of the dead.

But Pullman in some interviews has also explicitly rejected Tolkien's
worldview, offering his own trilogy as a critique of and an alternative to
Tolkien's. To one recent interviewer who asks about his relationship to
Tolkien, Pullman says:

> Tolkien also said didn't he—he was accused of escapism? and he said,
> this is a sort of proud banner. He said well if we are in prison it's the
> right thing to do to escape from it. He was like Lewis a sort of thor-
> oughgoing Platonist in that he saw this world, this physical universe
> as a fallen state created no doubt by God but marked and weakened
> and spoiled by sin and his imagined world was so much more truth-
> ful and full of beauty and what have you. Well I passionately disagree
> with this. The physical world is our home, this is where we live, we're
> not creatures from somewhere else or in exile. This is our home and
> we have to make our homes here and understand that we are physical
> too, we are material creatures, we are born and we will die. (Pullman,
> "Faith and Fantasy" interview)

In practice, Tolkien's rejection of the everyday world takes the form, first, of
a blanket erasure of the twentieth century in favor of a vaguely medieval
(and specifically North European, and almost entirely male) world of warrior kings, riders of the "mark," wizards, and goblins. Second, and partly as
a consequence of this medievalism, Tolkien's social world is deeply reac-
tionary, with monarchy as the only imaginable form of governance (thus, if
the king is weak and impotent, all is lost), and with women and 'umble ser-

vants like Sam Gamgee happily accepting their subordination to dominant males.[3] Finally, and most significantly, despite its Augustinian theological underpinnings, *The Lord of the Rings* is ultimately dualistic, positing a struggle between an Absolute Good and an Absolute Evil and inviting us to demonize the Other—Sauron, Saruman, the orcs, and all the vaguely African warriors that fight on Sauron's side—as deserving only annihilation, so that we cheer as they are slaughtered.[4]

In all three of the ways just noted (i.e., attitudes toward the contemporary world, toward hierarchical power structures, and toward the relationship of good and evil), *His Dark Materials* offers an alternative to *The Lord of the Rings*. Pullman's trilogy invokes a primordial Nordic world in some scenes, but the trilogy moves repeatedly into and out of the contemporary world. A computer plays a central role in the plot, and Will's Oxford is distinctly today's slightly grimy academic-industrial city, ringed by comfortable suburbs. Second, Pullman explicitly challenges Tolkien's hierarchical view of the world, rejecting, as in the interview quoted above, the Kingdom of Heaven in favor of, as Lyra puts it in the last line of the trilogy, "the Republic of Heaven" (*Amber Spyglass* [*AS*] 518), a phrase that Pullman has repeatedly quoted in interviews and has used as the title of an essay published in *Horn Book*. Pullman's world includes some putative kings and aristocrats, especially among the bears and the little people. Also, "Lord" Asriel plays a central role, and if Lyra's father is a lord, then presumably Lyra herself is a member of the aristocracy. But she prefers the company of the "gyptian" (i.e., gypsy or Roma) barge dwellers or of decidedly nonaristocratic children like Roger and Will, and several of these nonaristocrats rise to the status of heroes in the trilogy—Will, of course, but also John Faa, for example. Pullman has also challenged traditional gender hierarchies by giving women central roles in his trilogy: Lyra is our quest hero; throughout much of the book the principal villain appears to be Mrs. Coulter; in *The Amber Spyglass* Mary Malone moves into a central role; and witches (a few of them perhaps male, but most of them women) are important throughout the trilogy.

Above all, Pullman rejects Tolkien's metaphysical dualism. Every time we imagine that we've sorted out the good guys and the bad guys, Pullman pulls the rug out from under us. The first scene of *The Golden Compass* seems to establish Lord Asriel as a "good guy" and the Master of Jordan College, who is apparently attempting to poison Asriel, as evil—but then the Master gives Lyra the alethiometer. Throughout most of *The Golden Compass* we assume that Lord Asriel is one of the good guys; but then he kills Roger to advance his experiments, and the final scene of this volume suggests that in fact Lord Asriel and Mrs. Coulter may even be working together. Yet

despite his treatment of Roger, Lord Asriel does not move over definitively
to the Dark Side. Instead, throughout most of the trilogy the Dark Side is
represented primarily by Mrs. Coulter, so that we shudder with dread every
time she comes on stage. And yet in the third volume, as her maternal loyalty to Lyra begins to shape her choices, we also become uncertain about
the moral status of Mrs. Coulter herself. In Tolkien, a few characters (Saruman) move from the Light to the Dark Side, and Gollum, perhaps the most
interesting character in the trilogy, is torn between opposing impulses of
loyalty to Frodo and hunger for the ring. In fact, at the climax of the trilogy Gollum's mixed character allows him to play a decisive role in liberating Middle Earth from the curse of the ring. But most of Tolkien's characters are inherently Good or Evil, each of them choosing sides in the eternal
struggle between these two cosmic forces. Pullman, on the other hand, refuses to predicate Good and Evil as cosmic forces. Rather, for him the
words "good" and "evil" (lowercase now) describe certain potentials mixed
together in every human being, and the relationship between them is worked
out within the human heart. (It is perhaps for this reason that Pullman's
final battle seems so anticlimactic: in *His Dark Materials* the real battles are
internal, not fought with arms.)

Pullman's public statements about C. S. Lewis have been much more
critical than his comments about Tolkien, perhaps because Lewis asserted
his Christian commitments more aggressively than did Tolkien. In a series
of radio broadcasts and lectures delivered primarily in the 1940s and 1950s
and subsequently published as small books, Lewis established himself as an
influential spokesperson for what he called, in a book of that title, "Mere
Christianity," a set of fundamental doctrines that, he contended, anyone
who calls him/herself a Christian must accept: the essential goodness of
the world created by God, the Fall of human beings from an original state
of perfection as a result of their willful disobedience of God's commands,
Christ as the true and only Son of God, the redemption of humans from
their state of sin through Christ's death on the cross, hell as the destiny of
all unbelievers, eternal life in heaven as the reward of all who accept Christ
as their Savior. Lewis presented himself as a Christian ecumenicist, open to
fellowship with all who accepted what he saw as the basic principles of the
Christian faith. But in his insistence on the literal truth of these doctrines,
he was also a proto-Fundamentalist, and among contemporary Fundamentalists, at least in the United States, he remains a kind of cult figure even
today, with study groups and Web sites devoted to his life and teachings.
Along with his career as a religious polemicist, Lewis also published a series
of widely influential works of literary scholarship, most of them about the

literature of the Middle Ages and the Renaissance. *The Allegory of Love,* for example, remains the classic account of the development of the courtly romance from the Middle Ages through Spenser. While he did not use his scholarly writings as a means of proselytizing, Lewis always read the literature of the Middle Ages and the Renaissance as an expression of a Christian worldview. Like Tolkien, he longed for the presumed certainties of the Middle Ages, and in *The Discarded Image* he sought to reconstruct a picture of the universe that had—regrettably in his judgment—been destroyed by modern science. Most significantly for my purposes, Lewis, like many other twentieth-century scholars, saw Milton as the final, and in some way the greatest, spokesperson for the traditional Christian worldview.

Like his friends Tolkien and Dorothy Sayers,[5] Lewis recognized that the genres of popular fiction offer an effective new way of disseminating Christian beliefs. Lewis published three quasi-science fiction "adult" novels, *Out of the Silent Planet, Perelandra,* and *That Hideous Strength,* all of which present modern science as a vicious and dehumanizing mode of thought. Lewis's science fiction trilogy is so explicitly polemical that it now makes many readers uncomfortable, but his seven-volume series of fantasy novels for children, collected as *The Chronicles of Narnia,* is still widely read and admired. Lewis's religious views are not explicitly on display in the Narnia series, but with a little digging it becomes clear that he is again seeking to instill in his readers certain fundamental Christian principles. For example, *The Lion, The Witch, and The Wardrobe,* the first book in the series,[6] begins with a Fall, as one of the four principal characters, Edmund, eats a magical box of Turkish Delight offered him by the White Witch, who turns out to be a combination of Circe and Satan. Narnia is inhabited largely by talking animals, along with some creatures out of Ovid, such as fauns, naiads, dryads, centaurs, and unicorns. Lewis, an orthodox Christian in this respect too, presents these animals and woodland spirits as good. Evil has invaded Narnia from the outside, and most of the native inhabitants long only to see the last of the White Witch (only a few "unnatural" creatures like hags, incubuses, wraiths, specters, and minotaurs are on her side) and to welcome back their natural ruler, the great lion Aslan. Eventually Aslan does return (but we never learn why he has stayed away so long) to liberate Narnia from the spell of permanent winter that the White Witch has placed on the kingdom. However, the White Witch tells Aslan that ancient and inexorable laws dictate that Edmund belongs to her unless an innocent victim agrees to sacrifice his own life. Aslan agrees to die in order to redeem Edmund from the consequences of his sins, and he is brutally killed by the White Witch and her allies. But then Aslan rises from the dead, liberates the captives of the

White Witch, and proceeds to slaughter the witch and all of her allies. In this sequence of events, almost every reader will recognize that Aslan is both God and Christ (for Lewis the two are one), the creator (so we learn in *The Magician's Nephew*—*Chronicles* 64ff.) and natural ruler of the world, who also, however, gives himself over to death in order to release all believers from the burden of their sins but then returns in triumph at the Second Coming to purge the earth of evil.

Pullman has been outspokenly critical of Lewis's Narnia books. In a quickly notorious little essay titled "The Dark Side of Narnia," Pullman, after acknowledging that Lewis's "literary criticism is . . . effortlessly readable" and that Lewis "said some things about myth and fairy tale and writing for children which are both true and interesting," proceeds to denounce the Narnia cycle as "one of the most ugly and poisonous things I've ever read." Specifically, Pullman describes as "one of the most vile moments in the whole of children's literature" the final scene of the series, where the primary protagonists—Edmund, his brother Peter, and his sister Lucy—are on the verge of being reunited with their parents, after a separation that has extended over many volumes. At this moment Aslan reveals to the children that they and their parents are all dead, killed in a railway accident, thereby passing from the "Shadowlands" into the Kingdom of Heaven. "To solve a narrative problem by killing one of your characters is something many authors have done at one time or another," says Pullman. "To slaughter the lot of them, and then claim they're better off, is not honest storytelling: it's propaganda in the service of a life-hating ideology." Pullman also takes issue with Lewis's misogyny and his fear of adult sexuality. In *The Last Battle*, Susan, the fourth of the group of siblings that passes into Narnia at the beginning of the series, is denied salvation because "She's interested in nothing nowadays except nylons and lipstick and invitations. She always was a jolly sight too keen on being grown-up" (Lewis, *Chronicles* 741). "In other words," Pullman comments, "Susan, like Cinderella, is undergoing a transition from one phase of her life to another. Lewis didn't approve of that. He didn't like women in general, or sexuality at all, at least at the stage of his life when he wrote the Narnia books. He was frightened and appalled at the notion of wanting to grow up."[7]

However, I would propose that rather than simply rejecting Lewis as a model, Pullman has, in *His Dark Materials*, offered a kind of inverted homage to his predecessor, deliberately composing a kind of "anti-Narnia," a secular humanist alternative to Lewis's Christian fantasy. First, it seems to me worth noting that both *His Dark Materials* and the Narnia series begin with a young girl hiding in a wardrobe. Lewis's Lucy discovers in the wardrobe a doorway to an alternative universe, while Pullman's Lyra learns there some crucial information that will shape the rest of her life. Both works also emphasize the curiosity of their young protagonists. In this respect Pullman's opening scene establishes a long-term parallel between Lyra and the biblical Eve, whose curiosity leads her to taste the forbidden fruit; but Lewis, surprisingly, also seems to find Lucy's initial trust admirable: the title-page illustration of *The Lion, The Witch, and The Wardrobe* shows Lucy walking off into the woods, arm in arm with the faun that she meets when she first crosses over into Narnia; and surely, we feel, she should be a little uneasy, since a faun is at least a first cousin to a satyr. There is a good deal of vague medievalism in Lewis's fantasy world, much of it centered on Prince Caspian, a central character in two novels of the series. But Lewis's fantasy world, unlike Tolkien's but like Pullman's, also intersects with "our" world in many different ways. At the beginning of *The Lion, The Witch, and The Wardrobe*, Peter, Edmund, Susan, and Lucy (not yet dead, we presume) have been sent to the country to escape the wartime air raids, and they are living with an impossibly avuncular "Professor," who seems to be an only slightly ironic self-portrait of Lewis. The Professor's country home, like Pullman's Oxford, seems "real" enough, as does the thoroughly unpleasant "modern" co-educational school in which Jill Pole, the central character in *The Silver Chair*, is incarcerated at the start of that novel. But Lewis's "real" world contains some windows—at the back of the wardrobe in *The Lion, The Witch, and The Wardrobe*, a gate in a wall behind the gym in *The Silver Chair*—into alternative spaces. So too, beginning in *The Subtle Knife* Pullman's characters also begin to find or create and to pass through windows into alternative worlds. In particular, a scene at the end of Lewis's *Prince Caspian* strikingly anticipates the basic mechanics of Pullman's fantasy world. In this scene, Aslan "makes a door in the air" and invites the "Men of Telmar," citizens of "our" world who have wandered into Narnia by mistake and become trapped there, to pass through. They do so, to find themselves on a presumably uninhabited Pacific island. Then Peter and his siblings pass through too, to find themselves on a platform at a country station, waiting for a train—perhaps, although we are not told this at the time, the one that will carry them to their deaths.[8]

While the machinery of Pullman's fantasy world(s) is similar in important ways to Lewis's, Pullman puts that machinery to very different uses. Rather than simply enumerating these differences, however, I propose at this point to shift gears, and to devote the last part of this essay to a discussion of the role that Milton's *Paradise Lost* plays in Pullman's trilogy. This discussion grows naturally out of the issues I have pursued in the first part of this essay. Both Lewis and Pullman see Milton as a crucial figure in the English literary heritage, but they read *Paradise Lost* in radically different, even diametrically opposed ways, and I believe that the differences between Lewis's Christian worldview and Pullman's secular humanist worldview can usefully be measured by a comparison of their perspectives on Milton's epic. *Paradise Lost* retells the biblical story of human origins, the creation of Adam and Eve and their fall from a state of innocence. Like any origins myth, the biblical story encodes many of the basic assumptions of the culture that has created the story: in this case, assumptions about the relationship of human beings to the cosmos as a whole and to its presumed creator, as well as their relationship to one another—for example, are men created to rule over women, or not? But Milton elaborated this story far beyond what we find in the Bible, and he did so at a particular historical moment, the late seventeenth century. Milton was an enormously learned man, and he knew all the traditional lore surrounding the biblical creation myth, Jewish as well as Christian, heretical as well as orthodox. But Milton's life also overlapped with the lives of Spinoza, Locke, Liebniz, and Newton: with them, he stands on the cusp of modernity, and his poem shows the stress of the relationship between the old and the new. *Paradise Lost* reflects the tensions within Western culture at the moment of its creation, and as a result it lends itself to a variety of readings. In their readings of this complex and ambiguous poem, Lewis and Pullman position themselves within two sharply opposed interpretive traditions, and some discussion of these traditions is therefore in order here.

The "orthodox" reading of *Paradise Lost* and of the biblical creation story that lies behind the poem might be summed up as follows: (1) Before the beginning of time, a group of angels led by Satan and motivated by pure malice rebelled against God's rule and were condemned to Hell. (2) God then created the universe as a hierarchical structure with Himself at the top. In this hierarchy, humans were created to rule over animals, and men to rule over women. God designed the world for the enjoyment of humankind but set one rule: they must not eat the fruit of the tree of knowledge. (3) The original humans, encouraged by Satan, disobeyed God's one command, and at this point they and the world fell into a state of sin, with death as the proper punishment for sin. This Fall is a terrible thing. (4) However, God agrees to release human beings from the consequences of their sins—in effect, to undo the Fall—by offering his only Son as a blood sacrifice. (This last doctrinal principle does not come from Genesis itself but from the New Testament.) For a century after Milton's death, readers of *Paradise Lost* seem

generally to have accepted the poem as grounded in these orthodox Christian doctrines. However, beginning in the late eighteenth century this reading was challenged by a series of important poets and critics who, in the
words of Blake, saw Milton as "a true Poet and of the Devils party without
knowing it" (Blake 35). However, the "orthodox" reading has survived, and
the past two centuries have seen a lively and ongoing debate between what
we might call the "orthodox" and the "Romantic" readings of *Paradise Lost.*

In the twentieth century C. S. Lewis became a—in many ways *the*—
principal spokesperson for the "orthodox" viewpoint. In 1942 Lewis published a short book, *A Preface to "Paradise Lost,"* arguing that "as far as doctrine goes, the poem is overwhelmingly Christian. Except for a few isolated
passages it is not even specifically Protestant or Puritan. It gives the great
central tradition" (91). To Lewis, that is, Milton was a perfectly orthodox
Christian who presented God as Good and Satan as Evil, period, so that any
uncertainties on this point are in the minds of modern skeptical readers,
not in the mind of John Milton. Lewis also sees Milton as a man "enchanted by . . . the Hierarchical principle" (78), assuming without question
that Satan and Adam and Eve should have obeyed God, that Eve should
have obeyed Adam, and that their failure to obey their "natural" superiors
results only in misery for them and their heirs. Lewis's book was enormously popular among scholars and general readers alike, going through
nine printings by 1956, the date of my copy. By the 1960s some readers
were beginning to feel that Lewis oversimplifies the poem, but in 1967
Stanley Fish recast the "orthodox" reading in a more sophisticated form,
proposing that in *Paradise Lost* Milton is deliberately tempting the reader to
identify with Satan only to reveal to us the limitations of our own sinful
ways of thinking; and as Neil Forsyth has recently pointed out (71), for the
past half century the Lewis/Fish reading of *Paradise Lost* has enjoyed virtually hegemonic status among Milton scholars, at least in the United States.
In addition to his critical study of *Paradise Lost,* Lewis also wrote a fictional
adaptation of Milton's poem in one of his science fiction novels, *Perelandra,*
which describes an alternative planet (the one we call Venus) where that
planet's Adam and Eve live in a state of primordial innocence. Satan arrives
on the planet in the form of a physicist from Earth named Dr. Weston. But
with the advice of a visiting philologist from Earth who bears a remarkable
similarity to Lewis himself, the Adam and Eve of Perelandra are able to resist the temptation offered by Dr. Weston, so that this time the Fall never
occurs. In his novel as in his book on *Paradise Lost,* then, Lewis assumes that
the Fall was an unmitigated disaster, and that on this earth our one goal

should be to recover the state of innocence that we lost when our "first parents" committed the original sin that still taints us all.

But the "orthodox" reading of Milton's poem has not gone unchallenged. Like Blake, Shelley and Byron regarded Milton's God as an unjust and arbitrary tyrant, and they saw Satan the "true hero" of *Paradise Lost,* a gallant Promethean rebel fighting on in a cause that he knows is doomed but still insists is just. This interpretation enjoyed widespread popularity in the nineteenth century: Melville's Ahab, for example, represents a late version of the Romantic Promethean rebel, with distinct Satanic overtones. During the twentieth century, an increasing interest in Blake and a recognition of Blake's empathy with Milton have encouraged research into the potentially heretical dimensions of Milton's poem. As early as the 1920s, Dennis Saurat proposed that "the 'Puritan' Milton and the 'Swedenborgian' Blake" had more in common than was generally assumed: both were, he declared, radical heretics, drawing on a heritage of Kabbalism (v). Lewis devoted a good deal of energy to trying to refute Saurat's argument, but in the wake of Lewis's *Preface,* William Empson also forcefully challenged what he called the "neo-Christian" reading of *Paradise Lost,* arguing instead that the Romantics were quite right to see Milton's God as a cruel tyrant. And in less confrontational ways, many recent commentators have reopened the question of Milton's "heresies," offering us a Milton much more radical, much more engaged with the new social and intellectual possibilities opening up in the seventeenth century, than the proponents of the "orthodox" Milton have recognized. Many of these critics have also explored the ways in which within *Paradise Lost* God and Satan, Adam and Eve, are bound up with one another in relationships that are unstable because they are at once hierarchical and reciprocal, thus calling into question the neat dualisms that Lewis saw in the poem.[9]

No less than Lewis, Pullman is fascinated by *Paradise Lost.* He borrows the title of his trilogy and many of the epigraphs in *The Amber Spyglass* from Milton's poem. In one interview, Pullman says, "*Paradise Lost . . .* was the starting point for me. I've loved that poem ever since I was 16. . . . I found it intensely enthralling, not only the actual story—the story of the temptation and so on—but also the landscapes, the power of the poetry and the extraordinary majesty of the language, which excited me then and continues to excite me now" (Lexicon interview). Pullman is, I believe, fully aware of the quarrel between the neo-Christian and the Romantic, Blakean view of Milton; and in the trilogy he has developed what I take to be a Blakean redaction of the Miltonic mythos, directed against the neo-Christian readings of Lewis and others. The passage from *Paradise Lost* that Pullman selects as his epigraph, and that provides the title of his trilogy, provides an initial clue:

> Into this wilde Abyss,
> The Womb of nature and perhaps her Grave,
> Of neither Sea, nor Shore, nor Air, nor Fire,
> But all these in thir pregnant causes mixed
> Confus'dly, and which thus must ever fight,
> Unless th' Almighty Maker them ordain
> His dark materials to create more Worlds,
> Into this wilde Abyss the warie fiend
> Stood on the brink of Hell and look'd a while,
> Pondering his Voyage . . .
>   (Book II, lines 910–19)[10]

We stand here not at a moment of fixed certainties but of maximum potentiality. We are looking out at Chaos, which comes in some fashion "before" God Himself. In Chaos, light and darkness, male and female (note that Chaos has a "womb" and is "pregnant") have not yet been sorted out and classified as "good" or "evil." Out of this clash of opposites, not only our world but many worlds (and indeed, is it not possible that each of us has her own world?) may come. Pullman, like Blake and many other later readers of Milton, wants to recover this moment of infinite possibility, not the world for which Christians like Lewis long, in which Good and Evil stand against one another as clearly defined alternatives and implacable enemies.

In any theodicy, the status of the Other, of that which is *not* God, is primary. Thus, daringly, Milton begins his poem not with God or man but with Satan. So too, at the very beginning of Pullman's trilogy, we meet his "Satan," Lord Asriel, who is, we learn, in rebellion against the forces that claim to represent God, determined to break down the barriers that separate his world from the other worlds that he knows are, as Mulder of *The X-Files* would say, "out there." From the beginning Asriel has a distinctly Byronic aura of injured merit and defiance in the face of his enemies—and this Byronic role, historically, owes much to Milton's Satan. Like Milton's Satan in Books I and II of *Paradise Lost*, Lord Asriel builds his own kingdom apart from and in defiance of God, and like the Satan of Books V and VI he leads a rebel army in a battle against God's army—although in Milton the battle precedes the building of the kingdom apart, while in *His Dark Materials* Lord Asriel first builds his citadel and then leads his hosts into battle against God. We find ourselves rooting for Lord Asriel in the battle, but he is by no means an entirely positive figure. "Asriel" seems, to my ear, phonetically identical with "Azrael," the angel of death in many mythological traditions. My *American Heritage Dictionary* tells me that Azrael is "the angel that separates the soul from the body at death in Jewish and Moslem legend"—a definition that gives a very particular significance to the last scene of *The Golden Compass*, where Lord Asriel, in the attempt to open a pathway to other worlds, releases a burst of energy by severing the link between Roger and his daemon, killing the boy in the process. Here Asriel becomes a kind of Nietzschean *übermensch*, willing to go beyond good and evil in quest of his goals, yet we respond not with sympathy but with horror. And while Lord Asriel partly redeems himself for this murder by his final self-sacrifice for Lyra, he is not the "true hero" of Pullman's trilogy, just as, the Romantics to the contrary, Satan isn't the "true hero" of *Paradise Lost* either. Pullman's hero is Lyra, not her father, with Will in an important ancillary role. So too, I think that Pullman probably shares my belief that the "true hero" of Milton's poem is Eve, with Adam in an important ancillary role.

But what of Satan's great antagonist, God, the "Almighty"? Pullman follows Nietzsche in giving us a God who has been growing increasingly enfeebled for centuries, surviving only by being hermetically sealed in a crystal box, and who finally dies on page 410 of *The Amber Spyglass*. Milton's God is not yet dead, but some competent observers, including William Empson, have felt that he is at least moribund and deserves to die. While Satan is an active, energetic force moving about the cosmos, Milton's God remains immobile and invisible atop his mountain in heaven. Milton's God *does* speak, at length in Book II and more briefly later. However, his discourse is notoriously arid and unpersuasive—even Lewis, while defending Milton's presumed Christian theology, doesn't try to defend God as a character in the poem. Most readers still come away from *Paradise Lost* with a sense that "God" is auto-intoxicated with His own power, willing to tolerate enormous human suffering merely to prove that He was right in the first place. Midway between Milton's God and Pullman's senile Ancient of Days, we might put Blake's Nobodaddy (Blake 462–63), God as the voice of repression and denial. In this respect Pullman stands at the end of a tradition that extends from the seventeenth century, and his message seems remarkably straightforward. Once, surely, the word "God" named a powerful and vivid presence in people's lives—if we want to recover what that experience was like, we need only read the Bible. But this God has been dying for centuries, and all that is left is the machinery of repression and self-aggrandizement created in His name—the still-universal Church of Lyra's world, or the various churches of our world. Today, when people speak of God in anything except a historical sense, they are not talking about the ineffable Presence Who revealed Himself to Abraham. Rather, Pullman implies, they are talking about an idol that they have created in order to justify their power over others—a power that they seek, Pullman suggests, because they hate the life within themselves and want to destroy the life they see around them. Brutally and brilliantly, Pullman's portraits of Mrs. Coulter the opportunist and Father Gomez the fanatic reveal what "religion" has become in our time.

In Milton's world Satan claims to be the "opposite" of God. But monotheism says that there can be but one God, so Satan must be deluded. Yet Milton's God allows Satan the freedom to move about the world, and even to tempt Adam and Eve into sin. Is it possible that God is in fact not all-powerful? Are there two "gods" at work in the universe, one good and the other evil? Or if God is all-powerful, then is He Himself responsible for the Fall? Does He bring sin into the world? In the course of Milton's poem, an array of ambiguities assembles around these questions, for in practice, as such recent critics as Forsyth have suggested, God and Satan seem to need each other. Without Satan God's universe remains static, immobile—and, from a human perspective, intolerably dull. What sort of God would want to sit around for eternity as His angels sing hymns in His praise? The emergence of Satan thus initiates a dialectic that gives us the world of time and history in which we live, and if we love that world, then we must celebrate rather than lament the process that brought it into existence. Thus we arrive at the concept of the Fortunate Fall. In *Paradise Lost* Milton edges nervously around the heretical idea that the Fall might have been a good thing. But as we approach the end of the poem, Adam explicitly articulates the doubts that have been growing within the reader:

> . . . full of doubt I stand,
> Whether I should repent me now of sin
> By mee done and occasiond, or rejoyce
> Much more, that much more good thereof shall spring,
> To God more glory, more good will to Men
> From God, and over wrauth grace shall abound.
>   (Book XII, lines 471–78)

It must be acknowledged that Adam is here talking specifically about the redemptive work of Christ, which could not have happened had Eve and Adam not sinned. Yet Adam's words also allow us to acknowledge that the

Fall brings into existence humanity as we know it—and if we love the human, then we must affirm the Fall as well.

Ultimately, for Milton humans differ from all other beings in the universe in that they can choose between good and evil. God cannot choose
evil; the fallen angels, once fallen, cannot choose good. But Adam and Eve
can choose evil, repent, and choose good thereafter. Humans alone, then, are
moral beings, and for this reason they are the glory of the universe. If we
see the series of events that Milton narrates as having the ultimate purpose
of bringing into existence the possibility of human freedom, then it would
seem that the "true hero" of *Paradise Lost* is not the Son or the Serpent or
even Adam, but Eve. For it is Eve who, instinctively refusing even before the
Fall to accept a status as inferior (see the arguments that she presents for
going off on her own, in Book IX, line 206ff.), and curious about exactly
what "knowledge" eating the fruit might bring, causes the Fall. Does Milton blame Eve for all the ills that humankind suffers? Perhaps so, but we can
as easily see him praising her for making possible our entrance into a full
human estate. Further, after the Fall, when Adam vociferously blames Eve
for what has happened, it is Eve who begs forgiveness and who offers to kill
herself so that humankind will not have to suffer the consequences of her
sin. At this moment Eve becomes not only the prime mover of our entrance
into a fully human condition but also a proto-Christ, bearing the responsibility of all sin on her own shoulders. In these ways the logic of Milton's
poems carries us toward a definition of the uniquely human. We might say
that in Milton's universe God and Satan ultimately cancel each other out,
leaving us with Adam and Eve, our first parents, who in the last lines of the
epic leave Paradise to build the human world, the world of history that we
inhabit:

> The World was all before them, where to choose
> Thir place of rest, and Providence thir guide:
> They hand in hand with wandring steps and slow,
> Through *Eden* took thir solitarie way.
>   (Book XII, lines 646–49)

In the reading of *Paradise Lost* that I have here proposed, I have drawn on
many commentators on Milton, from Blake down to, most recently, Rumrich and Forsyth. But I have also had *His Dark Materials* in mind throughout,
for Pullman has given us, I am suggesting, a similar reading of Milton's
poem. By making the incorrigibly curious Lyra the center of his narrative,
Pullman acknowledges the dynamic and creative role of Eve in Milton's

poem, thus challenging not only Lewis but the feminist critics, most notoriously Sandra Gilbert, who basically accept Lewis's reading of the poem but turn that reading on its head, condemning rather than celebrating Milton's sense of male/female relations. And the logic of Pullman's narrative follows a dialectic that parallels Milton's. In *The Amber Spyglass*, at the very moment (or so it would seem) that Lyra and Will release God from his crystal cabinet, allowing him to dissolve into the cosmos, Lord Asriel, our Satan figure, and Mrs. Coulter are wrestling with Metatron, the angel who has claimed for himself the authority of God (*AS* 406–11). Mrs. Coulter has, of course, been an ambiguous figure throughout the trilogy, sometimes an opportunistic agent of the Church, sometimes a devoted mother to Lyra. But at the decisive moment in the battle, she chooses Lyra over everything else in the cosmos and hurls herself at Asriel and Metatron, sending all three of them down into the abyss. "God" and "Satan" thus perish together, leaving us with the human, Lyra and Will. Our young protagonists are, we should finally note, simultaneously "special," unique within the universe, potentially the initiators of a new stage in the evolution of humankind—thus the great fuss that everyone makes over them, especially Lyra, throughout the book—and also Everywoman and Everyman, for does not each of us pass through the great transition into full adult responsibility that Lyra and Will experience in the course of the trilogy? In their dual role as simultaneously unique beings, beings upon whom the entire future of the cosmos depends, and as Everywoman and Everyman, Lyra and Will are once again avatars of Adam and Eve. Thus, by invoking the great parallel of Milton's poem, Pullman reminds us that each moral choice changes the universe and that each one of us carries the future of the cosmos on our shoulders.

Notes

1. I will not here attempt to offer a full account of "the Inklings," a group of Oxford Christian academics centered on Lewis, Tolkien, and Charles Williams, also both a literary scholar and a novelist with theological interests. For a full biographical account of the group, which met regularly during the 1930s and 1940s to discuss their works in progress, see Humphrey Carpenter's *The Inklings*.

2. The phrase "secular humanism" has been a loaded term since the Reverend Jerry Falwell adopted it as a derogatory label to describe everything he sees as wrong with contemporary America. For Falwell and other fundamentalists, there is a "culture war" in America today between the Christians and the secular humanists. The phrase, however, was originally coined by John Dewey to describe the

belief that we can no longer look for divine guidance but must work out our destiny cooperatively on this earth. And the phrase seems to me to define quite precisely Pullman's avowed beliefs: "I think it's time we thought about a republic of heaven instead of the kingdom of heaven. The king is dead. That's to say I believe that the king is dead. I'm an atheist. But we need heaven nonetheless, we need all the things that heaven meant, we need joy, we need a sense of meaning and purpose in our lives, we need a connection with the universe, we need all the things that the kingdom of heaven used to promise us but failed to deliver. And, furthermore, we need it in this world where we do exist—not elsewhere, because there ain't no elsewhere" (Lexicon interview).

3. Tolkien does offer us a token woman warrior, but even in this respect Tolkien's social world remains safely traditional, for Eowyn has a direct Renaissance prototype in Spenser's Britomart. And by the end of the trilogy, Eowyn has returned to a more conventional female role.

4. The implications of this dualism are perhaps clearer in the film versions than on the page. In Tolkien's trilogy we are never invited to imagine what an orc might be thinking or feeling, but on the screen it is clear that the orcs are being played by human beings, whose humanity has, however, been effaced by makeup, so that we are free to rejoice as they are slaughtered—but leaving some of us feeling, afterward, a little sickened by our bloodlust.

5. Sayers, a longtime friend of Lewis but never an official member of the Inklings (an all-male group), was one of the great Dante scholars of the twentieth century and author of a still widely read translation of Dante's *Divine Comedy*. She was also a sometime theologian, author of a book titled *The Mind of the Maker*. But she is today best remembered as the author of a series of detective novels featuring Lord Peter Whimsey.

6. In the one-volume edition, *The Chronicles of Narnia*, *The Magician's Nephew* comes first, Lewis's preferred order because *The Magician's Nephew* gives some background information on Narnia. But *The Lion, The Witch, and The Wardrobe* was the first of the books to be published, and it introduces us both to the major symbolic patterns and to the four children who will remain the principal recurrent characters throughout the series, so many readers still regard it as the beginning of the series.

7. Lewis would probably defend himself by pointing to Jesus' statement that we must become as little children to enter the kingdom of God, but Pullman might respond that this statement is not to be taken literally—that Jesus isn't really telling us that we should try to die before puberty, to avoid the inevitable stains and compromises of adulthood.

8. Of course, Lewis did not invent the idea of "windows" or "portals" opening on alternative worlds. Dante passes through such a portal at the start of the *Divine Comedy*, and immediate precedents, certainly important to both Lewis and Pullman, are Lewis Carroll's Alice books. However, the parallels between the Narnia books and Pullman's trilogy seem to me sufficiently close as to suggest that Pullman has directly adapted this plot device from Lewis.

9. See, e.g., Hyman, Lieb, Schwartz, Belsey, Rumrich, and Forsyth.

10. Here as throughout I quote from *The Student's Milton*, which provides an original-spelling text.

Works Cited

Belsey, Catherine. *John Milton: Language, Gender, Power.* Oxford: Blackwell, 1988.

Blake, William. *The Poetry and Prose of William Blake.* Ed. David V. Erdman. Garden City, NY: Doubleday, 1965.

Carpenter, Humphrey. *The Inklings: C. S. Lewis, J. R. R. Tolkien, Charles Williams and Their Friends.* Boston: Houghton Mifflin, 1979.

Empson, William. *Milton's God.* London: Chatto and Windus, 1961.

Forsyth, Neil. *The Satanic Epic.* Princeton: Princeton UP, 2003.

Gilbert, Sandra. "Patriarchal Poetry and Women Readers: Reflections on Milton's Bogey." *PMLA* 93 (1978): 368–82.

Hyman, Lawrence W. *The Quarrel Within: Art and Morality in Milton's Poetry.* Port Washington, NY: Kennikat, 1972.

Lewis, C. S. *The Chronicles of Narnia.* (1950–56). New York: HarperCollins, 2001.

———. *The Discarded Image: An Introduction to Medieval and Renaissance Literature.* 1964. Cambridge: Cambridge UP, 1971.

———. *Mere Christianity.* 1952. London, Fontana, 1963.

———. *Perelandra.* 1944. New York: Macmillan, 1971.

———. *A Preface to Paradise Lost.* 1942. London: Oxford UP, 1956.

———. *That Hideous Strength.* 1946. New York: Macmillan, 1972.

Lieb, Michael. *The Dialectics of Creation: Patterns of Birth and Regeneration in Paradise Lost.* Amherst: U of Massachusetts P, 1970.

Milton, John. *The Student's Milton.* Ed. Frank Allen Patterson. Rev. ed. New York: Appleton-Century-Crofts, 1933.

Pullman, Philip. *The Amber Spyglass.* New York: Knopf, 2000.

———. "The Dark Side of Narnia." *The Guardian* (October 1, 1998). http://web.archive.org/web/20010628221443/http://riff.hiof.no./~steinabl/PULLMAN-LEW.HTML.

———. "Faith and Fantasy," Radio National Encounter Interview March 24, 2002. http://www.abc.net.au/rn/relig/enc/stories/s510312.htm.

———. *The Golden Compass.* 1996. New York: Knopf, 2002.

———. Lexicon interview with "TB" (October 2000). http://www.avnet.co.uk/home/amaranth/Critic/ivpullman.htm.

———. "The Republic of Heaven." *Horn Book* November/December 2001: 655–67.

———. *The Subtle Knife.* 1997. New York: Knopf, 2002.

Rumrich, John Peter. *Matter of Glory: A New Preface to Paradise Lost.* Pittsburgh: U of Pittsburgh P, 1987.

———. *Milton Unbound: Controversy and Reinterpretation.* Cambridge: Cambridge UP, 1996.

Rumrich, John Peter, and Stephan Dobranski, eds. *Milton and Heresy.* Cambridge: Cambridge UP, 1998.

Saurat, Dennis. *Milton, Man and Thinker.* New York: Dial, 1925.

Schwartz, Regina M. *Remembering and Repeating: Biblical Creation in Paradise Lost.* Cambridge: Cambridge UP, 1988.

Tolkien, J. R. R. *The Fellowship of the Ring.* New York: Ballantine, 1973.

————. "On Fairy-Stories." *Tree and Leaf.* Boston: Houghton Mifflin, 1965. 3–84.

————. *The Return of the King.* New York: Ballantine, 1973.

————. *The Two Towers.* New York: Ballantine, 1973.

6

Pullman's Enigmatic Ontology:
Revamping Old Traditions in *His Dark Materials*

CAROLE SCOTT

Pullman's assertion of a Milton-Blake ontological framework for his trilogy places him in a challenging force field whose energy crackles throughout the three novels. While both of his declared precursors produced works of compelling imagery—Milton's fantastic pictures created in words alone, Blake's both verbal and graphic—their theological approaches are highly divergent. In the creation of their ontological worlds, each danced with heresy. But while the Puritan writer Milton's approach was imbued with logical, even legal care, working strictly within biblical parameters as he sought in *Paradise Lost* to "justify the ways of God to men," Blake's wild visions of interactions with a fantastic and intricate hierarchy of good and evil are very personal. Pullman explicitly includes both writers in his trilogy: its title is taken directly from *Paradise Lost* (II: 916), and quotations from Milton's epic poem and Blake's works[1] are placed at the beginning of each chapter of the U.K. edition of *The Amber Spyglass*.[2]

This essay will explore how Pullman has used his three major literary sources—Milton, Blake, and the Bible—to reinterpret the ontology of humankind's moral and ethical universe, and to redefine humankind's quest for a meaningful purpose in life and the individual's responsibility in defining good and evil. In a work of remarkable ingenuity and power, he melds this wide continuum of philosophies and perspectives, old and new, into a unique world picture, creates a panoply of extraordinary characters representing many dimensions of the imagination, and boldly reshapes the biblical story with extraordinary new images and events. The intricate threads of relationship interweaving the three sources make the examination of Pullman's ontology remarkably complicated, incorporating a many-layered intertextuality. Not only did Blake decree that Milton was "of the Devil's party without knowing it,"[3] Blake also asserted that he wrote his poem titled

"Milton" because "Milton came back to earth and begged him to refute the errors of his own epic" (*William Blake* 48). Thus, while Pullman, Blake, and Milton all interpret the biblical themes and narratives in the context of contemporary thought and church doctrine, Blake also interprets Milton's interpretation, and Pullman reflects and re-creates them all. In this way, Pullman's trilogy becomes a triumph of intertextuality, with text quoting text and image quoting image in a metaphorical reflective hall of mirrors.

While Pullman may acknowledge his debts to these literary forebears, he has created an ontology at least as complex, and quite as singular, as theirs. He imports the relatively recent conviction that God is dead and that the divine structures have been usurped by wickedness. He depicts a debased church plagued by a Machiavellianism of the basest kind and asserts through Mary Malone that "the Christian religion is a very powerful and convincing mistake, that's all" (*Amber Spyglass* [*AS*] 464). He attacks the hierarchy of a Christian theology, replacing God with the Authority—a withered, decrepit old man in a glass box—and Metatron, the usurping spirit tormented by human lust who has seized tyrannical power for evil purposes. Nonetheless, albeit with imaginative reconstruction, Pullman continues to employ Christianity's humanistic ethics, traditions, and values; its biblical themes and narratives; its symbolism expressed in both the Bible and church rituals; and often its diction. Finally, we find a religious, even puritanical streak in his sense of every person's ultimate responsibility to humankind, even at the expense of their own happiness.

Especially cogent examples include Lyra's identification as the second Eve (though this title has usually belonged to the Virgin Mary) and pivotal events referring to Adam and Eve's Fall, Christ's Redemption of Humankind, and the Harrowing of Hell. Thus, after entering the world of the dead and freeing the lost souls, Lyra and Will share fruit and embark on the lovemaking that stops the disastrous loss of Dust from the world. Another allusion to the Fall occurs in the story of the *mulefa*'s momentous discovery of consciousness of self by means of the seedpod, which mimics Eve's apple. Not only is there a snake entwined in this fruit, but also its precious oil serves to give special sight both to the *mulefa* and to Mary Malone. This property suggests the holy oil of church ritual, which changes people's perception and marks entry into new life. Finally, Pullman's evocatively imagistic invention of the daemon to represent an aspect of humankind's psyche is carefully established in a trinity of body, soul, and spirit, thoughtfully explained in *The Amber Spyglass*.

As the anticipated "second Eve"—a young girl replacing the usual Christ figure as second Adam—Lyra's role focuses the book upon the battle of good and evil for the soul of humankind, the key theme of the biblical story, Milton's *Paradise Lost,* and most of Blake's work. This battle is expressed both externally, through church powers and supernatural forces (angels, devils, witches, imaginative figures), and internally, in the landscape of the soul, where innocence meets experience, and human emotions and thoughts interplay. Pullman states his vision of the battle in the deathbed speech of Will's father:

> There are two great powers . . . and they have been fighting since time began. Every advance in human life, every scrap of knowledge and wisdom and decency we have has been torn by one side from the teeth of the other. Every little increase in human freedom has been fought over ferociously between those who want us to know more and be wiser and stronger, and those who want us to obey and be humble and submit. (*Subtle Knife* [*SK*] 335)

Pullman, Blake, and Milton all share great cynicism regarding the church's part in this battle, perceiving corruption and a destructive use of power in which politics and debased practices have joined with the forces of evil to seduce and bully people from the truth. Pullman's vision of the church is not only represented by its multiple organizations—the Magisterium, its Consistorial Court of Discipline, Society of the Work of the Holy Spirit, and General Oblation Board, the latter experimenting with cutting apart children and their daemon-souls—but by the creation of well-defined individual characters. The passionately depraved priest, Father Gomez, receives advance "preemptive" absolution for the intended murder of Lyra, while in contrast the "tempter" who aids Lyra in her redemptive act is a former nun who has abjured a loveless and meaningless church for significant and joyful relationships with other beings and with the natural world.

Pullman acknowledges his consonance with Milton's sense of a debased church, referring to the "Reliques, beads, dispenses, pardons, bulls, the sport of winds" of *Paradise Lost* (III: 492–93). But he goes much further than either of his literary forebears in not only rejecting corrupt human beings but also in identifying depravity in the celestial powers. The Authority (also named God, the Creator, the Lord, Yahweh, El, Adonai, the King, the Father, the Almighty) lied to the other angels and assumed power, choosing Metatron as his Regent; he appears at the end of the trilogy as the anguished Ancient of Days, a withered figure in a crystal shell, mercifully released to disintegration by Will and Lyra. The allegiances of Pullman's figures are enigmatic and the reader often unclear on whom to trust. In this he differs from Milton and Blake, both of whom perceived a clear division between figures of good and evil: Milton's theologically hierarchical power structures distinguish "Thrones, Dominations, Princedoms, Virtues, Powers" (*Paradise Lost* [*PL*] V: 772) and their dim reflection in Hell's mimicry; Blake's symbolic and prophetic figures, based on his fanciful understanding of Hebraic-Christian models, are similarly divided into good and evil, though they are capable of change and transition.

We soon learn to identify the evil Mrs. Coulter and her colleagues, but our early faith in Lord Asriel is shattered when he destroys Roger, cutting apart body and daemon-soul to obtain the energy needed for his scientific experiment. This makes the reader wary of trusting Asriel's rebellion against the Authority, although we are led to believe his cause is just. While some grotesque figures are quite obviously evil—for example, the Specters and cliff-ghasts—ascertaining the good and evil powers, people, and actions is challenging, as is the slow, tantalizing accretion of information regarding the ontology that drives the trilogy. Mary Malone explains that she still believes in good and evil, but not in powers "outside us . . . good and evil are names for what people do, not for what they are" (*AS* 470). Lyra and Will become our only clear touchstones of value: those who love them and whom they truly trust—Iorek Byrnison, John Faa, Lee Scoresby, Serafina Pekkala, Balthamos and Baruch, Will's father, and Mary Malone—emerge as figures of worth, strongly defined by their capacity for love, which proves, through Lyra and Will's loving, to be the symbol of the world's redemption. Pullman's strong affirmation of love, both eros and agape, adds dimension to the biblical story, as well as echoing Milton's and Blake's interpretations of it.

Milton's influence is also seen in the architecture of Pullman's universe, the sense of the mythical/religious backdrop against which human life is played out, and, perhaps most pervasive, the sense of justification for humankind's purpose on earth. This involves explaining the rules; clarifying what is good and what is evil and how they are recognized, and revealing how sin, redemption, faith, and works are all landmarks and signs that guide and make sense of each individual's voyage through life's landscape, a terrain whose dimensions are limned in human, interactional, and psychic terms. Though the scope of Pullman's universe, unlike Milton's, is unbounded, both employ a spatial context: Milton's carefully constructed geographic cosmos establishes heaven above, hell below, while earth is suspended from heaven by a golden chain, all in a sea of chaos. Pullman takes the theoretical aspects of contiguous worlds, but concretizes them into tangible constructs as Will precisely manipulates the positions of his windows as though the worlds he transverses lie physically one against the other.

Half of the quotes Pullman chooses from Milton come from Book I of *Paradise Lost,* where Satan attempts to re-create in hell the pomp and magnificence of heaven. The grand scale of Milton's vision is very much an aspect of Pullman's trilogy, with the warfare an excellent example. Milton asks us "how shall I relate / To human sense th'invisible exploits / Of warring Spirits" (V: 564–66), and indeed his tumultuous war in heaven, with its divine weaponry and angels tossing mountains at each other, at times reminds the modern reader of an animated film. Pullman's battles are described in more immediate terms, and include the armored bears' duel and Lee Scoresby's sacrificial stand as sharpshooter, in addition to the overwhelming final war where the dead take on the Specters. Here the tumult of technologically advanced armaments creates the terrifying environment in which Will and Lyra seek the safety of their daemons.

Like Milton, who spent enormous effort on bringing the classical and Christian traditions into harmonious union, so Pullman unites spirituality with the study of the physical universe, conflating the two dynamically opposed ways of knowing—religious and scientific—into one: thus God's "Dark Materials" are allied to Mary Malone's Dark Matter Research Unit. Pullman accepts the spirit-science continuum as an expression of human striving for the truth. He begins by establishing the existence of "experimental theology," with its philosophical instruments of wire, porcelain, and other laboratory equipment in Lyra's Jordan College, a subject Will asserts that in his world "sounds like what we call physics" (*SK* 60). At Jordan this physics-theology has given rise to various theories, including those of the "renegade theologians," Barnard and Stokes, "who postulated the existence of numerous other worlds like this one, neither heaven nor hell, but material and sinful. There they are, close by, but invisible and unreachable . . . [and] there seem to be sound mathematical arguments for this other-world theory" (*Northern Lights* [*NL*] 31–32). Here, Pullman has clearly drawn on contemporary thought reflecting Heisenberg's principle, which suggests that "we live not in a single universe but an infinite number of parallel ones [with] matter continuously 'fluctuating' between one state of reality and another" (Berry). More recently, physicists who developed mathematically-based String Theory also postulate another dimension involving alternative universes.

The trilogy brings these theories into play by breaching the boundaries of the worlds, first by Asriel's release of energy from Roger's intercision, and then through the agency of the subtle knife, whose cutting power must be directed by Will's mind. At the heart of Pullman's cosmology lie deeper uses of science-soul. Lyra's alethiometer is an intricate mechanism that works with some level of her mind. It is paralleled in Will's world by Mary Malone's computer, a machine whose hardware and software are created by rational thought but whose ultimate power relies on aspects of the human mind similar to those Lyra brings to bear, aspects of intuitiveness and of spirituality. For Mary uses her computer as a medium in her search to understand Dust and the meaning of good and evil. Yet another example of this science-spirit alliance is the intention craft, the vehicle that Mrs. Coulter steals from Asriel, created by one aspect of human intelligence and guided by another, with the daemon-soul and the human being working in concert to direct it.

The second vital element of soul-self is represented by Dust, Shadows, or *sraf*. These "particles of consciousness" (*SK* 92) constitute the physical expression of an intelligent life force, one that is inherently moral both in human and in ecological terms and that supports the symbiotic nurturing of humankind and the natural world. Viewed as the essence of goodness, or the epitome of evil, depending on the character's allegiance and perspective, Dust is described by the angel Balthamos as "only a name for what happens when matter begins to understand itself. Matter loves matter. It seeks to know more about itself, and Dust is formed" (*AS* 33). Again the scientific-spiritual approach is evident as Mary notes that a colleague in archeology had discovered the increase in Shadows associated with human remains that began thirty thousand years ago, and "had to do with the great change in human history symbolized in the story of Adam and Eve; with the Temptation, the Fall, Original Sin" (235). Pullman creates the highly original *mulefa*, sentient beings whose self-awareness occurred in the same time period that Mary identifies. The history of their awareness mimics the Temptation in its involvement of seedpod and snake. And it is the oil of this fruit of the seedpod trees that bestows consciousness upon the *mulefa* and enables them to see the aura around all sentient creatures, the golden haze they term *sraf*. It is this oil upon the amber spyglass that enables Mary, too, to perceive the *sraf*, or Dust, she has sought so long.

This concept lies at the heart of Pullman's ontology and provides an opportunity to perceive Pullman's genius in partaking of and transforming the tradition in which he is working. In the King James Bible, "dust" is the word God uses to describe the essence of humankind: "for dust thou art, and unto dust shalt thou return" (Genesis 3:19). Milton continues this use when Raphael describes the Creation to Adam: "he form'd thee, *Adam*, thee O Man / Dust of the ground" (*PL* VII: 524–55), and in God's pronouncement after the Fall, "for thou / Out of the ground wast taken, know thy Birth, / For dust thou art, and shalt to dust return" (*PL* X: 206–08).

Blake's use of the word moves away from the biblical echo toward a more visionary understanding. In the U.K. edition of *The Amber Spyglass*, Pullman uses as a chapter heading Blake's line "Shew you all alive the world, where every particle of dust breathes forth its joy" (*Europe* 18; *AS* 472). Certainly Milton had lauded a Paradise described in sensuous terms, and within it the physical love of Adam and Eve "Imparadis't in one another's arms" enjoying their fill "Of bliss on bliss" (*PL* IV: 506–08), where thought is not seen to be degraded by sexuality as earlier church philosophers had averred. But Blake's vision of joyous love, emancipated from its fetters like the rose from its "invisible worm," is far more encompassing, permeating his work, and reversing the earlier tradition so that it becomes central to his sense of the way humankind may achieve freedom. Pullman's trilogy moves even further in this direction, so that Dust is the central life force of an intelligent and caring universe, affecting not only humankind but the entire natural world as well. The sickness of the world, as Pullman sees it, is not simply one of a corrupt power structure, but one where the Dust has been leaking into the Abyss of nothingness. To correct this malady, Asriel and Coulter must sacrifice their own lives to destroy the evil Metatron. But this is insufficient: Will and Lyra must return alone to their separate realms after breaking the knife that creates Specters and causes Dust to leak each time it is used to move from world to world.

It is particularly interesting to trace some of the quite specific features that Pullman has taken and transformed from his earlier models. Milton melded classical and Judeo-Christian traditions in constructing *Paradise Lost*. He used epic similes from classical tradition, such as the first descriptions of the fallen angels; and he ironically patterned Satan's creation of Sin on the birth of Athene from Zeus's head. Pullman similarly took the classical boatman who rows the dead to the underworld to ferry Lyra across the water to the land of the dead as well as incorporating the classical harpies to torture the lost souls. Milton brings the angels to describe the Creation and the war in heaven and to give advice to Adam; Pullman brings angels to explain the warring elements to Lyra and Will and to describe the long battle between good and evil; they also support Will and Lyra in their quest and destroy Father Gomez.

Pullman goes further than Milton in taking figures not simply from the classical tradition but from other legends. Thus Pullman draws witches into his trilogy in a significant way, not only as actors in events but also as beings with their own lore and philosophy. We learn about their relationships with human beings, their sense of time, their deaths when Yambe-Akka comes, their values, their use of cloud pine, and their spells and medicines. He introduces shamanism through the experiences of Will's father. And added to these extant legendary figures are the beings he, like Blake, creates from his own imagination: Iorek Byrnison and the armored bears, with their straight-forward loyalties; the Gallivespians, with their intelligence, their gallantry and the sense of honor that informs their brief lives; and the *mulefa*, whose peaceful collaborative existence, tending the environment in a long and significant symbiosis, has led to the vision of a right life. However, while Blake's figures remain visionary and cloudy, the conceptions of Pullman's creatures are highly developed with characterization created through telling particulars as well as in general terms. When we see Iorek Byrnison involved in his ironwork, Tialys tending the chrysalis that will hatch into his dragonfly mount, or the *mulefa* maintaining their wheels, they become as real as the more traditional characters.

Where Milton defends God (Milton's vision of Adam and Eve as "Sufficient to have stood, though free to fall" [*PL* IV: 99]), Blake leads Pullman from the Miltonic structured universe into a realm where creativity knows no bounds, where heresy is laughable, where emotions and intuition rise above reason, and where all that is emotional, sensuous, and joyful is an aspect of "the body divine." While both Blake and Milton saw the fruits of the earth as a divine gift, Blake's drafted images—for example, the graphic poetry of *Songs of Innocence*, with verbal text and picture intertwined—express a consonance between humankind and the natural world that Pullman frequently asserts, including the botanical garden of Lyra and Will's future virtual meetings.

As Milton provides inspiration for the grand vision and the scope of the trilogy, so Blake's legacy can be found most evidently in the rebellious socio-politico-religious stance and the perception of innocence and experience in Pullman's trilogy. This view harmonizes strongly with Blake's sense of humankind's entrapment by the forces of Satan, "'the Miller of Eternity' [whose] mills of reductive intellect attempt to grind down creation and so destroy the minute particulars that constitute the human" (Harold Bloom, in Blake, *Complete Poetry* 910); the figure of Urizen (destructive reasoning) is a role for Satan himself. And Pullman is completely in accord with Blake's sense of a corrupt church. Pullman's description of the church court's cruel torture of the young witch gives substance to the appalling vision of Metatron's threatened "permanent inquisition" (*AS* 393) and echoes the passionate hatred expressed in Blake's writings. Blake's dark picture in *Songs of Innocence and of Experience* of priests "binding with briars my joys & desires," crescendos to real virulence in *The Marriage of Heaven and Hell* [*MHH*] with pronouncements such as, "As the caterpillar chooses the fairest leaves to lay her eggs on, so the priest lays his curse on the fairest joys" or "Prisons are built with stones of Law, Brothels with bricks of Religion" (Blake, *Complete Poetry* 36, 37). And certainly Pullman's notion of a Republic of Heaven, toward which Will and Lyra will be working here on earth, is closely allied to Blake's desire to see "Jerusalem builded here, / Among these dark Satanic mills," where humankind can create a just and free society that incorporates the values that religion and the church have perverted. Blake also uses real English place-names in his prophetic works, providing an exact geography for Pullman that balances Milton's generalized picture of the cosmos.

Especially important is Blake's perception of innocence, experience, and higher innocence as stages of maturity, both physical and spiritual. Blake's work holds special significance for critics of children's literature because of the question of dual audience and cross-writing. For Pullman's work speaks both to youngsters and adults, while Blake's *Songs of Innocence and of Experience* are read to children but challenge adults in their enigmatic simplicity. And both carry strong aspects of the didactic, as does Milton's work. Since the Bible itself speaks to a variety of ages and intellects, it is not surprising that the three authors continue this tradition.

Lyra's facility with the alethiometer is the clearest evidence of the comparability of Pullman's vision of innocence to that of Blake's, giving her an intuitive ability to employ the instrument's truth-telling in a way that adults must dedicate untold hours and effort to achieve. Her loss of this gift as she reaches maturity asserts the impact of experience, and is in accord with the innocence, or lack of Dust, that keeps children safe from Specters; it is this situation that has led the misguided religious forces to suppose that Dust equates with original sin. For Blake, experience is not wrong but an inevitable stage of human maturity and, he believes, a necessary step on the path to higher innocence. Where Milton has teamed knowledge and experience with sin and the Fall, Blake has led the way for Pullman's redefinition of good and evil so that freedom, wisdom, and strength are humankind's goal, replacing the obedience, humility, and submission that should be abhorred. The path from innocence through experience to higher innocence is clearly evidenced in *The Amber Spyglass* when the angel Xaphania explains to Lyra, who is distressed by her loss of the skill to read the alethiometer: "You read it by grace . . . and you can regain it by work. . . . Your reading will be even better then, after a lifetime of thought and effort, because it will come from conscious understanding. Grace attained like that is deeper and fuller than grace that comes freely, and furthermore, once you've gained it, it will never leave you" (520). The assertion of grace, with its religious overtones, lends a special Romantic aura to the understanding of innocence, though it does also connect to the idea of ignorance as an unspoiled state.

Another compelling feature of Pullman's work in which Blake's influence may be found is his creation of the terrifying Specters, first discovered in Cittàgazze, which feed on the Dust-attracting adults, killing them from within. They are created by the mysterious subtle knife or Aesahaettr (God destroyer) each time it is used to open a window from world to world, a side effect that demands the ultimate separation of Will and Lyra, confined to their respective worlds. As an instrument of power, it has both an intentional and unintentional aspect, as Iorek Byrnison first warns Will. The Specters are its evil emanation. As noted, Pullman heads chapter 30 with a quote from Blake's *Jerusalem* (*J*), beginning, "Each Man is in his Spectre's power" (*J* 37). "Spectre" is a word that Blake employs frequently in *Jerusalem*. Los's specter is described as "Hung'ring & thirsting for Los's life" (*J* 8 l.28), a characteristic it shares with Pullman's figures, and roundly declares itself in the ranks of evil: "The Almighty hath made me his Contrary, / To be all evil, all reversed & for ever dead: knowing / And seeing life, yet living not" (*J* 10 56–58). Similarly, though classical influences clearly predominate in Pullman's anguished depiction of the dead, we may also find echoes of Blake's words from his Notebooks, "A fathomless and boundless deep / There we wander there we weep" (*Complete Poetry* 73).

Pullman perceives himself above all as a storyteller, but one who challenges his young readers to think and to learn: "Thou shalt not is soon forgotten, but Once upon a time lasts forever" ("Carnegie Speech"). His inventive and resourceful redefinition of the biblical themes and narratives, and their earlier interpretations, has created a trilogy of enormous impact, a fantasy as "truthful and profound" as he judges Milton's *Paradise Lost* to be ("ACHUKA Interview"). Infused with aspects of classical mythology as well as with elements of popular legend and folktale, Pullman's artistic innovations support a replay of Temptation, Fall, and Redemption that offers an exciting new perspective on old systems of belief. And the descent into the underworld that parallels the Harrowing of Hell, and releases the spirits to merge once again with the energy of the universe, melds religious, classical, and folk traditions in a modern idiom consonant with Pullman's vision of the diligent creation of a harmonious universe.

Notes

1. *Songs of Innocence and of Experience; The Marriage of Heaven and Hell; Auguries of Innocence; Jerusalem; A Song of Liberty; America: A Prophecy;* and *Europe: A Prophecy.*
2. Blake is represented most fully with ten chapter headings, followed by six quota-

tions apiece from the Bible and Milton's *Paradise Lost.* Emily Dickinson merits three mentions, Andrew Marvell two, while thirteen others are represented by one quotation apiece: Pindar, Spenser, Webster, metaphysical poets Donne and Herbert; Romantics Coleridge, Byron, and Keats; Ruskin and Christina Rossetti.

3. "The reason Milton wrote in fetters when he wrote of Angels & God, and at liberty when of Devils & Hell, is because he was a true poet and of the Devil's party without knowing it." *MHH* 5 in Blake, *Complete Poetry* 35.

Works Cited

Berry, Adrian. "How to Swap Universes," *Sunday Telegraph* (London) June 12, 1994.

Blake, William. *William Blake.* Ed. Alfred Kazin. New York: Viking, 1946.

———. *The Complete Poetry and Prose of William Blake.* Ed. David V. Erdman. With commentary by Harold Bloom. Berkeley: U of California P, 1982.

———. *Jerusalem* (facsimile edition). New York: Beechhurst, 1955.

Milton, John. *Complete Poems and Major Prose.* Ed. Merritt Y. Hughes. New York: Prentice Hall, 1957.

Pullman, Philip. ACHUKA Interview no. 18 (1998). *ACHUKA Children's Books UK.* Archived on a CD available at http://www.achuka.co.uk/index2.php.

———. *The Amber Spyglass.* London: Scholastic, 2000.

———. "Carnegie Medal Acceptance Speech" (1996). *His Dark Materials.* http://www.randomhouse.com/features/pullman/philippullman/speech.html.

———. *Northern Lights.* London: Scholastic, 1995.

———. *The Subtle Knife.* London: Scholastic, 1997.

7

"Without Lyra we would understand neither the New nor the Old Testament": Exegesis, Allegory, and Reading *The Golden Compass*

SHELLEY KING

Introduction: The Text as Alethiometer

When Martin Luther pronounced that "without Lyra we would understand neither the New nor the Old Testament,"[1] he was referring to Nicholas of Lyra (c. 1279–1349), a late-medieval textual scholar whose commentaries on the Bible and principles of literary criticism helped to form the basis for the subsequent reexamination of received scriptural interpretation central to the Reformation movement. For readers of Philip Pullman's *His Dark Materials* trilogy, however, the phrase linking a name more readily associated with the child heroine Lyra Belacqua to issues of scriptural authority possesses a curious resonance, and provides a key to responding to the complex intertextuality of the novels. One of the defining features of Pullman's art is its uncompromising celebration of the textual experience, whether revealed through the difficulty of the carefully documented epigraphs to the novels from writers ranging from Milton and Blake to Rilke and Ashbury, or through more indirect means, such as the allusive description of Lyra as a "little girl lost" (*Subtle Knife* [*SK*] 160), a silent evocation of the title of two poems from Blake's *Songs of Innocence and of Experience*, featuring the near-homophone protagonist "Lyca."[2] As Millicent Lenz points out, the *Dark Materials* trilogy draws heavily on Milton, Blake, and von Kleist in structuring the "'big' metaphysical questions" (123) in the series, but in addition to being about such questions, *The Golden Compass* is also very much about the act of reading itself. Or perhaps more accurately, it is about reading in the broader sense of the process of textual interpretation and the role it plays in the framing of metaphysical questions within a culture. The fantasy world of *The Golden Compass* is a world as clearly shaped by texts and their interpretation as our own, where attitudes toward sexuality are colored by inherited cultural values based on Scripture.

The primary device within the novel for focusing the reader's attention on the process of reading itself is the alethiometer, a "golden compass" marked by thirty-six symbols, each capable of signifying multiple levels of meaning, in infinite combinations. As Farder Coram explains to John Faa, "All these pictures round the rim, . . . they're symbols, and each one stands for a whole series of things. Take the anchor, there. The first meaning of that is hope, because hope holds you fast like an anchor so you don't give way. The second meaning is steadfastness. The third meaning is snag, or prevention. The fourth meaning is the sea. And so on, down to ten, twelve, maybe a never-ending series of meanings" (*Golden Compass* [*GC*] 126). The device is equipped with three hands that can be set to ask questions by pointing to specific symbols, and a needle that offers a response by pointing in turn to a sequence of symbols. As Pullman explains, "In short the alethiometer supplies the semantic content of a message, and the mind of the enquirer supplies the grammatical connections between the various elements. Only when the two work together does the full meaning of the message become apparent" ("How to Read the Alethiometer"). Reading the alethiometer is thus cast as a complex interpretive act, one requiring the ability to entertain multiple strata of symbolic meaning while actively working to construct the relationships connecting them. It is, as Farder Coram tells Lyra, "a subtle art" (*GC* 144).

The interpretive process is figured in *The Golden Compass* in two ways: first, through readers, and second, through the dual "text" being read: the alethiometer, which is the subject of reading within the novel, and the text of the novel itself. Only two categories of reader can interpret the symbolic language of the instrument: Lyra, an intuitive child who instinctively possesses the necessary skills for understanding, and a body of trained Scholars, who, with the aid of years of study supplemented by books of critical commentary produced by previous Scholars, can come to a difficult conscious reading of the alethiometer. This pairing is duplicated, of course, in Pullman's own readership of engaged child readers and literary critics, who similarly come to the text with differing modes of engagement. It is important to note here that Pullman's text validates both approaches. If Lyra at the outset of the novel regards the Scholars and their work with pitying scorn, it is nevertheless the career path she is set upon at the conclusion of *The Amber Spyglass:* she is destined to embody both types of reader. Thus the novel suggests that there are two ways to understand the mysteries posed by the alethiometer/text: the way of youth and innocence, which possesses direct intuitive access to meaning, and the way of maturity and experience, which through consciousness and cognitive effort can reach the same goal.

This chapter will explore the notion of the novel itself as a kind of alethiometer, a self-reflexive reader's guide to its own interpretation and to the process of producing meaning. Beginning with the construction of Lyra as reader/interpreter of the alethiometer, I will examine Pullman's dual implied reader in the text—the child and the scholar—and the importance of the exegetical tradition exemplified by the work of Nicholas of Lyra to an understanding of the production of meaning within the text.

The Child Reader: Pullman, MacDonald, and Interpretive Faith

The narrative of *The Golden Compass* is riddled with moments of interpretive uncertainty for its characters. Lee Scoresby and Serafina Pekkala puzzle over the meaning of Lyra's quest, and when the aeronaut asks, "That's how you read it, huh?" the witch replies, "That is how it seems. . . . But we can't read the darkness, Mr. Scoresby. It is more than possible that I might be wrong" (*GC* 310). Her awareness of the potential for error in her interpretation seems to set her above the Scholars of Jordan College, who, like stereotypical academics, are better with texts than with children. When they witness Lyra's interaction with her Oxford companions, they interpret it as "Children playing together: how pleasant to see! What could be more innocent and charming," though the narrator quickly assures us, "In fact, of course, Lyra and her peers were engaged in deadly warfare" (35). The difficulty of reading the significance of lived experience has its counterpart in the difficulty of reading the symbolic language of the alethiometer. After identifying the device as "a symbol reader," Farder Coram explains to Lyra "to read it fully I'd need the book" (126), and at the novel's conclusion, Lord Asriel similarly asserts that the alethiometer "would be no use to me without the books" (378). Like a complex text, the alethiometer's statements are accessible to Scholars only with the aid of glosses and references. *The Subtle Knife* provides a scene of explication readily recognizable to textual scholars:

> Serafina Pekkala looked around carefully and saw someone else in the room as well: a thin-faced man with a frog daemon, seated to one side of a table laden with leather-bound books and loose piles of yellowed paper. She thought at first that he was a clerk or a secretary, until she saw what he was doing: he was intently gazing at a golden instrument like a large watch or a compass, stopping every minute or so to note

what he found. Then he would open one of the books, search laboriously through the index, and look up a reference before writing that
down too and turning back to the instrument. (*SK* 34)

Apart from the frog daemon, the scene at the table is familiar to all textual
critics and has been since the dawn of exegetical criticism begun by Hebrew
scholars and the early Patristic commentators of the Christian Church: the
painstaking line-by-line examination, the multiple reference texts, the piles
of notes slowly accumulating the information necessary to pronounce upon
textual meaning—together they epitomize the traditional ways in which
scholars have worked with texts.

Lyra, however, is a different kind of reader. When the Master of Jordan College first presents her with the alethiometer, he says only, "It tells
you truth. As for how to read it, you'll have to learn by yourself" (*GC* 73).
Even the name of the instrument is puzzling to her, as she later asks Pan,
"What did he call it?" and when given the proper term, thinks, "There was
no point in asking what that meant" (78). From this seemingly inauspicious
beginning, however, Lyra emerges as a skilled interpreter of the device.
Though interpretation of the alethiometer is primarily the preserve of
Scholars who develop facility only following long years of study, Lyra's success as a reader stems from her intuitive ability to assemble the multiple as-
sociative levels of connection into a meaningful narrative. As she explains,
"I kind of see 'em. Or feel 'em rather, like climbing down a ladder at night,
you put your foot down and there's another rung. Well, I put my mind down
and there's another meaning, and I kind of sense what it is. Then I put 'em
all together. There's a trick in it like focussing your eyes" (151). This state
of awareness is described in *The Subtle Knife* as embodying Keats's "negative
capability," when a person is "Capable of being in uncertainties, mysteries,
doubts, without any irritable reaching after fact and reason" (88)—a state,
in fact, opposed to the conscious struggle of scholarship. The unique nature of her ability is emphasized in her interview with Dr. Lanselius, who
tells her the history of the alethiometer's creation and asks, "Without the
books of symbols, how do you read it?" Lyra explains that she "just makes
[her] mind go clear" (174). Pullman's creation of the alethiometer and its
readers, then, suggests to us two modes of engagement with the text: one
the result of careful interpretive scholarship, the other the intuitive, sponta-
neous perception of the meaning underlying the mysteries.

That Lyra, the child reader, succeeds relatively easily where adult
Scholars in the novel struggle suggests that Pullman as a writer of children's
literature belongs to that group of authors best exemplified by George

MacDonald, who trust in the ability of the child to interpret meaningfully texts beyond simple comprehension. When Lyra asks Serafina Pekkala about the relationship between men and witches, Serafina responds, "You are so young, Lyra, too young to understand this, but I shall tell you anyway and you'll understand it later" (*GC* 314). This insistence on the necessity of disclosing information beyond the immediate understanding of the child echoes MacDonald's belief in both the richness of the text's meaning and the deferred fulfillment of comprehension. In his *The Princess and the Goblin,* the powerful wise woman figure explains to Irene that she is her "father's mother's father's mother." Confused by the progression of possessives, the little princess replies, "Oh dear! I can't understand that," to which her great-great-grandmother responds, "I daresay not. I didn't expect you would. But that's no reason why I shouldn't say it" (13–14). By refusing to limit her discourse with the child to that which meets Irene's current limited understanding, she reflects MacDonald's broader insistence on the need for children's texts that encourage—or rather *require*—interpretive efforts to construct meaning on the part of the child reader. In "The Fantastic Imagination" MacDonald offers an exchange between an author and his anxious reader-interpreter that clearly establishes the premises on which his fantasies are constructed. Seeking assurance that reading consists simply of a measured decoding, the interpreter asserts that "words . . . are meant and fitted to carry a precise meaning," only to find that the author is more than willing to unsettle this certainty:

> It is very seldom indeed that they carry the exact meaning of any user of them! And if they can be so used as to convey definite meaning, it does not follow that they ought never to carry anything else. Words are live things that may be variously employed to various ends. . . . Is the music in them to go for nothing? It can hardly help the definiteness of a meaning: is it therefore to be disregarded? They have length, and breadth, and outline: have they nothing to do with depth? Have they only to describe, never to impress? . . . The greatest forces lie in the region of the uncomprehended. (52–53)

MacDonald advocates a literary art that transcends the certainties of immediate comprehension, substituting for the complacency of easy understanding the invigorating stretch of mind offered by interpretive acts. Disavowing the comforting fiction of a language that invariably carries "a precise meaning," he asserts instead the power of a language clothed in mystery. "The greatest forces" do indeed "lie in the region of the uncomprehended," for it is only when confronted with such textual mysteries that readers reach within and without to produce meaning. Pullman, too, advocates this type of readerly challenge. In an interview with ACHUKA, he is asked, "[W]ere you at any stage concerned that the uncondescending references to Church lore and Milton might alienate some children?"; he responds:

> No. I knew I was telling a story that would be gripping enough to take readers with it, and I have a high enough opinion of my readers to expect them to take a little difficulty in their stride. My readers are intelligent: I don't write for stupid people. Now mark this carefully, because otherwise I shall be misquoted and vilified again—we are all stupid, and we are all intelligent . . . I pay my readers the compliment of assuming that they are intellectually adventurous." ("ACHUKA Interview")

Like MacDonald, Pullman implies that age is not a necessary barrier to or instrument of textual understanding: each reader will find the meaning that results from personal engagement with the text, constructing it through what is brought to the text and the possibilities that the novel itself offers.[3] Pullman imagines a complex audience for his novel, one that ranges from child to textual scholar.

Within *The Golden Compass,* Lyra's name provides the link between these two types of readers; if the alethiometer tells us that interpretation involves holding multiple levels of meaning in tension, then we are implicitly directed to consider the polyvalent meaning suggested by names within the text. Many names yield their meanings readily: Mrs. Coulter is recognized by crossword buffs, students of medieval technology, and readers of rural background as someone immediately connected with knives and cutting, "coulter" being the name for the vertical blade segment of a plow, that slices the ground so that the share may turn the sod with less resistance. Her cutting comments and involvement with the intercision project come as no surprise to the verbally astute. Lord Asriel's name seems even more suggestive: as an alternative form of Azrael, the name carries a complex history. One of the fourteen angels of death in the rabbinical tradition, Azrael is also the archangel of Islamic lore who at each individual's death must sever the soul from the body. Thus, here too the character's potential for involvement in intercision is predicated by the name assigned. With Lyra, however, the nominal associations seem more allusive, and Pullman himself provides no explanation as he does for other characters:

> As for the names, some come with their names already attached, like Lyra. I don't know why. Others you have to find, like Lee Scoresby, the

balloonist. This came from two places: "Lee" from the actor Lee Van Cleef, who worked alongside Clint Eastwood in the spaghetti westerns of the 1960s. As for the "Scoresby," this is from the Arctic explorer William Scoresby—which gives you the Texan explorer who I imagine my character to be. Others you have to find wherever you can. Serafina Pekkala, the witch, came straight from the Helsinki Telephone Directory . . . not that they have a Yellow Pages section for witches! (Pullman, "CLC Pupils interview")

Thrown on our own resources, as readers we seek some aptness in Lyra's name and find that it suggests the brightest star in the constellation Vega in the northern sky, and is thus appropriate to the dominant setting of *The Golden Compass*, or *Northern Lights* as the British edition is titled. Phonetically, the name is the "liar, liar" of the harpy's accusation in *The Amber Spyglass* (293), a fitting appellation for the girl who excels in weaving duplicitous tales.

There is, however, a further association that anchors Lyra specifically as a reader and interpreter: she shares her name with Nicholas of Lyra, a thirteenth-century scholar celebrated for his contributions to both the theory and practice of textual exegesis, the interpretation of sacred texts through the application of increasingly complex levels of meaning. And if Lyra's first name were insufficient to point in this direction, her last name, Belacqua, evokes a character from the *Divine Comedy*, and therefore Dante, a proponent of exegesis for vernacular secular texts.[4] Lyra Belacqua thus models Pullman's two modes of interpretation: she is both Lyra the intuitive child reader, and Lyra the theological scholar-exegete. Pullman's comment that he "do[es]n't know why" his protagonist bears this name may be disingenuous (imagine explaining to the media that the name of your child protagonist is a clever evocation of a sophisticated textual practice dating to the Middle Ages), or the name may simply be the trace of a forgotten memory, or even merely serendipitous. Whatever its source, Lyra's name effectively symbolizes complementary approaches to the act of reading. *The Golden Compass* thus invites us to choose our method of engaging the text, assuring us that naive and scholarly readings are means to the same end.

The Scholar-Reader: Allegory and Exegesis in *The Golden Compass*

If the child Lyra represents the empowerment of intuitive reading, both her name and her fate direct our attention to the long tradition of textual exegesis. Nicholas of Lyra occupies a central position in the history of biblical criticism. Given the soubriquet "doctor planus et utilis" (the plain and useful doctor), Lyra has been called "the greatest biblical exegete of the fourteenth century" (Krey, *Apocalypse Commentary* 1) and is recognized as a scholar whose approach to textual interpretation was instrumental in establishing a balance between what contemporary critics would recognize as historical criticism of the text as literary object and an emphasis on the figurative meaning of divine Scripture as the revealed intention of God. As the central text of the Christian Middle Ages, the Bible was the object of intense scholarly study and by the thirteenth century had accumulated a considerable body of commentaries offering interpretations designed to reveal the meaning of the text. Beginning with St. Augustine, who famously interpreted St. Paul's pronouncement that "the letter killeth but the spirit setteth free" as an injunction to move beyond the literal meaning of a text in order to reveal the inner or hidden meaning of the words, the early patristic writers and their medieval heirs had labored to develop a set of strategies designed to help the reader interpret Scripture. Indeed, by the latter part of the century, scholars were becoming increasingly insistent upon complex allegorical readings and the importance of the academically trained reader to any understanding of the Bible. Nicholas of Lyra is important as a scholar whose ideas served to moderate this trend. His *Literal Postill on the Whole Bible*

> was a running commentary on the Old and New Testaments, intended primarily for theologians as a basis for dogmatics and as a reform of the over-allegorization of the Bible employed by Lyra's contemporaries. Nicholas tried to discover the intention of the human authors in the literal sense of the Bible by looking at grammar, philology, historical context, and the place of the passage in the whole outline of the Biblical book. (Krey, *Apocalypse Commentary* 9)

The *Postills* were justly famous, and considered so essential to interpreting Scripture that throughout late-medieval Europe the text of the Bible was frequently published accompanied by Nicholas of Lyra's commentaries. As Philip Krey points out, "The combined texts of these inclusive editions are a marvellous record of the development of exegesis in the Middle Ages, and they remind us that medieval scholars themselves read more widely and held more opinions and strata of interpretation in their heads than our modern desire to draw distinctions and pigeonhole sometimes wishes to acknowledge" (*Apocalypse Commentary* 12). The concept of exegesis as holding "strata of interpretation in their heads" precisely describes the experience of reading the alethiometer.[5]

Exegetical critics of the Middle Ages were in general agreed that interpretation involved reading on a variety of levels or senses. As A. J. Minnis and A. B. Scott note, "The authorities seem to differ on this question, two, three, four, or indeed five senses having been postulated. Yet all our schoolmen . . . come to same basic conclusion, however much they vary in emphasis: there is a single literal sense and a threefold spiritual sense (tropological/moral, allegorical/Christological, and anagogical)" (203). Lyra is sometimes credited with a popular mnemonic rhyme cited in the general prologue of the *Literal Postill on the Bible* outlining this fourfold interpretation:

Littera gesta docet
Quid credas allegoria
Moralia quid agas
Quo tendas anagogia

The letter teaches history;
Allegory, what you must believe;
The moral sense, what you must do;
The anagogical, your future destination.[6]

Thus texts could be interpreted according to four levels of meaning: the literal, the allegorical, the moral or tropological, and the anagogical. Nicholas of Lyra offers the following succinct explanation:

And it is the common intention of all books that their words should signify something, but it is a special quality of this book [i.e., the Bible] that the things signified by the words should signify something else. We understand by the first signification, which is that conveyed by the words, the literal or historical sense. We understand by the second signification, which is that conveyed by the things, the mystical or spiritual sense. This is in general threefold. If the things signified by the words are taken as referring to the essential elements of belief to be found in the New Law, this is understood to be the allegorical sense. If they are taken as referring to those things which we ourselves must do, this is the moral or tropological sense. But if they are taken as referring to that which we must hope for in our future blessed state, this is the anagogical sense. (266–67)

Not all levels of meaning are active in every passage of a text, but awareness of multiple levels of interpretation allows the reader to be alert to the potential for meaning in the text.

If we consider how this model of layered reading might apply to Pullman's text, we can see that Lyra Belacqua is, of course, always to be understood literally as the child protagonist who experiences the adventures that form the basis of Pullman's narrative. As Pullman insists in a number of interviews, we must never lose sight of the importance of story, of the primacy of the literal narrative in responding to his work. Nevertheless, Pullman also asserts:

> My aim is to tell a story which does have other resonances, if you like, some of them being moral. . . . That's not to say I set out to preach: I'm in the wrong trade if I set out to preach. When you undertake a task of any sort of intellectual weight, when you set out to write a book that's going to take you seven years to finish—as I did with "His Dark Materials"—then necessarily you do have some sort of moral commitment to it. You do it because you think it's a good thing to do. (Brown 8)

This comment suggests the possibility of a moral/tropological reading that directs us to "those things which we ourselves must do." Perhaps the most powerful example of literal conduct as moral exemplum in *The Golden Compass* appears in Lyra's encounter with Tony Makarios, the severed child. Although initially sickened and repelled by the boy as "something unnatural and uncanny that belonged to the world of night-ghasts, not the waking world of sense" (214), Lyra responds with courage and with love: "In Lyra's heart, revulsion struggled with compassion, and compassion won. She put her arms around the skinny little form to hold him safe" (216). To point the moral even more clearly, Pullman draws attention within the text itself to the potential of her actions to offer moral guidance. When the gyptians draw back from Tony, Iorek chides them: "Shame on you! Think what this child has done! You might not have more courage, but you should be ashamed to show less" (216–17). In the context of Pullman's secondary world, Lyra acts literally to save the boy, and in so doing serves as an example to the gyptian men. As readers belonging to our own primary world, we will never be faced literally with responding to a severed child, but we understand that Tony Makarios stands not just for himself but for all of those "hideously mutilated creature[s]" (216) who merit our courage and compassion. The moral qualities expressed by Lyra throughout the trilogy have meaning beyond their function in the narrative, and encourage readers to reflect on aspects of their own lives that could benefit from similar conduct.

More complex is the possibility of reading Lyra allegorically, which is to say in a specifically typological sense, though I would argue that Pullman invites us to do precisely that in his challenge to traditional theology. Medieval exegetes argued, for example, that Christ should be read as a type of Adam—if our first father's transgression brought sin and death into the world, then the new Adam, Christ, brought the promise of salvation through his incarnation and redemptive Grace, which offered forgiveness of sin and eternal life. Exegetical readers of Pullman's narrative might see Lyra as a second Eve, one who also brings a form of salvation to her world. Inverting the patriarchal model of Christian theology, Pullman offers a second mother, rather than a second father, who redeems not the soul but the body.[7] Her passion provides a kind of redemptive carnality, which necessarily complicates the final level of exegesis, the anagogical, which refers "to that which we must hope for in our future blessed state." As Sarah Lyall notes, "Mr. Pullman argues for a 'republic of heaven' where people live as fully and richly as they can because there is no life beyond, [saying] 'I wanted to emphasize the simple physical truth of things, the absolute primacy of the material life, rather than the spiritual or afterlife'" (E7). For such a text, anagogy as the medieval theologians imagined it can have no function: in a world with no "future blessed state" the text can only affirm the value of the physical and material. This is not, of course, to say that Pullman rejects ideas of human virtues such as love and courage that have been traditionally understood as aspects of an immortal soul; rather, he suggests that such "spiritual" qualities are manifested only through material, incarnate existence. Thus Pullman presents the traditional binary of body and soul as a type of doctrinal error. Such a binary is itself a metaphorical intercision highlighted by anagogical readings that insist upon the eventual severance experienced by all souls. The evocation of Nicholas of Lyra's fourfold method of reading through the protagonist's name thus offers a complex reassessment of exegetical interpretation, one whose working out establishes a complex interplay between received authority and innovative practice.

Nicholas of Lyra is also pertinent to the present discussion as an exegetical scholar who nevertheless defended the ability of the lay reader to interpret Scripture. In his commentary on the Book of Ruth, Lyra suggests that the woman gleaning in the fields "signifies the devout person who searches the Scripture for the food of life" (Smith, "Rewards" 55). In offering this interpretation,

> Nicholas is adding his opinion to the debate which begins in the first
> half of the thirteenth century about who could understand and inter-

pret the Bible: did it take a university education, or was this sort of knowledge accessible to all? Did knowledge of God necessarily entail academic interpretation of the Bible, or was such knowledge available to the less-educated, in other ways? . . . Nicholas hold[s] out for a more inclusive option. (55)

This insistence on the accessibility of meaning to all readers, naive and scholarly alike, finds its counterpart in Pullman's Lyra, who embodies both approaches to textual study. Nicholas of Lyra thus offers a model for Pullman's dual readership, affirming both the necessity of careful scholarship and the availability of meaning to the untrained reader.[8] This is perhaps best illustrated by the way Pullman's text can be seen as illuminating Nicholas of Lyra's "duplex sensus litteralis" (the double literal meaning), a difficult concept scholars of medieval literary theory see as one of his most subtle contributions to textual criticism.

For all of its usefulness, Nicholas of Lyra, along with a few other late-medieval scholars, found the fourfold method inadequate to explain one type of discourse: prophecy. Earlier in the Middle Ages, theorists held that prophets were "the passive mouthpieces for mysterious divine messages," but by the fourteenth century scholars rather held that "all kinds of figurative language, including proverbs, parables, likenesses, ironies, and metaphors, are part of the literal sense of Scripture" (Minnis and Scott 205). Thus emerged the term "duplex sensus litteralis" or "twofold literal sense," of statements, both aspects of which were controlled by the human author. As David C. Steinmetz explains in "The Superiority of Pre-Critical Exegesis,"

> If the literal sense of Scripture is the meaning which the author intended (presupposing that the author whose intention finally matters is God), then is it possible to argue that Scripture contains a double literal sense? Is there a literal-historical sense (the original meaning of the words as spoken in their first historical setting) which includes and implies a literal-prophetic sense (the larger meaning of the words as perceived in later and changed circumstances)? (31)

Pullman offers something analogous to this in the prophetic statements offered by Will's mother in *The Subtle Knife*. Early in the novel she assures him, "One day, you'll follow in your father's footsteps. You're going to be a great man too. You'll take up his mantle" (12). Will has no literal grasp of the phrase "take up his mantle" (i.e., cloak), but nevertheless "he understood the sense of it, and felt uplifted with pride and purpose. All his games were going to come true. His father was alive, lost somewhere in the wild, and he was going to rescue him and take up his mantle. . . . It was worth living a difficult life, if you had an aim like that" (12). Pullman returns repeatedly to the prophecy throughout the text. Will repeats the phrase to Lyra: "And my mother used to tell me that I was going to take up my father's mantle. She used to say that to make me feel good. I didn't know what it meant, but it sounded important" (263). Eventually, the question of meaning is confronted directly in another exchange between the protagonists:

> "Will," she said, "d'you know why you have to find your father?"
> "It's what I've always known. My mother said I'd take up my father's mantle. That's all I know."
> "What does that mean, taking up his mantle? What's a mantle?"
> "A task, I suppose. Whatever he's been doing, I've got to carry on. It makes as much sense as anything else." (307)

In this discussion, Lyra poses the direct question relevant to a strictly literal reading of the phrase "what's a mantle?" but Pullman withholds the definition: Will can only articulate his understanding of the figurative meaning. The prophecy comes to its double literal fulfillment only after Will's father's death, when the boy both figuratively and literally "takes up his father's mantle": "Then he noticed his father's feather-trimmed cloak trailing behind his body on the ground, heavy and sodden but warm. His father had no more use for it, and Will was shaking with cold. He unfastened the bronze buckle at the dead man's throat, and swung the canvas pack over his shoulder before wrapping the cloak around himself" (324). The layers of readerly satisfaction evoked in this scene are multiple: even the most literal of naive readers can recognize that Will has some tangible memento of the significant encounter with his father, while the intuitive child reader posited by MacDonald, though lacking like Will and Lyra the vocabulary skills necessary to interpret the figurative language, will also like them recognize the powerful forces at work cloaked in the mystery of language. The reader whose vocabulary includes the connection between mantle and cloak recognizes in the action the fulfillment of the word game of figurative and literal meaning; and the scholar of medieval literary theory finds in the fulfillment of Will's mother's prophecy an illustration of Nicholas of Lyra's double literal sense. The point, of course, is that satisfaction is available to readers at all levels, and as George MacDonald advises, "Everyone . . . who feels the story, will read its meaning after his own nature and development: one man will read one meaning in it, another will read another" ("Fantastic Imagination" 51).

Scripture and Interpretation in *The Golden Compass*

Finally, the evocation of Nicholas of Lyra within Pullman's text focuses attention on the role that exegesis and Scripture play within the culture of the novel. In its critique of puritanical attitudes toward human sexuality, *The Golden Compass* engages directly with the fundamental impact of one text—the Bible—upon Western culture. Historically, the Bible is perhaps the most mediated text in the history of the world, its influence the result not merely of the words of Scripture themselves, but of the interpretations of those words produced by a special class of textual scholars. Pullman's readers inside the text are equally the product of centuries of exegetical criticism, and the preparation for the climax of the action in the novel brings that process vividly to the foreground. When Lord Asriel explains to Lyra the significance of Dust, he begins by reading the story of the Fall of Man from the Book of Genesis, explaining to her, "And that was how sin came into the world, . . . sin and shame and death. It came the moment their daemons became fixed" (*GC* 372). As a child reader confronted by a complex sacred text, Lyra struggles to comprehend its nature, saying, "but it en't *true*, is it? Not true like chemistry or engineering, not that kind of true? There wasn't really an Adam and Eve?" (372). Resistant to the implications of the literal reading of the text, Lyra seeks to classify it as "just a kind of fairy tale," a pleasing fiction (372). In the parallel world of Pullman's text, however, the yoking of empirical scientific truth and textual scholarship results in the intercision project. Lord Asriel sends her back to the Genesis text, directing her to read the words documenting the role of dust: "In the sweat of thy face shalt thou eat bread, till thou return unto the ground; for out of it was thou taken: for dust thou art, and unto dust shalt thou return. . . ." Nevertheless, he makes clear that the biblical text is resistant to interpretation, and that the meaning assigned is the product of generations of textual debate:

> Church scholars have always puzzled over the translation of that verse.
> Some say it should read not "unto dust shalt thou return" but "thou
> shalt be subject to dust," and others say the whole verse is a kind of
> pun on the words "ground" and "dust" and it really means that God's
> admitting his own nature to be partly sinful. No one agrees. No one
> can, because the text is corrupt. But it was too good a word to waste,
> and that's why the particles became known as Dust. (373)

The world of Pullman's fiction is bound not only by one foundational text, but also by the weight of scholarly traditions brought to bear upon it.

Within this culture, interpretation is far from free. One of the Bolvangar experimenters comments of Lord Asriel, "I think he's got an entirely
different idea of the nature of Dust. That's the point. It's profoundly heretical, you see, and the Consistorial Court of Discipline can't allow any other
interpretation than the authorized one" (*GC* 274). The distinction between
interpretations that are "heretical" and those that are "authorized" demonstrates that scholarship can become an instrument of institutional authority, complicit in the disciplining of human experience: what begins as free
inquiry into meaning can become altered to a mechanism for reinforcing existing power relations, especially in a culture where the discourses of science
and theology combine to determine truth.

Perhaps for this reason it is salutary to remember that the equation of
Dust and Original Sin also has an antecedent in John Bunyan's *The Pilgrim's
Progress*. One of the most influential didactic works of Christian literature,
The Pilgrim's Progress runs counter to the dominant Puritan suspicion of fiction as lies and figurative language as deceptive. In a scene that establishes
the importance of allegorical readings, the protagonist, Christian, enters the
House of the Interpreter, where he is shown a series of tableaux and asked
to explicate their meaning. An interpretive neophyte, Christian at first must
turn to the Interpreter himself to receive understanding. After first being
shown the picture of Evangelist, or the word of God active in the world,
Christian turns to the next room in the House of the Interpreter:

> Then [the Interpreter] took him by the hand, and led him into a very
> large *Parlour* that was full of dust, because never swept; the which, after
> he had reviewed a little while, the *Interpreter* called for a man to *sweep:*
> Now when he began to sweep, the dust began so abundantly to fly
> about, that *Christian* had almost therewith been choaked: Then said
> the *Interpreter* to a *Damsel* that stood by, Bring hither Water, and sprin-
> kle the Room; which when she had done, was swept and cleansed with
> pleasure. (24–25)

If the text is to offer more than a literal lesson in seventeenth-century domestic science, it must be read allegorically. The Interpreter subsequently
explains that "This Parlour, is the heart of man that was never sanctified
by the sweet Grace of the gospel" and that "the *dust,* is his Original Sin"
(25). Themselves anxious concerning the role of a scholarly priestly class
that had been established as necessary mediators between the individual
Christian and Scripture, Puritan writers emphasized the need for each
reader to interpret Scripture personally. Thus, Bunyan's protagonist, before
he can set forth on his way to the Celestial City, must first be educated in

interpretive strategies. From the perspective of Pullman's text, however, Bunyan does not go far enough—though he recognizes the necessity of personal engagement with the interpretation of the text and the pleasures of allegorical reading, he fails to question the basic premise of Original Sin: that task is left to Lyra.

If the exegetes of the Consistorial Court of Discipline serve as reminders of the potential for the abuse of the power that resides in the interpretation of sacred texts, Lyra reminds us of the potential for naive understanding to transcend flawed scholarship. At the conclusion of *The Golden Compass*, Pantalaimon tells her, "We've heard them all talk about Dust, and they're so afraid of it, and you know what? We believed them, even though we could see that what they were doing was wicked and evil and wrong. . . . We thought Dust must be bad too, because they were grown up and they said so. But what if it isn't?" (398). The intuitive understanding of the mystery of Dust shared by Lyra and her daemon contests the received interpretation of the Consistorial exegetes and the scientists. By reading in the right spirit, Lyra forges her own humane understanding of Dust as well as of the alethiometer.

In "Darkness Visible," Pullman discusses his debt to Kleist's essay "On the Marionette Theatre" and the importance of acquired grace. The essay, Pullman comments, "was written a year or so before [Kleist] committed suicide in about 1812, [and] tells of a conversation he had with a friend who was a dancer" ("Darkness Visible"). The pair exchange stories concerning the nature of physical grace and its destruction by self-consciousness, and they speculate on the superiority of the unconscious grace of the non-human tame bear, or even the inanimate marionettes, to that of the human being who has become self-aware. Pullman continues,

> We live in a dark valley, on a spectrum between the unconscious grace of the puppet and the fully conscious grace of the god. But the only way out of this impasse, [Kleist and the dancer] agree, is not back towards childhood: as with the Garden of Eden, an angel with a fiery sword guards the way; there is no going back. We have to go forward, through the travails and difficulties of life and embarrassment and doubt, and hope that as we grow older and wiser we may approach paradise again from the back, as it were, and enter that grace which lies at the other end of the spectrum. ("Darkness Visible")

It is this grace that Lyra comes to as a reader at the conclusion of *The Amber Spyglass*. The Master looks at her and sees "how the child's unconscious grace had gone, and how she was awkward in her growing body" (514) and advises her, "make the alethiometer the subject of your life's work, and set out to learn consciously what you could once do by intuition" (515). As a reader, Lyra must "enter that grace which lies at the other end of the spectrum," and to recognize that, as Pullman notes elsewhere, "the grace of human dancer [reader] who has lost the initial grace but regained it through training is actually a more valuable thing to have, because when you look at the dancer [reader], not only do you see the grace and beauty, but you also look into her eyes, and you see wisdom as well" (Parsons and Nicholson 118). Lyra's fall into scholarship merely renders her aware of the process of her own production of meaning and, like her namesake Nicholas of Lyra, she is poised to embrace the full complexity of textual signification to the adult mind.

Notes

1. Quoted by E. M. White in "Formatting the Word of God/Text with Commentary." The debt owed by Luther to Nicholas of Lyra's textual practice is also registered in an oft-repeated tag with a number of variations: "If Lyra had not piped/played/plucked his lyre, Luther would not have danced, and the whole world would have gone to perdition."

2. Blake wrote "The Little Girl Lost" for *Songs of Innocence* and "A Little Girl Lost" for *Songs of Experience;* the preliminary lines of the latter poem are particularly apt for Pullman's text:

   Children of the future age,
   > Reading this indignant page,
   > Know that in a former time
   >> Love, sweet love, was thought a crime.

   (ll.1–4)

3. Consciously or not, Pullman echoes MacDonald with surprising vividness. Compare his comment—"We all negotiate the meanings of things as we read them. . . . My reading of the book, while no less valid than anybody else's, is no more valid. If I were to say, this means that, or you must read it in that way, this would seem to have a particular authority that I don't want" (Lyall)—with MacDonald:

   > Everyone . . . who feels the story, will read its meaning after his own nature and development: one man will read one meaning in it, another will read another.
   >> [Questioner]"If so, how am I to assure myself that I am not reading my own meaning into it, but yours out of it?"
   >> Why should you be so assured? It may be better that you should read your meaning into it. That may be a higher operation of your intellect than the mere reading of mine out of

it: your meaning may be superior to mine. ("Fantastic Imagination" 51)

4. In his *Convivio* and *Epistle to Can Grande della Scala*, Dante "attempt[s] to elevate vernacular poetry through the appropriation (and adaptation) of scholastic literary theory" (Minnis and Scott 383).

5. Perhaps, Lyra's parallel Oxford, like our own, possesses manuscript copies of Nicholas's *Postills*, and perhaps in that world, too, his was the first biblical commentary to be printed. Minnis and Scott list Merton College MSS 163–65, New College MSS 8–13, and Bodleian Library MS Canon, Bib. Lat. 70 among the manuscript copies of Lyra's works held at Oxford (7–11).

6. Minnis and Scott provide the translation and discuss this rhyme at greater length (267).

7. In "Talking to Philip Pullman" Parsons and Nicholson ask about the necessary nature of the Fall. Pullman offers that "if we had our heads straight on this issue, we would have churches dedicated to Eve instead of the Virgin Mary" (119).

8. In negotiating the needs of these distinct readerships, Pullman practices what U. C. Knoepflmacher and Mitzi Myers have termed "cross-writing," "a dialogic mix of older and younger voices [that] occurs in texts too often read as univocal" ("From the Editors: 'Cross-Writing' and the Reconceptualizing of Children's Literary Studies," *Children's Literature* 25 [1997]: vii).

Works Cited

Brown, Charles N., and Tanya Brown. "Philip Pullman: Storming Heaven." *Locus* 45.6 (2000): 8, 80–82.

Bunyan, John. *The Pilgrim's Progress.* Ed. N. H. Keeble. Oxford: Oxford World's Classics, 1986.

Hunt, Peter, and Millicent Lenz. *Alternative Worlds in Fantasy Fiction: Ursula K. Le Guin, Terry Pratchett, Philip Pullman, and Others.* London: Continuum, 2001.

Knoepflmacher, U. C., and Mitzi Myers. "From the Editors: 'Cross-Writing' and the Reconceptualizing of Children's Literary Studies. *Children's Literature* 25 (1997): vii–xvii.

Kvam, Kristen, Linda Schearing, and Valarie Zingler, eds. *Eve and Adam: Jewish, Christian, and Muslim Readings on Genesis and Gender.* Bloomington: Indiana UP, 1999.

Krey, Philip. *Nicholas of Lyra's Apocalypse Commentary.* Trans. with introduction and notes. Kalamazoo: Medieval Institute, 1997.

Krey, Philip, and Lesley White, eds. *Nicholas of Lyra: The Senses of Scripture.* Studies in the History of Christian Thought. Leiden: Brill, 2000.

Lenz, Millicent. "Philip Pullman." *Alternative Worlds in Fantasy Fiction: Ursula K. Le Guin, Terry Pratchett, Philip Pullman, and Others.* Ed. Peter Hunt and Millicent Lenz. London: Continuum, 2001.

Lyall, Sarah. "The Man Who Dared Make Religion the Villain; In British Author's Trilogy, Great Adventures Aren't Pegged to the Great Beyond." *New York Times* November 7, 2000: E1, E7. http://www.nytimes.com/2000/11/07/arts/07-

PULL.html.

MacDonald, George. "The Fantastic Imagination." *The Heart of George MacDonald: A One-volume Collection of His Most Important Fiction, Essays, Sermons, Drama, Poetry, Letters.* Ed. Rolland Hein. Wheaton: Shaw, 1994. 49–54.

————. *The Princess and the Goblin.* 1872. Ed. Roderick McGillis. Oxford: Oxford UP, 1990.

Minnis, A. J., and A. B. Scott, with David Wallace, eds. *Medieval Literary Theory and Criticism, c. 1100–c. 1375.* Oxford: Clarendon, 1998.

Parsons, Wendy, and Catriona Nicholson. "Talking to Philip Pullman: An Interview." *Lion and the Unicorn* 23.1 (1999): 116–34.

Patton, Corrine. "Creation, Fall, and Salvation: Lyra's Commentary on Genesis 1–3" *Nicholas of Lyra: The Senses of Scripture.* Ed. Philip Krey and Lesley Smith. Leiden: Brill, 2000. 19–43.

Pullman, Philip. ACHUKA Interview #18, 1998. *ACHUKA Children's Books UK.* Archived on a CD available at http://www.achuka.co.uk/index2.php.

————. *The Amber Spyglass.* New York: Knopf, 2000.

————. "C[heltenham] L[adies'] C[ollege] Pupils interview celebrated author Philip Pullman" (November 2003). http://www.cheltladiescollege.org/news/pullman.asp.

————. "Darkness Visible: An Interview with Philip Pullman." Part Two. http://www.amazon.com/exec/obidos/tg/feature.

————. *The Golden Compass.* New York: Random House, 1995.

————. "How to Read the Alethiometer." http://www.randomhouse.com/features/pullman/alethiometer/index.html#howto.

————. *The Subtle Knife.* New York: Knopf, 1997.

Smith, Lesley. "The Rewards of Faith: Nicholas of Lyra on Ruth." *Nicholas of Lyra: The Senses of Scripture.* Ed. Philip Krey and Lesley Smith. Leiden: Brill, 2000. 45–58.

Steinmetz, David C. "The Superiority of Pre-Critical Exegesis." *Theology Today* 37.1 (1980): 27–36.

White, E. M. 1998. "Formatting the Word of God: The Text with Commentary." http://www.smu.edu/bridwell/publications/ryrie_catalog/3_2.htm.

8

Rouzing the Faculties to Act: Pullman's Blake for Children

Susan Matthews

Children's literature is a form of writing often designed by the adult purchaser to induce sleep in the younger child or silence in the older one: one of its most useful functions for the parent is to buy a moment's peace. In its debt to Blake (credited as one of the three key influences at the end of *The Amber Spyglass*) Pullman acknowledges a writer committed to challenging his reader. As Blake wrote to a dissatisfied patron, Dr. Trusler, in 1799: "You say that I want somebody to Elucidate my Ideas. But you ought to know that What is Grand is necessarily obscure to Weak men. That which can be made Explicit to the Idiot is not worth my care. The wisest of the Ancients considered what is not too Explicit as the fittest for Instruction because it rouzes the faculties to act" (702). Yet despite his commitment to a kind of difficulty that provokes "the faculties to act," Blake announces in the same letter: "I am happy to find a Great Majority of Fellow Mortals who can Elucidate My Visions & Particularly they have been Elucidated by Children" (703). Pullman's popularity suggests the ability of children to elucidate his narrative—despite the ambition of his rewriting of one of the grand narratives, the myth of the Fall, which in its articulation in *Paradise Lost* is far from accessible to the contemporary child, adolescent, or even adult reader. Rather than rouzing "the faculties to act," Mrs. Coulter attempts to keep her daughter, Lyra, asleep and thus prevent her from meeting the temptation, the fall that is prophesied. The name of Lyra's mother clearly puns on "culture," signaling the culture that encodes a rigid image of femininity, of authority, and of religious conservatism. Pullman sets out to counter the force of a culture that tries to keep the child asleep.

Lyra's name recalls Lyca, Blake's "The Little Girl Lost" from "Songs of Experience," a poem that provides the epigraph to the first chapter of *The*

Amber Spyglass. This novel opens with Lyra asleep in a cave, and not just sleeping but kept asleep by her mother, Mrs. Coulter, who drugs her to protect her from the experience that is prophesied. Pullman's trilogy uses Blakean images and references throughout, but "The Little Girl Lost" is, as the epigraph suggests, a key point of reference. In this poem, Lyca sleeps free from harm though lost in "the southern clime," carried to safety in a cave, and guarded by a watching lion and lioness:

> Sleeping Lyca lay;
> While the beasts of prey,
> Come from caverns deep,
> View'd the maid asleep
> (Blake 20–21)

Here, sleep is protection from danger, and the journey of the little girl, though terrifying to her parents, takes her to a place of delight where leopards and tigers play. It is a Song of Experience that reads strangely as a vision of innocence. And although Lyca stays asleep in the cave in this poem and in "The Little Girl Found," it is prefaced by a vision of a time in which the "earth from sleep . . . Shall arise" (20). Lyca is the little girl who "In futurity" it seems, will herald the waking of the earth and the time when "the desart wild / Become a garden mild." (20). But this poem can also be read as a Song of Experience by focusing on the fear of Lyca's parents, who "dream they see their child / Starv'd in desart wild" (21). In Pullman's narrative, Mrs. Coulter is the anxious parent who misreads this poem, fearing the loss of the child and the innocent sensuality of her experience:

> Leopards, tygers play,
> Round her as she lay;
> While the lion old,
> Bow'd his mane of gold.
>
> And her bosom lick,
> And upon her neck,
> From his eyes of flame,
> Ruby tears there came;
>
> While the lioness,
> Loos'd her slender dress,
> And naked they convey'd
> To caves the sleeping maid.
> (Blake 21)

The Innocence reading of the poem turns it into a tale of exploration, in which the child's wandering allows her to hear "wild birds song" and in which the child's sleep, at peace with herself, is dependent on her parents trusting and not weeping. But in Mrs. Coulter's experienced reading, the parent intervenes to try to keep the child from knowledge, including knowledge of her own sexuality.

Another Experience poem, "A Little GIRL Lost" takes the narrative of the child's awakening further, telling of the love of "Youth and maiden bright" and of their terror as "her father white" appears in the garden. In this poem, the father's arrival seems to echo the appearance of God in Genesis after the Fall. But the poem also addresses a future time:

> Children of the future Age,
>   Reading this indignant page;
>   Know that in a former time.
>   Love! sweet Love! was thought a crime.
>
> (29)

It might seem that, writing in the last years of the twentieth century, Pullman's audience is precisely the "Children of the future Age," for whom love is no longer a crime. The first book invokes the "former time" as a parallel world, an anachronistic world where religion dominates science, where there are elaborate religious rituals. This is a world that the Enlightenment never reached, one where Oxford scholars have political power and where the cultural power of the clerisy remains unchallenged. Pullman's return to Blake therefore echoes a writer now culturally enshrined as an authority and source of inspiration. But it also writes from a very different space, one where sexuality is endlessly celebrated by consumer culture, a culture that is aimed as much at children and adolescents as at adults. If Pullman's trilogy is retelling the story of Lyca as Lyra, echoing and re-creating the two poems from *Songs of Innocence and of Experience*, meanings change in this retelling. Even though the sexuality of the child is still, and rightly, a difficult subject for the society from which the trilogy emanates (end-of-the-millennium Oxford), sexuality has changed its meaning since the late eighteenth century. And as Pullman's narrative suggests, the society from which it emanates and to which it speaks is not unitary. Just as Pullman's characters cut through to other worlds, so even the globalized culture to which it hopes to speak contains a diverse range of cultural practices.

The trilogy develops a rereading of Blake that suggests a commentary on the "future Age" imagined in "A Little GIRL Lost"—the future age of now. Despite the prophecy of the Experience poem, the repression of sexuality suggested by the practice of intercision is explained not only as con-

tinuing the historic practices of the church ("A castrato keeps his high tre-
ble voice all his life, which is why the Church allowed it: so useful in Church
music.") (*Northern Lights* [*NL*] 374) but also as offering a parallel to practices that still persist in some cultures. The witches in *The Subtle Knife* talk
of things that happen "in the south lands":

> Sisters, you know only the north: I have travelled in the south lands.
> There are churches there, believe me, that cut their children too, as the
> people of Bolvangar did—not in the same way, but just as horribly—
> they cut their sexual organs, yes, both boys and girls—they cut them
> with knives so that they shan't feel. That is what the church does, and
> every church is the same: control, destroy, obliterate every good feel-
> ing. (52)

Lord Asriel also explains Mrs. Coulter's plan as a result of her travels in
Africa: "The question was whether it was possible to separate daemon and
body without killing the person. But she's travelled in many places, and seen
all kinds of things. She's travelled in Africa, for instance. The Africans have
a way of making a slave called a *zombi*. It has no will of its own; it will work
day and night without ever running away or complaining. It looks like a
corpse" (*NL* 375). This motif seems to invite the reader to draw a parallel
with the practice of female circumcision. Indeed the references to the south
lands and to travel in Africa seem to raise the possibility that the book
imagines other cultures negatively. The use of a plurality of worlds is potentially open to a multicultural reading. But the visible range of cultural
reference is limited and often seems to invoke cultural stereotypes of the
darkness and savagery of other cultures. The utopian world of the *mulefa*
has been compared by Pullman to California (though they are also clearly a
version of Swift's Houyhnhnms, with their "sweet horse-like smell") (*Amber
Spyglass* [*AS*] 245), and the somewhat *Lord of the Flies* world of children who
roam in packs through Cittàgazze seems to belong in Italy, but the extreme
north and the south lands are both associated with forms of oppression. It
seems as if Pullman is trying to approach the question of religious fundamentalism as well as the abuses of technology and science. It then becomes
understandable that he should dodge the attempt to represent other cultures
and societies, moving out from a recognizable version of contemporary Oxford (complete with Botanical Garden and Covered Market) to other
stranger, more fantastic lands. The parallel worlds in which religion dominates science become a comment on contemporary practices. Although the
book's energy and narrative depend (after the first novel) on the device of
cutting through to other worlds, the trilogy ends with an insistence on the

need to live in your own world. Will and Lyra have to accept that their lives will be shortened if they attempt to live outside their own worlds. Although travel and adventure drive the plot, there is also a fear of other worlds in this trilogy, and the action of opening up worlds (a positive action in Blakean myth) is one that is fraught with danger, leading in the end to the appearance of Specters.

Yet the willingness of the narrative to engage with difficult topics is also its strength. Pullman can suggest the abuses of sexuality as well as repression. In *The Amber Spyglass* Will encounters what is clearly a pedophile priest (107). And in tackling abuses and distortions of sexuality resulting from oppression (within narratives and images that are open to the child reader), Pullman is as insistent as Blake that innocence is not ignorance. The books, just like Lyca in the Experience poem, are able to confront danger and difficulty, resisting the attempt of Mrs. Coulter (or culture) to censor and simplify. "Darling, these are big, difficult ideas, Dust and so on. It's not something for children to worry about" (*NL* 283), she tells Lyra, but Pullman can find images and words that contain "big, difficult ideas."

The most powerful imaginative device that Pullman uses in the trilogy is the figure of the daemon—an animal companion, usually but not always of the opposite sex, who acts as a metaphorical extension of the self, as soul, and as sexuality. The child's daemon continually changes shape (is clearly polymorphously perverse) until puberty, when it settles into the shape of one kind of animal, becoming a single identity in the adult. The insistence on the device of the daemon, and the intensity of the passages in which characters lose or are momentarily separated from their daemons, comes from the attempt of the novel to stress the unity of the soul, body, and sexuality. The writing about separation and loss can be paralleled in Blake's poetry—as well as speaking to the fears of loss associated with the child's growth and separation from the parent. The pronunciation of the word, "DEE-muhn," which Pullman insists upon, encourages us to see a link with the demons who populate Blake's poetry of the 1790s. *The First Book of Urizen* describes the fall as a splitting or division and does so in language that provides an analogue to the threat of intercision. For the demon in Blake, as in Pullman, is a figure of desire:

> 9. Los wept howling around the dark Demon:
> And cursing his lot; for in anguish,
>   Urizen was rent from his side;
>   And a fathomless void for his feet;
> And intense fires for his dwelling.
>   (Blake 73–74)

But this passage also suggests something of the difference between Pullman and Blake. Even though Blake's notebook contains a fragment, "The Island in the Moon," which reads as a parody of a novel, it is impossible to imagine Blake as the author of a novel. And this is in part because the notion of identity, of character, which is central to the rise of the novel in the eighteenth century, is antithetical to the way that Blake's poetry deconstructs individuality through concepts such as the emanation, states, and specters. Identity, from the early *The Marriage of Heaven and Hell* through to the long prophetic books, is always subject to change and redefinition, to what Saree Makdisi has recently described as an "unequivocal challenge to the very concept of the sovereign individual" (41). To some extent the concept of the daemon has a similar function in Pullman, introducing an idea of the constant flux of identity (in the child at least). One of the most powerful passages is the one in which Lyra's daemon, Pantalaimon, changes shapes in his attempt to escape forcible separation from Lyra: "But Pantalaimon, in answer, had twisted free of those hateful hands—he was a lion, an eagle; he tore at them with vicious talons, great wings beat wildly, and then he was a wolf, a bear, a polecat—darting, snarling, slashing, a succession of transformations too quick to register, and all the time leaping, flying, dodging from one spot to another as their clumsy hands flailed and snatched at the empty air" (*NL* 277). Pantalaimon's changes here are strongly reminiscent of those of Blake's Orc of the Preludium to *America:*

> Sometimes an eagle screaming in the sky, sometimes a lion,
> Stalking upon the mountains, & sometimes a whale I lash
> The raging fathomless abyss, anon a serpent folding
> Around the pillars of Urthona, and round thy dark limbs,
> On the Canadian wilds I fold, feeble my spirit folds.
> For chaind beneath I rend these caverns; when thou bringest food
> I howl my joy! and my red eyes seek to behold thy face
>   (51)

Yet in Pullman the narrative works toward a stable kind of identity as the individual matures into adulthood. The refusal to recognize the process of settling, which Pullman sees as inevitable, marks the gulf between Blake's poetry and the Pullman trilogy, which ends with Lyra in school.

As a child, Lyra's instinctual power is imaged in her ability to read the alethiometer, a skill that she will have to laboriously relearn as she grows up. Pullman once again alludes to Blake when, in *The Subtle Knife* [*SK*], we are told that "Without the alethiometer, she was . . . just a little girl, lost" (167). Of course, in Blake's poem Lyca is not a "little girl, lost," as her parents fear, but is safe and secure in her wandering, cared for by the lion and lioness. The alethiometer therefore functions as a symbol for the visionary confidence of the child of innocence. Or indeed for the power of prophecy that Blake defines when he writes: "Every honest man is a Prophet he utters his opinion both of private & public matters / Thus / If you go on So / the result is So / He never says such a thing shall happen let you do what you will. a Prophet is a Seer not an Arbitrary Dictator" (617). Pullman uses a similar formulation when he explains that "the alethiometer does not *forecast*; it says, '*If* certain things come about, *then* the consequences will be—' and so on" (*AS* 71). What is different here is Pullman's use of symbolic objects: the alethiometer, the subtle knife, and the amber spyglass. Blake's writing, which focuses so centrally on the human form, is remarkably lacking in objects. In his wholesale rejection of consumer culture, Blake creates an imagined world populated by people, by animals, but not by objects—except where these are the tools and instruments of the laborer, those of the engraver or the builder. The compasses with which Urizen divides the abyss after the fall seem to limit the fall into disorganization but not to enable vision. Yet Pullman's novel is perhaps not so different: it takes the reader out of worlds where there are passing references to cola and a Swiss Army knife into those of the *mulefa*, in which technology is intimately linked to the natural world. The imagined worlds of the trilogy make little reference to commerce, consumption, or the media, even if the struggle to awaken the earth takes place through the new physics rather than the work of the laborer.

It is perhaps in the representation of women and of Nature that Pullman appears to be furthest from Blake—mirroring the largest cultural shift in "the future age" of now. It is not the male figure of the poetic genius, Los, but the girl Lyra and the female scientist, Mary Malone, who work to bring about the Republic of Heaven. There seems to be a new emphasis on nature and ecology in Pullman that are difficult to match in Blake's long poems, though they could be found in the visionary lyrics. But these differences may represent more shifts in emphasis rather than in underlying assumptions. In many ways the figure of Mrs. Coulter recalls Blake's Vala, for both represent a socially constructed femininity that is alluring, entrapping yet destructive. In her most negative form in *Jerusalem* Vala appears as a hardened form of conventional femininity:

> On her white marble & even Neck, her Heart
> Inorb'd and bonified: with locks of shadowing modesty,
>   shining
> Over her beautiful Female features, soft flourishing in

beauty
Beams mild, all love and all perfection, that when the
lips
Recieve [*sic*] a kiss from Gods or Men, a threefold kiss
returns
(224)

In *Northern Lights*, Mrs. Coulter presents Lyra with an image of femininity that is quite new to her, of women "so unlike female Scholars or gyptian boat mothers or college servants as almost to be a new sex altogether, one with dangerous powers and qualities such as elegance, charm and grace" (82). In many ways the two figures are similar: delusive, ideological, and alluring. Yet there is also a difference in that Vala is often associated in *Jerusalem* with the corporeal and with the veil of the created world. This might be taken to mean that whereas Vala is corporeal, Jerusalem is spiritual. Blake would therefore be suggesting a turning away from the body and from nature. In Pullman's (I think correct) reading of Blake, this negative feminine figure is associated with culture (by her punning name) rather than with nature or the body. Both Mary Malone and Lyra are associated not only with the natural world but also with an awareness of the body. In *The Amber Spyglass* Mary's story gives to Lyra a new sense of her body: "She felt as if she had been handed the key to a great house she hadn't known was there" (468). In the writing about closeness, separation, and touch, Pullman achieves a reading of Blake's account of separation in *The Book of Urizen* that uses the ability of the novel to map space and proximity in a very different way from poetry.

Pullman's fiction has been criticized for its occasional didacticism. Yet many readers of Blake have argued that his work energetically resists establishing authority: it is insistently dialectical, working with contraries that oppose each other and that undo and reform meanings that shift continually. The spiritual building of Golgonooza in *Milton* is characteristically "ever building, ever falling" (99). As Heather Glen argues of Blake's "The Shepherd": "Where readers . . . would have expected the poet's controlling voice to direct their attitudes to the material presented, here there is no obvious controlling voice and no such direction" (5). Pullman's trilogy conveys a sustained attack on moral authority, culminating in the fall of the Authority, an aged figure like Blake's Urizen or his Ancient of Days. Yet, at least initially it might be argued that Pullman is less willing to give up his own narrative authority. Often, in *Northern Lights*, the narrative voice is both knowing and wise: "'Yes; I can't prevent it,' said the Master, and Lyra didn't notice *at the time* what an odd thing that was to say" (74, my italics). Even though the narrative voice is challenged by the nonstandard speech of the gyptians and of Lyra, the sometimes-didactic control of the narrative remains. Yet as the trilogy develops, the narrative method also shifts. In the second novel, movement between worlds disrupts the temporal flow of the narrative and forces the reader to shift perspective and assumptions. In the third novel the fragmentary voices of the dead Roger and the sleeping Lyra float up between the chapters, questioning the formal shaping of the novel. In this novel also, key narratives belong within the voices of characters rather than the narrator. Milton's serpent takes the form of the scientist (and former nun) Dr. Mary Malone, who tells Lyra the story of a meeting that ended her religious vocation. The voice of the tempter is located as that of a specific character; her story has a clearly didactic function, but it is one that is registered in Lyra's bodily response, her physical reaction to the tale: "As Mary said that, Lyra felt something strange happen to her body. She felt a stirring at the roots of her hair: she found herself breathing faster" (*AS* 467). If Mary Malone still has a slightly Mary Poppinsish blandness, her tale of sensual awakening still marks an attempt to give over authority to a female voice—replacing Proust's madeleine with her own taste of marzipan.

The third novel also focuses the reader's attention on intertextuality through the use of epigraphs to each chapter. These are set into a kind of memorial tablet at the opening of each chapter (using slightly varied forms of typography, but echoing visually an artist like John Hamilton Finlay). The epigraphs come from a canonical range of authors (Keats, Marvell, Emily Dickinson, Webster, the Bible, Blake, Milton). The size of Pullman's adult and child readership convincingly establishes him in the realm of the popular. But the use of high cultural epigraphs seems also to be a claim for the status of children's literature. It could be argued that the epigraphs also suggest a lack of confidence in the status of his text, functioning like the epigraphs from Shakespeare in Anne Radcliffe's novels. Perhaps children's literature shares the concerns about authority *and* the emergent ambition and confidence that marked writing for women at the end of the eighteenth and early nineteenth centuries. It is inhabited by parallel worries about the readers and their desires—their innocence or otherwise. In Pullman's version the writing comes to some extent from outside the sphere of cultural authority, drawing in its imaginative energy on the soaring movement of comic heroes in its battles and journeys, but also, like Blake's writing, demanding access to the key myths of its culture.

The ending of the book speaks of loss and the need for work. The final point—the move from the kingdom of heaven to the Republic of Heaven is a nice one, but it's one that sounds like the end of an essay—it is the end of an argument that is controlled by a single voice. And if the control is clear throughout, perhaps that is what makes it children's literature (even if adults read it). There are different languages and worlds, but the flow of the narrative is controlled despite the echoes of popular literature and the imaginative power of the writing. The trilogy rereads Blake's multiple, worrying, and often contradictory narratives into a single linear narrative, which in its ending asserts the inevitable need for the openings between worlds to be closed and for lovers to part. The change results in part from a reading of Blake that maps the move from innocence to experience onto the process of growing up. This linear reading is of course appropriate to a novel for children. But it is one that loses some of the dialectical power of opposition and contraries. As the trilogy ends, Lyra enters a school, having closed up the hole between the worlds opened by the male overreacher, her father, Lord Asriel. The wild child is imagined and valued, but there is no doubt in this book that innocence ends, the connection between worlds must be lost, daemons must stop changing, and the adult world must be entered.

Works Cited

Blake, William. *The Complete Poetry and Prose of William Blake.* Ed. David V. Erdman. New York: Anchor Press/Doubleday, 1965. Rev. 1982.

Glen, Heather. *Vision and Disenchantment: Blake's "Songs" and Wordsworth's "Lyrical Ballads."* Cambridge: Cambridge UP, 1983.

Makdisi, Saree. *William Blake and the Impossible History of the 1790s.* Chicago: U of Chicago P, 2003.

Pullman, Philip. *The Amber Spyglass.* London: Scholastic, 2000.

———. *Northern Lights.* London: Scholastic, 1995.

———. *The Subtle Knife.* London: Scholastic, 1997.

9

Tradition, Transformation, and the Bold Emergence:
Fantastic Legacy and Pullman's *His Dark Materials*

KAREN PATRICIA SMITH

In the acknowledgments section of *The Amber Spyglass*, Philip Pullman says: "I have stolen ideas from every book I have ever read. My principle in researching for a novel is 'Read like a butterfly, write like a bee,' and if this story contains any honey, it is entirely because of the quality of the nectar I found in the work of better writers" (520). As the winner of the prestigious Whitbread Award, a Carnegie Award, a Guardian Fiction Award, and such distinctions as the American Library Association's notable book mention, ALA Best Book for Young Adults, Pullman is being overly modest.

I am fascinated by the process of "literary digestion" suggested by the butterfly/bee similes. In this process, elements that remain in the mind of an author—either consciously or unconsciously—are assimilated and combined with that author's inventiveness, ultimately rendering the final product so different, so worthy of the distinction of an original contribution, and ultimately profoundly unforgettable. I shall concentrate my attention on these elements in the *Dark Materials* trilogy.

First, a brief overview of those elements in *His Dark Materials*, which may be described in one of three ways: in this writer's view, the trilogy is primarily fantasy but also a combination of science fiction or science fiction fantasy. In any case, the elements are universal. They are the same ones I encountered at about age eight, when reading my first works of British fantasy. I preferred stories containing invented worlds and anthropomorphic creatures. For me, the quintessential fantasy had to be set in a well-constructed world, complete with its own conventions. I liked it best when the action first began in the real world, and I reveled in the rural setting of an English countryside. The major players had to be real children, who very often were involuntarily exiled from a city environment. And these children had to possess heroic qualities and be capable of doing great things. Much to my pleasure, I discovered that there was an entire body of literature that met these qualifications, and so I read my way through my childhood—and continue to do so through my adulthood. I suspect that Philip Pullman and I read many of the same books, for I see in his writing echoes of authors like Lewis Carroll, Edith Nesbit, Rudyard Kipling, J. R. R. Tolkien, even C. S. Lewis (whose *ideologies* were vigorously contested by Pullman), Susan Cooper, Alan Garner, and a host of others, some of whom I shall mention in this discussion.

Five Key High Fantasy Conventions

For purposes of this essay, five key fantasy conventions are identified and utilized as frameworks within which to view aspects of Philip Pullman's literary contributions in the trilogy. These are:

1. Young protagonists (sometimes greatly troubled) who have an important life mission that may be addressed through a crucial, otherworldly adventure;

2. An excursion into an invented world that may have well-defined boundaries (possibly mappable) or more abstract configurations;

3. Perilous journeys that provoke mind- (and life-) altering events and consequences;

4. Adult (and other) guides who offer information and assistance to major characters;

5. A return to the primary world with new information, insights, and abilities to address the problems that the protagonist(s) left behind.

These are not just conventions of fantasy but more specifically of "high fantasy," a type of serious fantasy that has mythic overtones, life and death battles between good and evil, and critical tasks for young protagonists to undertake. These tasks are accomplished through some form of magic, mystery, and not a little mayhem. High fantasy appeals to an audience who sometimes is a little atypical, sometimes the quiet, the introverted, the thoughtful child who has a great deal more going on inside him or her than most people might ever imagine. In the Anne Carroll Moore Lecture for 1988, given at the New York Public Library, Susan Cooper spoke of the child's need (in this case, the *American* child) for stories of fantasy and the importance of an understanding of inherited mythic patterns:

> We need to make sure that our children are given an early awareness
> of the timeless, placeless archetypes of myth. And since we have no

one single myth, that has to mean all the different—and yet similar—
mythic patterns we inherit, collectively, in this country from our very
diverse beginnings. I am speaking not only of ancient myth but of the
modern fantasy which is its descendant, its inheritor. Like poetry,
these are the books which speak most directly to the imagination.
("Fantasy in the Real World" 70)

Here Cooper summarizes the key aspects of high fantasy, stressing the need
for fantasy in the lives of young people, the role of ancient myth, and the
fact that the essence of myth gave rise to high fantasy. Not mentioned in
this excerpt, however, is the fact that high fantasy is often more difficult to
read and absorb than other types of writing. It can make incredible demands upon the mind, because of its intertextuality. If one has some understanding of the Bible, northern mythology, Greek mythology, classic
fairy tales, and William Shakespeare, one will find the *Dark Materials* trilogy
even more accessible. But even if this knowledge is not second nature, if one
is willing to do a little extra thinking and a bit of research there are great
possibilities for beginning to appreciate Pullman's work.

Convention I: Troubled Young People
with an Important Life Mission

Pullman's young people—Lyra Belacqua and, later, Will Parry—begin in a
state of sophisticated innocence. They are children, below the age of thirteen, who have had dysfunctional upbringings. Lyra has been raised in a
college where she was placed by the man she initially believes to be her
uncle, Lord Asriel. She does not immediately know the identity of her
mother, who later turns out to be Mrs. Coulter. Lyra roams the halls of
Jordan College, within an Oxford run by Scholars. Will Parry has been
raised by his mother, a woman who suffers from periods of schizophrenia.
His father, an explorer lost on an expedition, vanished some time ago. During episodes of her illness, his mother must rely upon her son for care.
Readers derive a sense of Will's necessary sophisticated innocence at the
very beginning of *The Subtle Knife* when we learn that Will has to arrange
for a caretaker for his mother while he is away on what will turn out to be
a life-changing adventure.

Both Will and Lyra possess a certain self-assuredness and a sense of
their life missions at the outset. They do not shrink from confronting the
unknown, even though they do not know what will be required of them.
British fantasy has earlier models for such protagonists: Curdie and Irene in

George MacDonald's *The Princess and the Goblin* (1872) and *The Princess and Curdie* (1883). Younger than Lyra and Will, these children are at risk from conniving goblins and savvy adults as they make their perilous journeys. *Alice in Wonderland* (1865) and *Through the Looking-Glass and What Alice Found There* (1872), though not representative of the high fantasy genre, feature a heroine who, while she doesn't start off on a perilous journey, must use her wits to maneuver through alien territory—humorously alien territory, but alien all the same. Moving ahead in time, we can look to the children in C. S. Lewis's "The Seven Chronicles of Narnia," published between 1950 and 1956. The children in these novels (Peter, Susan, Lucy, and Edmund—and later, Jill Pole, Eustace Scrubb, and Polly and Digory) are all preadolescents. The first four live in wartime England and have been sent off to the home of an old professor in the English countryside for safety. Eustace Scrubb (first met in *The Voyage of the Dawn Treader*) is the truly obnoxious relative who comes to stay with the four Pevensie children. (He has been reared via the questionable methods of "progressive schooling.") All of these major protagonists have difficulties that are resolved by the conclusions of the stories. And then there is Susan Cooper's Will Stanton, the hero of her "Dark Is Rising" sequence—which consists of five books: *Over Sea, Under Stone,* published in 1965 (Will doesn't appear in this one); *The Dark Is Rising* (1973); *Greenwitch* (1974); *The Grey King* (1975); and *Silver on the Tree* (1977)—who could well serve as a model for Pullman's Will Parry: Will Stanton is eleven and Pullman's Will Parry is twelve years old. (Note also the significance of their names: Will Parry's last name is defined as a verb, "to parry": "To ward off or deflect [a blow, the thrust of a sword, etc.]"—and also "to counter or ward off [criticism, a prying question, etc.] by a clever or evasive response" [*Webster's New World College Dictionary* 984]). Will Stanton in Cooper's books stands tall in the face of danger, his name indicative of his tendency to "stand up" in the face of adversity. This old tradition of "stock" names has its roots in allegorical literature and also in the fairy tale. Dickens, of course, used it widely in his novels (e.g., Mr. Gradgrind in *Hard Times*), as did other British writers of Victorian and earlier times.

The relatively young ages of Will Stanton, Will Parry, Lyra Belacqua, and many other protagonists in fantasy novels are significant. Part of the fantasy tradition embraces the concept that a person is particularly accessible to the wiles of the fantastic *before* adolescence. Youth offers a rationale for ignoring or denying the logic associated with adulthood. The richest fantasies tend to reveal that the "rules" established by the fantastic world make more sense, are more sophisticated, and offer more opportunities than those of the "real" world. Therefore, one ultimately matures in age and understanding during one's fantastic adventures in a way that can provide unique advantages when one returns to the "real" world. But these advantages are not always agreeable in context. Similarly, coming of age in fantasy is not without its dangers. Will and Lyra, for example, have to watch out for the dread Specters, who can be seen only by those past puberty and who, in fact, ingest only adolescents and adults. Children are of no interest to them. Pullman informs readers that coming of age and the subsequent attainment of wisdom and understanding come at a heavy price. Cooper's Will Stanton similarly has a heavy task: to assemble certain objects in *The Dark Is Rising* in order to thwart the powers of evil and deliver the world from destruction. In order to do this, he undertakes excursions back in time and to other fantasy dimensions.

Pullman thus works within a preexistent literary tradition, but his characters undergo heightened anguish and endure injuries more serious and more devastating than their fantastic predecessors. Will Parry, for example, loses several of his fingers in *The Subtle Knife,* and those bloody stumps bleed on and off in a horribly realistic manner during the remainder of the narrative. Lyra Belacqua narrowly misses execution when she is subjected to the torture of almost being separated from her daemon by the silver guillotine in *The Golden Compass.* The stakes are far higher in Pullman's trilogy than in previous stories for young people.

Convention 2: Excursions into Invented Worlds

The nature of the excursion is one of Pullman's most interesting extensions of an existing fantasy convention. In Victorian England, which is where the fantasy travel narrative first began in earnest, such trips were well defined by physical boundaries. So well defined in fact, that one could create actual maps to illustrate the journey. However, in the works of such authors as Susan Cooper and Philip Pullman, the reader encounters "complications" and more abstract places. Pullman's *The Golden Compass* is set in a fantastic Oxford, which geographically occupies the same site as the Oxford in the realistic contemporary world, but it is an Oxford that occupies another dimension in time. In *The Subtle Knife* protagonists travel from one world to another. The landscape of the first world Will enters, Cittàgazze, is very earthlike, essentially Italian, with characters named Paolo and Angelica. The time is indeterminate, and the location at first does not seem to be magical—quite ordinary, in fact. Until, that is, the reader encounters Angelica's older brother, who is fending off invisible Specters who are trying to consume him. But how does Will first enter Cittàgazze? Though he has not yet

learned to use the knife, he gains knowledge of the "rules" of entry by simply observing an innocuous-looking feline walk through a door in the air.

> Will, still watching, saw the cat behave curiously.
>
> She reached out a paw to pat something in the air in front
> of her, something quite invisible to Will. Then she leaped backward,
> back arched and fur on end, tail held out stiffly. Will knew cat behav-
> iour. He watched more alertly as the cat approached the spot again,
> just an empty patch of grass between the hornbeams and the bushes
> of a garden hedge, and patted the air once more . . .
>
> The cat stepped forward and vanished. (*Subtle Knife* [*SK*] 15).

What Will sees, it turns out, is an opening into another world. The passage
describing his entry into the parallel world is indeed very C. S. Lewis–like,
resembling the last chapter in *Prince Caspian* (1951), titled "Aslan Makes a
Door in the Air," allowing the children to leave Narnia. The deceptively
simple construction proves to be the entry into an afterlife: "At one end of
the glade Aslan had caused to be set up two stakes of wood, higher than a
man's head and about three feet apart. A third, and lighter, piece of wood
was bound across them at the top, uniting them, so that the whole thing
looked like a doorway from nowhere into nowhere." A "burly, decent-look-
ing fellow," one of the Telmarine soldiers, chooses to take Aslan's offer and
enter the opening. Aslan responds,

> "It is well chosen. . . . And because you have spoken first, strong
> magic is upon you. . . . Go through it, my son," said Aslan, bending
> towards him and touching the man's nose with his own. . . . Then he
> [the man] squared his shoulders and walked through the Door.
>
> Everyone's eyes were fixed on him. They saw the three pieces
> of wood, and through the trees and grass and sky of Narnia. They saw
> the man between the doorposts: then, in one second, he had vanished
> utterly. (284–85)

In Susan Cooper's *The Dark Is Rising* (1973), Will Stanton enters his fantasy
world through two giant doors on a hilltop disconnected from any reality
that he knows:

> And before him, standing alone and tall on the white slope, lead-
> ing to nowhere, were two great carved wooden doors. Will thrust his
> cold hands into his pockets, and stood staring up at the carved panels
> of the two closed doors towering before him. . . . There were no han-
> dles on the doors. Will stretched his arms forward, with the palm of

each hand flat against the wood, and he pushed. As the doors swung open beneath his hands, he thought that he caught a phrase of the fleeting bell-like music again; but then it was gone, into the misty gap between memory and imagining. And he was through the doorway, and without a murmur of sound the two huge doors swung shut behind him, and the light and the day and the world changed so that he forgot utterly what they had been . . .

"Come in, Will Stanton," he [Merriman Lyon] said, "come in and learn." (26–28)

It is interesting, perhaps ironic, that Pullman is no advocate of the work of Lewis, an author whose work he regards as a return to the past of conservative and stereotypic views of women and minorities. However, despite this viewpoint (however valid), there are certain conventions that are very much a part of British fantasy and frequently appear in the work of imaginative and inventive authors, and Pullman, like Lewis, employs them.

The British (and, later, Americans following in their footsteps) have always been intrigued by routes of entry into fantastic lands. And these routes, many and varied, are fascinating in and of themselves. In an article titled "The Weak Place in the Cloth," published in the October 1973 *Horn Book,* Jane Langton examined the various methods utilized by fantasy characters (and eventually the audience) to enter other worlds. Overlays of natural worlds upon fantastic ones and dream sequences are noted, among other portals. In *The Subtle Knife,* however, Will Parry's methods of ingress become sharp in context. Here, he learns to literally carve his way into new worlds via the use of the knife. The knife is subtle (an ironic designation) only inasmuch as one cannot actually *see* the cuts it makes. One *feels* them. The knife also does not look very different from other knives, but its power is tremendous and horrific. Such an instrument is not owned without sacrifice. In fact, the old man who teaches Will Parry how to use the knife lost his fingers in the process of owning and using it. Will Parry suffers the same fate. Ah, but what a knife! Will makes numerous incisions into the body of this fantastic dimension and with its help enters many worlds. He is not the only "innocent" mortal to enter fantastic universes.

The first entry of Dr. Mary Malone, the scientist investigating dark matter in *The Subtle Knife,* into worlds of the "improbable" takes place through the common ordinary vehicle of a tent, set up in the middle of a street in Oxford, supposedly erected to protect electrical repairs. It is a deliberately understated entryway, whose simple construction is fraught with irony. This portal, quietly amazing in its mundane quality, is juxtaposed against the complexity of the person of Dr. Malone and her mission in life. A former nun now disillusioned with her faith, Mary (her name, further evidence of the irony and also emblematic of her original mission) turns to science. She becomes involved in the quest to discern the nature of dark matter, which, it is eventually discovered, is a pseudonym for Dust or Original Sin. Unable to resist the call to her "displaced" inner consciousness, she sets out on a mission that her computer, referred to as "the Cave" (in reference to Plato), indicates to her is the way to the scientific answers she seeks. But, Pullman implies, it is as much scientific answers as those originally sought in her earlier religious quest that Mary seeks as she "continues" her journey by walking through that tent on Sunderland Avenue. The tent surrounds the entrance to another world, a world permeated by darkness and degrees of darkness that Mary tried to flee when she first abandoned her religious life in the convent. It is an otherworldly adventure, a spiritual trip to realms of darkness wryly suggested by Pullman through the use of the word "Sunderland" (sounding very like "under the land"). When Mary walks through that tent and into Cittàgazze, she leaves whatever innocence she had and, drawn by destiny, leaves the earth as we know it—and also the book. We do not see her again until she reappears in *The Amber Spyglass*.

After tasting the mysteries of Cittàgazze (which apparently she has been doing for a week before the reader meets her again) Mary encounters another window or portal, and travels through it, Lewis-style, into yet another world:

> She approached the little patch of air with passionate curiosity, because she hadn't had time to look at the first one: she'd had to get away as quickly as possible. But she examined this one in detail, touching the edge, moving around to see how it became invisible from the other side, noting the absolute difference between *this* and *that*, and found her mind almost bursting with excitement that such things could be.
>
> The knife bearer who had made it, at about the time of the American Revolution, had been too careless to close it, but at least he'd cut through at a point very similar to the world on this side: next to a rock face. But the rock on the other side was different, not limestone but granite, and as Mary stepped through into the new world she found herself not at the foot of a towering cliff but almost at the top of a low outcrop overlooking a vast plain. (*Amber Spyglass* [*AS*] 82–83)

Pullman's description of Mary's entry into the new world is initially feline, comparable to the earlier entry made by the cat and observed by Will. But

Mary's second entry is accompanied by further evidence of intellect, signaling the fact that she is growing in knowledge. Pullman as omniscient observer, also reserves (and exercises) the right to furnish the reader with detached but helpful explanations. He provides a historical context dating back to the American Revolution as the period of creation of this portal. In so doing, Pullman generates a sense of *reality* about this entryway. The reference to the American Revolution is indisputably a pragmatic event, not just dramatic in implication for Americans but for the world; not simply an event occurring at a given point in time but one resonating into the future. Mary's entrance into the new world, while based upon an entry provided by someone else in the past, has about it the air of purposefulness, an entrance crucial to the events that will follow. The fact that she is also a scientist lends credence and import to her excursion. In this way Pullman extends the context of the simple curiosity demonstrated by the cat. Mary has gone beyond basic curiosity and has acceded to the pull of destiny and a scientist's natural inclination toward experimentation.

But it is evident that failure to seal up the "windows" made by the knife has created a terrible dilemma, comparable to misuse of the environment in our own world. At the end of *The Amber Spyglass*, the reader discovers that all the knife cuts, the creation of windows into other worlds, are actually draining the worlds of energy or "Dust." The only way to stop this draining is to seal up the openings that have been left by careless knife bearers. Such a turn in story line is evidence of Pullman's ability to go beyond established conventions, find threads undeveloped by previous fantasy authors, and create a realistic and rational literary fabric. While other authors show us how to get into magic worlds, there are generally few consequences that result from *paving the way*. There *are* dangers in store for those who pass through the door and must deal with what is encountered in the new world, but there are *not* dangers resulting from paving the way. Pullman uses conventional means for entry into new worlds but goes beyond the fact of entry by posing the questions: What are the *consequences* of creating portals? And what can (and should) be done about portals once they have been created? Ultimately, it is the need to seal up all of these openings that separates Lyra and Will, who have discovered their mutual love. The reader's psyche is challenged; the limitations of potentially derivative devices are surmounted.

Convention 3: Perilous Journeys

Pullman's perilous journeys are devastating. While all works of fantasy involve some form of journey, many of those in earlier fantasies were delightful, almost tourlike in context. The trips made by the children in Hilda Lewis's *The Ship That Flew* (1939), Mary Norton's *The Magic Bed-Knob; or How to Become a Witch in Ten Easy Lessons* (1943), or the relatively mild excursions made by the children in Barbara Sleigh's *Carbonel* (1955), *The Kingdom of Carbonel* (1960), and the final sequel, *Carbonel and Calidor: Being the Further Adventures of a Royal Cat* (1978), are all examples of early prototypes. These adventures, while not without danger, when compared to those in Pullman's *Dark Materials* and the works of other authors of high fantasy, may be judged as relatively innocuous. In high fantasy, traveling becomes a perilous affair. Irene and Curdie in George MacDonald's Victorian fantasies are chased by frightening, meat-eating goblins in his *The Princess and the Goblin* (1872), one of the earliest examples of high fantasy. In C. S. Lewis's stories, which may be categorized as "early" high fantasy, the excursions are filled with some danger and a great deal of adventure. Will Stanton's journeys in Cooper's "Dark Is Rising" sequence often threaten life and limb. We find the same in works like Alan Garner's fantasy novels, *The Weirdstone of Brisingamen* (1960) and *The Moon of Gomrath* (1963). However, Pullman's journeys are so perilous that the reader may wonder whether or not the children will actually make it back. In fact, one child, Roger, has already lost his life in *The Golden Compass.* Loyalty, a quality both prized (between and among friends and compatriots) and questioned (when applied to faith and doctrine) stimulates Lyra's journey to Hades in *The Amber Spyglass* to bring Roger back to the world of the living. Here the reader finds interesting borrowings and allusions as well.

The journey to the world of the dead is the most terrifying excursion that the children make in the story. The surprising and rather unpredictable nature of Pullman's narrative art indicates to us that it is possible that they will not return, even though the tradition in fantasy literature is that the heroes and heroines always return to their environment, or at least go someplace else eminently better. Fantasy offers varying levels of escapism dependent upon the depth of the writer's imaginative prowess. A journey to the world of the dead is formidable and is one rarely undertaken in children's literature. In classical tradition this is an Orpheic journey. Readers will recall that in the Greek myth, Orpheus is instructed not to look back. Unable to resist, he does look back, and Eurydice vanishes. The story has haunting resonances and obviously haunted Pullman as well. He pushes the analogy further by having the children ferried over by a boatman, who resembles Charon, the boatman of Hell who ferries the dead across the river Styx. Visiting Hell is an expensive excursion. Orpheus found the price (to avoid looking back) too heavy for him and ultimately fails the test. The price for Pullman's children? They must leave their individual souls behind, or as Pullman calls them (somewhat ironically), their *daemons*. For Lyra, parting from her daemon means a separation so wrenching that some readers may in fact ask themselves whether this is appropriate for a middle-grade children's or young adult book. (Will is mercifully still unaware of his daemon.) However, Pullman's respect for the intellectual, emotional, and physical potential of young people will not permit less fidelity to the art of storytelling and narrative direction. Thus, he expects his readers to make a leap in understanding and acquire emotional strength (if they are not already in possession of it), just as his protagonists must do. Children who make the intellectual journey in reading Pullman gain substantial education through a rich though noncondescending story line. Any young person who takes the time to assimilate such writing will be well prepared in later years to confront Dante Alighieri's "Inferno" in *The Divine Comedy.*

Convention 4: Adult (and Other) Guides Proffer Information and Assistance

Numerous guides proffer information and assistance during the traversing of perilous landscapes by Pullman's protagonists. Once again he borrows liberally from many sources.

Pullman's Oxford training afforded him an enviable classical/literary education. His knowledge of early texts, mythology, and previously discussed conventions are freely drawn upon, as are the works of individuals like William Shakespeare and John Milton. He utilizes this knowledge in nongratuitous ways that effectively aid or inform the protagonists in the trilogy. For example, his reference to the ancient Chinese text *I Ching, Book of Changes* in *The Subtle Knife*, a poster of which is hung emblematically in Mary Malone's office, is symbolic of the changes she has undergone and will undergo in the future. As Mary prepares for her most life-changing journey, she includes this text among her belongings, and later, in *The Amber Spyglass*, uses it as a guide in her attempt to understand her current situation. It is a precious parcel she carries; Pullman notes that she has wrapped it in silk. This is both a tribute to the Chinese origins of *I Ching* as well as to the preserving qualities of the fabric. Pullman demonstrates how possessing reverence and respect for the past can be of great use to one in "present" circumstances:

> She read:
>   Turning to the summit

For provision of nourishment
Brings good fortune.
Spying about with sharp eyes
Like a tiger with insatiable craving
(81)

Mary has already entered Cittàgazze in a combined state of curiosity, destiny, and her own natural desire for scientific experimentation. The ancient text advises her that she can no longer afford her initial luxury of happenstance; she must now be vigilant and calculating in her moves. In so doing, Pullman raises Malone's broad knowledge base to a higher level. *I Ching* serves as a crucial training guide for what Mary must do to both survive and complete her mission successfully.

When Mary Malone first arrives in Cittàgazze, she is aided by an elderly couple who help to psychologically ease the way as she prepares to negotiate the unfamiliar terrain of that place. The couple is modeled on Baucis and Philemon, together a paradigm of hospitality in Greek myth. The myth indicates that during the times when the gods roamed the earth, Zeus and Hermes came to the house of Baucis and Philemon and were greatly impressed with the hospitality they received there. In payment for their kindness, the gods ensured that when the couple died, instead of merely having their bodies go into the earth, they would be remembered in perpetuity. Their bodies would be transformed into trees that would live forever outside the cottage, which had been a haven of hospitality. In fact, that cottage ultimately served as a temple for passersby. Pullman's benefactors offer Mary "wine and cheese and bread and olives" (*AS* 79), apparent direct references to Greek landscape and hospitality. Later, Will and Lyra encounter their counterparts in the "suburbs of the dead" (258) just prior to making their painful journey to the underworld. This couple welcomes them (and others), offering the children stew and, later, bread and tea.

Another unique form of assistance is that offered by the strange "horses" encountered by Mary Malone in *The Amber Spyglass*. This episode is reminiscent of the passage in Jonathan Swift's *Travels into Several Remote Nations of the World* (1726) in which Gulliver encounters the horselike Houyhnhnms. Pullman's "*mulefa*" are horselike, but they also have trunks—so they are elephant-like as well. When first seen, they appear to be grazing. They mobilize themselves by hooking claws through seedpods, which they manipulate like wheels. In Gulliver's first encounter with the Houyhnhnms, they stand and observe each other, in much the same way that Mary Malone and the *mulefa* do. Eventually, Swift's Gulliver decides that the Houyhnhnms have an intelligence of their own and possess a way of communicating—even though it is alien to him. Mary Malone discovers the same thing about the *mulefa*, and eventually they learn to communicate with one another. Gulliver is astounded by the intelligence of the Houyhnhnms, and Mary Malone, in turn, is amazed by the intelligence of the *mulefa*.

The *mulefa* offer much assistance to her, and Mary reciprocates by offering help to Lyra and Will. In fact, Mary makes a commitment to serve as a caregiver, an offer that conveys both affection and loyalty. At the very end of the story, when Mary and Will travel back to their world of Oxford, she agrees to take Will and his mother in until they can get other assistance. Thus, the availability of help in the parallel world continues into the "real" environment.

In addition to the alethiometer given to Lyra in *The Golden Compass,* and other forms of assistance rendered to Lyra and Will by humanlike contacts during their quest, additional assistance is offered by beings not conventionally viewed as helpful. Such is the case of assistance offered by the witches, whom the reader soon learns can be as helpful or as unhelpful as any humans or humanlike beings encountered. In this context, Pullman does not neglect a Shakespearean model. When the witches gather in *The Subtle Knife* to create a spell designed to cure Will's battered hand, the chant reminds one of the witches' chant in *Macbeth.* Many ingredients go into Pullman's brew, including "entrails." But while *his* witches are able to discern the origins of the knife and the historic damage that it has done, their more human state precludes their effectiveness in the manipulation of magical arts. There is promise and hope and potential power in the incantation they utter, but the magic fails. Unlike Shakespeare's witches, they lack a crucial ingredient—in this case, bloodwort—and this makes all the difference. Ironically, it is Will's father, whom he meets briefly, just prior to his death, who holds the powerful restorative. Once again, Pullman appears to be traversing creative roads paved earlier by gifted literary minds. But once again the reader is offered surprises congruent with the situation at hand, unanticipated by the reader, yet in retrospect eminently plausible within the context of the narrative.

Yet another significant example of guidance rendered occurs in *The Amber Spyglass.* Pullman transplants harpies from the world of Greek myth into the fantasy construction. Initially, they seem demonic, but they surprise the reader by evolving into humanized figures who raise for the reader the possibilities of forgiveness and character transformation. Initially, they are the last beings that anyone would want to consider as possible guides or assistants:

> As the travelers saw her more clearly, she became even more repulsive.
> Her eye sockets were clotted with filthy slime, and the redness of her

lips was caked and crusted as if she had vomited ancient blood again
and again. Her matted, filthy black hair hung down to her shoulders;
her jagged claws gripped the stone fiercely; her powerful dark wings
were folded along her back; and a drift of putrescent stink wafted
from her every time she moved. (*AS* 290)

Yet, through Lyra's kindness and real humanity, the harpies are assigned an
important task that establishes for them a sense of self-worth (that is, the
task of guiding the dead to the upper world, where their souls will become
dispersed matter in the living realm), and their hearts are softened. In fact,
it is a harpy who ultimately saves Lyra's life. Lyra's renaming of the harpy
signals an interesting (and ironically, almost religious) conversion:

> "I am going to call you Gracious Wings. So that's your name now,
> and that's what you'll be for evermore: Gracious Wings."
>
> "One day," said the harpy, "I will see you again, Lyra Silver-
> tongue."
>
> "And if I know you're here, I shan't be afraid," Lyra said.
> "Good-bye, Gracious Wings, till I die."
>
> She embraced the harpy, hugging her tightly and kissing her
> on both cheeks. (386)

Convention 5: Return to the Primary World
with New Information, Insights, Abilities

In *The Amber Spyglass*, the final volume of the trilogy, Lyra and Will return
to their primary worlds with new information, insights, and abilities. A ma-
turing Will and Lyra discover their love for each other. Part of that maturity is acknowledgment of pain, in this case the pain of separation. Lyra has
also lost both of her parents, but this is a fact that Pullman chooses not to
share with her. Unlike previous works of British fantasy for children and
young adults, the return to the primary world in his *Dark Materials* trilogy
is not without great sadness. The only way Will can remain with Lyra is to
be permanently separated from his mother in the "real" world as well as the
life's work that he must do. Painful choice is often conceived of as an adult
predicament; but in reality, young people can easily be placed in such situations. Pullman provides his protagonists with such a growth opportunity.
Part of Will's ongoing task is to *discover* the nature of that work.

> "What work have I got to do, then?" said Will, but went on at
> once, "No, on second thought, don't tell me. *I* shall decide what I do.
> If you say my work is fighting, or healing, or exploring, or whatever

you might say, I'll always be thinking about it. And if I do end up doing that, I'll be resentful because it'll feel as if I didn't have a choice, and if I don't do it, I'll feel guilty because I should. Whatever I do, I will choose it, no one else." (496)

This is a significant change in perspective from earlier fantasies, where essentially, the work is done by the conclusion of the novel. This is not to say that protagonists have not learned lessons that will affect them in later life. Rather, the primary object of their journeys has been achieved by the conclusion of the story. This is certainly the case in the Narnian chronicles, though we note the heavy biblical implications of Lewis's final story, *The Last Battle* (1956), in which all of the children are told by Aslan that they are dead and now residents of the Shadowlands. The point, however, is that they are *dead together*. Some readers may interpret this as Lewis's attempt to spare us the heartbreak of having the children grieve for parents, siblings, and friends they will never see again. There will be no separations:

> Lucy said, "We're so afraid of being sent away, Aslan. And you have sent us back into our own world so often."
> "No fear of that," said Aslan. "Have you not guessed?"
> Their hearts leapt, and a wild hope rose within them.
> "There *was* a real railway accident," said Aslan softly. "Your father and mother and all of you are—as you used to call it in the Shadowlands— dead. The term is over: The holidays have begun. The dream is ended: this is the morning." (524)

It is interesting to note that Pullman has taken vehement exception to this passage, calling the act of having all of the protagonists die at the end "propaganda in the service of a life-hating ideology" ("Dark Side of Narnia"). However, it is important to remember that Lewis and Pullman stand diametrically opposed on the issue of Christianity and the afterlife. While Lewis views death as an opportunity for the faithful to gain an everlasting life, Pullman views death as an end, with no consolation save perhaps becoming a part of nature. This renders Pullman's separations—those that embody the death experience as well as the act of saying farewell to loved ones whom you know (or doubt) you will see again—more absolute, heartrending, and, in a sense, less compromising than endings such as Lewis's.

At the end of Cooper's *Silver on the Tree* (1978), which concludes her "Dark Is Rising" sequence, we are privy to a successful battle, in which we witness the triumph of good over evil, a triumph that functions as a familiar model in high fantasy. However, it is a triumph just narrowly achieved, showing the small opportunity that good may have in many cases in winning the final battle. In the final scene, both forces strive to retrieve the silver blossom on the tree, which will signal the winner of the conflict. It is an exciting struggle, leaving the reader breathless at the conclusion. However, readers during the seventies would have been shocked had the battle been lost or won with the major protagonists suffering a major mishap. But in the twenty-first century, child audiences and child protagonists are expected to be made of sterner stuff. It is this "stuff" that Pullman calls upon in his work. Ironically, the resolute British nature of earlier times, witnessed in works for adults and young adults, takes over in a series for children and young adults that could have been written only at the beginning of the twenty-first century. Now, that resolution, that need to maintain courage in the face of discomfort or tragedy applies to the young in a genre once viewed as primarily escapist and is well demonstrated through Pullman's contributions to the genre.

Conclusion

In his *Dark Materials* trilogy, Philip Pullman functions as narrative "magician" in his ability to interweave the unique strands of narrative elements at once familiar yet simultaneously fresh, innovative, and inspiring. Marcel Mauss has stated in *A General Theory of Magic* (1950) that "the art of the magician involves suggesting means, enlarging on the virtues of objects, anticipating effects, and by these methods fully satisfying the desires and expectations which have been fostered by entire generations in common" (142). The dark materials that function at the core of Pullman's stories not only investigate the original sin that so concerns the protagonists in the stories, but they also serve as metaphor for the dark excursions undertaken by them. Through such inventively crafted excursions and the power of allusions conveyed in an original and convincing way, Pullman forces us to examine our own hearts and reconsider those things that in some cases we try to ignore and in others have come to take for granted. Through casting new enchantments upon old conventions, Pullman encourages the reader to move forward, confront previously held expectations, and consider new possibilities. We are entranced by some of the images presented, chastened by the sobering significance of others, and repelled in still other instances. But regardless of individual comfort levels, Pullman demands that the reader think, digest, and consider the possibilities and consequences of human behavior in general, and ultimately that which lies within the core of our individual beings.

Works Cited

Cooper, Susan. "Fantasy in the Real World." *Dreams and Wishes: Essays on Writing for Children.* New York: Margaret K. McElderry, 1996. 57–71.

Lewis, C. S. *The Complete Chronicles of Narnia.* London: Collins, 1998.

Mauss, Marcel. *A General Theory of Magic.* Trans. Robert Brain. 1950. New York: Norton, 1972.

Pullman, Philip. *The Amber Spyglass.* New York: Knopf, 2000.

———. "The Dark Side of Narnia." *The Guardian* October 1, 1998. http://web.archive.org/web/20010628221443/http://riff.hiof.no./~steinabl/PULLMANLEW.HTML.

———. *The Golden Compass.* New York: Knopf, 1995.

———. *The Subtle Knife.* 1997. New York: Dell Yearling, 2001.

Webster's New World College Dictionary. 3rd ed. New York: Simon and Schuster, 1997.

Additional Works

Carroll, Lewis [Charles Lutwidge Dodgson]. *Alice's Adventures in Wonderland.* London: Macmillan, 1866.

———. *Through the Looking-Glass, And What Alice Found There.* London: Macmillan, 1872.

Cooper, Susan. *The Dark Is Rising.* New York: Atheneum, 1973.

———. *Greenwitch.* New York: Atheneum, 1974.

———. *The Grey King.* New York: Atheneum, 1975.

———. *Over Sea, Under Stone.* 1965. New York: Harcourt, Brace & World, 1966.

———. *Silver on the Tree.* New York: Atheneum, 1977.

Garner, Alan. *The Moon of Gomrath.* 1963. London: Lions, 1978.

———. *The Weirdstone of Brisingamen.* 1960. London: Lions, 1979.

I Ching; Book of Changes. New York: Bantam, 1969.

Langton, Jane, "The Weak Place in the Cloth." *Horn Book* 49.5 (1973): 433–41.

Lewis, Hilda. *The Ship That Flew.* Oxford: Oxford UP, 1939.

MacDonald, George. *The Princess and Curdie.* London: Chatto and Windus, 1883.

———. *The Princess and the Goblin.* London: Strahan, 1872.

Norton, Mary. *The Magic Bed-knob; or How to Become a Witch in Ten Easy Lessons.* New York: Hyperion, 1943.

Sleigh, Barbara. *Carbonel.* 1955. Harmondsworth: Puffin, 1961.

———. *Carbonel and Calidor: Being the Further Adventures of a Royal Cat.* Harmondsworth: Kestrel, 1978.

———. *The Kingdom of Carbonel.* 1960. Harmondsworth: Puffin.

Swift, Jonathan. *Gulliver's Travels: An Account of the Four Voyages into Several Remote Nations of the World; Now Written Down by Jonathan Swift.* New York: Heritage, c. 1940.

III
PULLMAN AND THEOLOGY, PULLMAN AND SCIENCE FICTION

The five essays in this final section raise a number of key questions in the interpretation of Pullman's *His Dark Materials*, such as, what is his novelistic stance vis-à-vis theology or, more specifically, Christianity? More broadly, how do his narratives relate to some of the ultimate questions raised by philosophers and theologians? Does he really, as one commentator has argued, identify religion as the villain in the human condition? (See Sarah Lyall, "The Man Who Dared Make Religion the Villain; In British Author's Trilogy, Great Adventures Aren't Pegged to the Great Beyond." *New York Times* [November 7, 2000], late ed.: EI.) One thing seems certain: Pullman's perspective is subtle and complicated, as witnessed by the five essays that follow, all of which offer much food for serious thought in their differing interpretations of both the explicit and implicit religious, antireligious, or agnostic views emanating from the narratives of the trilogy. *His Dark Materials*—like fantasy and its closely related genre, science fiction (or its close kin, "speculative fiction")—often concerns itself with ultimate values and theological/philosophical questions. Some of the questions raised by reading Pullman's trilogy are, for example, What sort of Supreme Being (if any) exists in our own universe? and What is the relationship of humankind to this higher power (or in Pullman's terms, the "Authority")? Similarly, if the Authority is dead, where does humankind find an alternative theological vision, a basis for defining the meaning of human life? *His Dark Materials*, as Anne-Marie Bird writes, posits consciousness (Dust in Pullman's terms) as "The central presence in the trilogy . . . the *logos*," and it is created through the shaping of stories, as Lyra finds in her visit to the underworld: thus the creation of stories gives shape and meaning to human life. But what about the perennial mystery of the suffering of the innocent—such as the hapless Roger, for whom Lyra risks all? How do human beings deal with the age-old problem of evil (metaphorically, one could say, the Specters)? What is the nature of "sin" and guilt? How can contemporary readers find meaning and significance in biblical stories, and especially the story of Eve and Adam—the original parents—and what does the "Fall" mean in relationship to the destiny of humankind? In the absence of belief in God, who can define what the catechism calls "the whole end of man" (clearly we can no longer take refuge in the traditional catechized answer, "to glorify God and enjoy him forever")? Or if God is dead or silent, why are we here and what is the meaning of our lives? What about the ultimate question facing every individual—is death the end of life? If this must remain a mystery, how shall we prepare ourselves to enter, in Shakespeare's words, "The undiscovered country from whose bourn / No traveller returns"? (*Hamlet*, III, i, 79–80). It is naive, of course, to expect Pullman to answer these questions, nor should a novelist be expected to do so, but what he can and has done is to dramatize them and present them for our contemplation and as subjects of academic discourse.

In the opening essay, "'And He's A-Going to Destroy Him': Religious Subversion in Philip Pullman's Trilogy *His Dark Materials*," Bernard Schweizer finds *His Dark Materials* to be an "anomaly" among fantasy novels in its subversion of "the most basic tenets of Christianity." Though Pullman seems to dismantle biblical teaching on "theism, creation, original sin and divine Providence," Schweizer points to a puzzling complacency on the part of both critics and the general reading public. Why have Pullman's bold theological musings raised few eyebrows, despite the firestorm of religious indignation elicited by some current fantasy books? The complacency may stem from an inability to "account conceptually and historically for Pullman's religious heresy." Schweizer places the trilogy in a broad historical, literary, and philosophical framework in order "to define more precisely the nature of Pullman's provocative theological premises." He reviews critical response, ranging from the negative critiques of Alan Jacobs and Cynthia Grenier to the chiefly congratulatory reviews from mainstream journalists. Of particular interest are the diametrically opposed readings of the Hitchens brothers, Peter and Christopher. Pullman's anticlericalism, the "moral authority" of the witches' pronouncements, Asriel's open warfare against god, and the depiction of the Authority as "a fraud and a liar" are all examined. Texts ranging from William Empson's *Milton's God* to works of Tennessee Williams, Elie Wiesel, and others are invoked to show Pullman's "elaboration of an intellectual tradition" of misotheism (etymologically, based on the Greek root "misos" for hatred and "theos" for deity). Pullman's receptivity to "a different kind of deity, notably a female one," may reveal leanings toward feminist ideology, suggesting "a feminine understanding of grace as fusing both sex and wisdom." Significantly, Pullman writes in an often-neglected genre in today's world, the novel of ideas. The question of the trilogy's suitability for an audience of children is also broached. Ultimately, Schweizer affirms the "liberating and positive" side of Pullman's iconoclasm.

From quite another perspective, Andrew Leet incorporates perspectives from science fiction criticism to support his view that Pullman's trilogy does not exclude or devalue some form of Christianity and religious values. Leet begins "Rediscovering Faith through Science Fiction: Pullman's *His*

Dark Materials" by affirming the role of science fiction in theological speculation; he then shows how *His Dark Materials* treats three theological
themes: popular conceptions of the afterlife, heaven, and hell; the role of
the soul as a marker of humanity and individuality, drawing upon Paul
Tillich's concept of faith as "ultimate concern"; and compassion and mystery as "the ultimate cores of religious belief." His essay critiques the
Church of Lyra's world as basically "non-Christian," contrasting its corruption with the morally and religiously based values of the "gyptian" community. He draws upon Pullman's own statements relating to the influence
of religion upon his formative years. Leet traces Lyra's spiritual journey
from innocence toward the realm of mature rediscovery of "natural truth"
through "conscious understanding." His close reading of the novels cites
textual evidence for their ultimate reaffirmation of the theological concept
of "mystery." Defending Pullman against the charge that he is an atheist or
God-killer, Leet reads Pullman's trilogy as an affirmation of a religious
stance in the broadest and deepest sense of the meaning of *faith:* faith comprehends "questioning the role of organized religion," as well as examining
"popular perceptions of heaven and hell . . . [and] examining the importance of the soul." Pullman's accomplishment finally is made possible
through his "appreciation of theological mystery."

Working from still different premises than the more traditional theological framework of Andrew Leet, Anne-Marie Bird similarly arrives at an
alternative theological vision with mystery at its core in "Circumventing the
Grand Narrative: Dust as an Alternative Theological Vision in Pullman's
His Dark Materials." Drawing on theories of postmodernism and poststructuralism—in particular, Derrida's theory of Deconstruction—Bird explores Pullman's attempt to construct an alternative theological vision that
is particularly attuned to the secular humanistic climate of the late twentieth century. As her analysis shows, the key to Pullman's alternative vision is
his rich and paradoxical concept of Dust, which she finds to be the "central presence in the trilogy," "the *logos* or 'Total Being,' the ultimate cause or
'ground,'" "a First Cause." Initially, she places Pullman within a tradition of
dissent (represented by modernist thinkers such as Nietzsche, Marx, and
Freud), but then distinguishes him from the likes of Nietzsche, for Pullman
believes in the "joy and enchantment of everyday life." Further, her textual
evidence demonstrates how the "instability" of Dust enables Pullman to
build "an alternative theological vision with Dust at its center" (the "logocentric quest" being at the core of the trilogy) yet allows him to avoid constructing "a new grand narrative." Though he constructs a "'system' of

sorts," the free play of meaning surrounding Dust renders his vision open and egalitarian, not totalizing and authoritarian. Dust thus functions as a "new focus for our spirituality," without which humanity would lack meaning, purpose, and "a sense of wonder and mystery."

Pat Pinsent brings her knowledge of feminist theology to bear upon *His Dark Materials* in "Unexpected Allies? Pullman and the Feminist Theologians." As she convincingly demonstrates, despite the fact that the views Philip Pullman espouses in the *His Dark Materials* trilogy have shocked and worried many Christians, notably Evangelicals and right-wing Catholics, readers familiar with the insights of feminist theologians, on the other hand, may have felt quite at ease with the challenges to established religion which Pullman poses. His critique of the Church, in particular, recalls much of the work of Rosemary Radford Ruether and Ursula King; his rejection of the traditional image of God is likely to be congenial to readers of Sallie McFague and Mary Grey; while his suggestion that the Fall should not be seen as disaster but as, effectively, a coming of age is foreshadowed in the theological approach of Anne Primavesi. His creation of an enterprising and spiritually questing female protagonist in Lyra is likely to be welcome to all who have been inspired by the rereading of Scripture presented by writers such as Elisabeth Fiorenza and Elisabeth Moltmann-Wendel. Readers who resonate to the themes of feminist theology and spirituality are, Pinsent affirms, "likely to have felt that in many ways Pullman is a kindred spirit," though on the other hand she notes that "the debunking of religion that he has undertaken should ideally be part of a positive process, not to establish the somewhat debatable 'Republic of Heaven' but to revalue the more profound spiritual insights" already "latent within religious and spiritual sources." In such an undertaking, the feminist theologians "could be seen as allies." Pinsent may provoke the intriguing thought that Lyra (imagining her future extra-novelistic academic life) might acquire a profound knowledge of religious and spiritual literatures (assuming these exist in her universe), and that perhaps in such "stories" might find a more enduring and trustworthy "myth" than the "Republic of Heaven."

The book closes with "'Eve, Again! Mother Eve!': Pullman's Eve Variations" by Mary Harris Russell, a study of the Eve of traditional religion, the alternative Eves of some non-Scriptural, non-canonical writings of both Hebrew (e.g., Enochic) and early Christian authors (including the "dissident" Gnostics), and finally Pullman's Eve variations—Marisa Coulter, Mary Malone, and Lyra herself, tracing "this [last] new Eve" through all three volumes, in her quest for both intellectual and emotional knowing and in her initiation into sexual knowing. In the non-canonical traditions,

an alternative Eve—mother of all and sometimes associated with knowledgeable serpents—is "above all an insistent seeker of knowledge." Not
until the fourth century C.E. did Eve's quest for knowledge begin to be
viewed as (like Pandora's curiosity) the source of humanity's woes. All of
Pullman's Eves seek knowledge, and the older two, Marisa and Mary, give
context to Lyra's search for self-knowledge. Marisa Coulter incorporates the
femme fatale elements of Lilith (the apocryphal first woman who chose to
leave Adam to escape domination), hence the first "alternative" Eve. Despite Coulter's morally flawed nature, her combination of knowledge and
beauty at first mesmerizes Lyra; later, her latent motherhood begins to
emerge, and she and Lord Asriel ultimately give their lives to save Lyra.
Mary Malone models the "serpent mother, the initiator into knowledge,"
both rational and sensual. Pullman's new Edenic myth portrays Lyra as an
Eve who is a knowledge seeker and a maker of important decisions who will
shape the future of humankind. Understanding her role illuminates the link
between two major plot events in *The Amber Spyglass*—namely, "the sexual
knowing that takes place between Will and Lyra" and "the disintegration of
the Authority." Russell puts it succinctly: "when the new Eve is ready for
the new creation, built on truth, the old Authority, built on a lie, must vanish." Russell emphasizes that no deicide is involved; rather, there is a transition "between deceit seen as 'aged' and true knowledge embodied as
'youth.'" Lyra, in a new garden at the close of *His Dark Materials*, signals
hope for a new era of human life.

10

"And He's A-Going to Destroy Him": Religious Subversion in Pullman's *His Dark Materials*

Bernard Schweizer

The end of the twentieth and the beginning of the twenty-first century brought with it a sense of doubt, uncertainty, and searching. At the same time, science fiction and fantasy books with a religious slant were burgeoning. From Theodore Beale's "The Eternal Warriors" series, to Octavia E. Butler's "Earthseed" novels, to the grimly apocalyptic "Left Behind" blockbusters (coauthored by Tim LaHaye and Jerry Jenkins), the hunger for "speculative fiction—and particularly for adaptations of Christianity to new and undreamed-of possibilities—was a remarkable thing during the period of millennial transition. In an article for *Publishers Weekly*, Kimberly Winston noted that "in the past couple of years, authors and publishers have been producing more SF/fantasy titles that in some way incorporate religion or religious themes than they have since the days of George Mac-Donald and C. S. Lewis." Speaking of C. S. Lewis, his pious "Narnia Chronicles" as well as Tolkien's epic battle between Good and Evil in *The Lord of the Rings* were, of course, also enjoying a sustained and even spectacular revival.

Enter *His Dark Materials*, which appears to occupy the same hybrid genre of religious fantasy novel and to tap into the same market. But there is a remarkable difference here: although the above-named fantasy writers stretched and modified biblical teachings in their tales of other worlds and future times, they still affirmed the basic tenets of Christianity. Philip Pullman, on the other hand, chips away at the very basis of Christian doctrine. In his fictive world, religion is mass deception; God is a grizzled, tottering liar; his prince-regent a kind of devil; and the servants of the Church as corrupt as they are tyrannical. What's more, a band of children under the leadership of a prepubescent girl put God out of his misery, help defeat the heavenly powers that be, and proclaim their intention to establish a "Republic of Heaven."

Despite virtually dismantling the biblical teachings about theism, creation, original sin, and divine Providence, Pullman's series garnered much critical acclaim and generated a swiftly growing readership in the late 1990s and into the new millennium. This enthusiastic reception took some astute reviewers and industry experts by surprise. Shannon Maughan from *Publishers Weekly* wondered why "Pullman's bold theological musings have hardly raised an eyebrow." Similarly, Alona Wartofsky's review of *The Amber Spyglass* in the *Washington Post* of February 2001 was subtitled "Philip Pullman's Trilogy for Young Adults Ends with God's Death and Remarkably Few Critics." Wartofsky went on to say that the scarcity of critical comments about Pullman's trilogy "is particularly surprising given that religious fundamentalists have criticized the relatively innocuous Harry Potter series as a glorification of 'pagan' witchcraft." How should one account for this complacency vis-à-vis Pullman's radical theological subversion? Is it a sign that religious fundamentalism is on the retreat? That would be too good to be true, though, and indeed an unconvincing explanation. More to the point, I will argue that the author of *His Dark Materials* tapped into a stream of antitheistic rebellion (with roots in Thomas Paine, Nietzsche, Swinburne, and anarchists like Bakunin) that has simply not been promoted to the status of a major intellectual tradition to date. In situating *His Dark Materials* in such a historical, literary, and philosophical context, I will focus less on institutional and liturgical aspects of Pullman's religious provocation than on the fundamental theological implications of his argument.

The full scale of Pullman's religious subversion emerged only with the third and concluding volume of the trilogy, *The Amber Spyglass* (2000). Shortly after its publication, Alan Jacobs published what might be the first article condemning the heretical underpinnings of the work. Pullman is taken to task because "the theological freight of his books . . . turns out to be a distinct *anti*-theology" (40), something Jacob considers to be "a reductive and contemptuous ideology" (40). Jacobs is particularly piqued by Pullman's "*truly* anti-theological point that whether God lives or dies is not in the long run a very significant matter" (42), an attitude he rightly contrasts with that of Blake and Milton (from whom Pullman draws much inspiration) because both of them, though declared anticlerics, were not antitheologians. Jacobs's negative response, however, remained by and large a minority view, as mostly congratulatory reviews kept appearing in the *Times Literary Supplement*, the *Boston Globe*, the *New York Times*, and so forth. But in October 2001, another religiously inspired critique of Pullman's literary undertaking appeared. Cynthia Grenier, of the Catholic monthly magazine *Crisis*, lamented that "few Christians or Jews seem even to notice, much less care about, the all-out attack on their faith just underneath the skillful narration and imaginative fantasy that the critics have praised in *His Dark Materials.*" According to Grenier, the view "that Pullman's trilogy is a 'critique of organized religion' is an understatement." Indeed, Pullman's God is not so much defeated in heroic battle as withering away unceremoniously in *The Amber Spyglass.* Although Grenier admits that "Pullman's theology [is] on the creative side," she cautions readers to stop "their Potter-bashing to examine the far worse threat the Pullman books present to the faith of young readers."

The issue came to a head when *The Amber Spyglass* received the prestigious Whitbread Award in 2001. Now conservative Christians had no choice but to make their protest heard. In *The Mail on Sunday* of January 27, 2002, Peter Hitchens published a withering denunciation of Pullman's work under the inflammatory title "This Is the Most Dangerous Author in Britain." Hitchens opined that "[Pullman] is the anti-Lewis, the one the atheists would have been praying for, if atheists prayed." Besides inviting readers to think of Pullman as the anti-Christ, Peter Hitchens discharges another broadside against Pullman's work on the basis that "political correctness creeps in leadenly. There is a brave African king and a pair of apparently homosexual angels." Thus, Hitchens's religious critique is at bottom a political concern, and now we have the concoction from which full-blown ideological controversies are made. It did not take long before Peter Hitchens's leftist brother, Christopher, joined in the fray. His review for *Vanity Fair* of October 2002, titled "Oxford's Rebel Angel," is wholly and enthusiastically in favor of Pullman's work, not despite Pullman's religious radicalism but precisely because of it. Christopher Hitchens writes approvingly that "Pullman's daring heresy is to rewrite the Fall as if it were an emancipation, and as if Eve had done us all a huge favor by snatching at the forbidden fruit. Our freedom and happiness depend on that 'first disobedience'" (178). According to Christopher Hitchens, Pullman's departure from the pious standards set by C. S. Lewis, Lewis Carroll, and J. R. R. Tolkien is a liberating rather than a deplorable act of innovation.

It is clear from Christopher Hitchens's favorable review that he shares more than a superficial similarity of opinion with the writer of "that fabulous trilogy" (178). Indeed, in his *Letters to a Young Contrarian* (2001), Christopher Hitchens reveals himself to be Pullman's ideological alter ego: "Imagine a state of endless praise and gratitude and adoration, as the Testaments ceaselessly enjoin us to do, and you have conjured a world of hellish nullity and conformism" (25). This statement would sit comfortably on the pages of *His Dark Materials*; moreover, Hitchens's advocacy "of Promethean revolt and the pleasures of skeptical inquiry" (66) could serve very well as the motto for Pullman's muse. It would be easy to label these views as "leftist" or "liberal" (Peter Hitchens's term) and be done with it. Yet, such a reaction would foreclose a potentially enlightening debate that needs to be started instead of ended. Indeed, the views propounded by Christopher Hitchens and Pullman have been insufficiently conceptualized, let alone historicized, even by these intellectuals themselves.

The most conventional aspect of Pullman's religious subversion is his declared anticlericalism, which is buttressed by fervently anti-ecclesiastical outbursts. The story of *His Dark Materials* is set in motion by evil machinations of the hegemonic Church, whose leaders have plotted to abduct children from the streets of Oxford to whisk them to a secret location in the far north (all recognizable locations set in an estranged alternative universe); it turns out that the servants of the Church experiment on these children in order to separate them from their "daemons" (Pullman's Jungian concept of the soul). This daemon, which takes the form of various animals, is linked to a person by an invisible, quasi-magnetic attraction, and the Church is developing methods to sever the connection, which, if accomplished, leaves behind a zombielike body that will shortly die of emotional atrophy. It is a hideous plan, concocted with the intention of solving the problem of "Dust." This elusive substance, which is fabled to be a kind of "dark matter" imbued with self-consciousness, settles on adults only, not on children. Solving the mystery attached to these omnipresent particles would be comparable in our world to the Vatican's having the only nuclear weapons arsenal in the world.

The captive children, who eventually manage to escape from the clutches of the Church, find powerful allies in a tribe of benevolent "witches," who at one point debate the prehistory of the conflict they have been drawn into:

> For there is a war coming. I don't know who will join with us, but I know whom we must fight. It is the Magisterium, the Church. For all its history—and that's not long by our lives, but it's many, many of theirs—it's tried to suppress and control every natural impulse. And when it can't control them, it cuts them out. . . . They cut their sexual organs, yes, both boys and girls; they cut them with knives so that they shan't feel. That is what the Church does, and every church is the same: control, destroy, obliterate every good feeling. So if a war comes, and the Church is on one side of it, we must be on the other, no matter what strange allies we find ourselves bound to. (*Subtle Knife* [*SK*] 50)

By thus condemning the antisexual bias of the "Church," the witches not only reject the concept of Catholic celibacy and its potential perversions of the sexual impulse; but they also further undermine St. Augustine's teachings about original sin, which have for ages tainted the sexual with the odium of shame and defilement. By depicting the witches as the supernatural helpers of Lyra Belacqua, the story's precocious heroine, the witches' pronouncements are invested with a moral authority that reveals them to be Pullman's own beliefs. Indeed, even readers who don't know that Pullman calls himself an atheist will sense that the systematic voicing of anti-ecclesiastical views comes with authorial approval.

At the witches' council just mentioned, the subject of Lord Asriel is also introduced. This character, whose name recalls the archangel Ariel (i.e., one of the "Atheist crew" overthrown by Abdiel in Book IV of *Paradise Lost*) is the very prototype of a Blakean rebel against divine conformity: "Lord Asriel has never found hisself at ease with the doctrines of the Church," says a wise old man named Thorold: "I've seen a spasm of disgust cross his face when they talk of the sacraments, and atonement, and redemption, and suchlike" (*SK* 45). When asked about the nature of Asriel's insurrection against heaven, Thorold explains that Asriel "turned away from a rebellion against the Church not because the Church was too strong, but because it was too weak to be worth the fighting" (46). It is at this point that Pullman's conventional anti-ecclesiasticism turns into something that is both less familiar and more radical than other religious heresies. Indeed, we are told that Lord Asriel "is aiming a rebellion against the highest power of all. He's gone a-searching for the dwelling place of the Authority Himself, and he's a-going to destroy Him" (46). Thus, the declared aim of the plot is not ecclesiastical reform or even the demolition of the established Church; it is, rather, open warfare against God, and that is quite a different matter.

Surely, the epic struggle against "the God of the Church, the one they call the Authority" (45) is motivated by much more than simply a rejection of His ecclesiastical representatives on earth. Indeed, the heroes of the story act on the belief that God is not a champion of mankind but rather its enemy, since He is opposed on principle to what is beautiful, enlightened, and pleasurable in life. It is in keeping with this divine hatred for mankind that "the agents of the Authority are sacrificing children to their cruel God," and that "the rebel angels fell because they didn't have anything like the knife," which is "the one weapon in all the universe that could defeat the tyrant. The Authority. God" (319–20). Now, although we have heard the charge of God's cruelty before, it is a topic not frequently raised. In fact, it may fail to register properly when it *is* raised.[1] But in Pullman's case, it would be difficult to overlook his enormous resentment of God. Indeed, besides overturning God's attribute of divine omnibenevolence, he further demolishes the other major theistic attributes—namely, God's supposed omnipresence, omniscience, and omnipotence.

As for omnipotence, it becomes increasingly clear in the trilogy's last installment that God's fabled status of a powerful tyrant is quite a fallacy. Although God succeeded by main force to turn the realm of the dead into "a prison camp. . . . The Authority established it in the early ages" (*Amber Spyglass* [*AS*] 33), God's power in *His Dark Materials* is neither unconditional nor absolute. In *The Amber Spyglass,* Will is informed by the insurgent angels Baruch and Balthamos that

> The Authority, God, the Creator, the Lord, Yahweh . . . was never the creator. He was an angel like ourselves—the first angel, true, the most powerful, but he was formed of Dust as we are. . . . He told those who came after him that he had created them, but it was a lie. One of those who came later was wiser than he was, and she found out the truth, so he banished her. We serve her still. And the Authority still reigns in the Kingdom, and Metatron is his Regent. (31–32)

By undermining God's claim to have created the universe *ex nihilo* (while Himself being uncreated), this passage establishes God as a fraud and a liar. Moreover, His moral integrity is called into question by his association with Metatron, the sexually repressed, brutal, and power-hungry Regent installed by God.

Pullman not only desecrates God by placing Him in the company of such an ugly tyrant, he also emphasizes God's gradual descent into senility. One character seems to have intelligence that God is "at some inconceivable age, decrepit and demented, unable to think or act or speak and unable to die, a rotten hulk? And if that is his condition, wouldn't it be the most merciful thing, the truest proof of our love for God, to seek him out and give him the gift of death?" (*AS* 328). This gift is indeed granted God shortly afterward. By chance, Will and Lyra stumble upon His crystal litter (a sort of divine preservation machine), which has gone missing during a botched attempt to transfer Him to a safe location to escape Asriel's wrath. When the two children try to liberate God from his absurd contraption, they witness a puzzling spectacle: "Demented and powerless, the aged being could only weep and mumble in fear and pain and misery, and he shrank away from what seemed like yet another threat" (410). So frail is this decrepit former "Authority" that once "in the open air there was nothing to stop the wind from damaging him, and to their dismay his form began to loosen and dissolve. Only a few moments later he had vanished completely, and their last impression was of those eyes, blinking in wonder, and a sigh of the most profound and exhausted relief" (411).

Such a disoriented, feeble God has obviously no claim to omnipotence or omniscience. It could therefore be argued that the earlier pronouncements about His tyrannical nature cannot be true either. But this would be a misreading, since it is perfectly consistent that a former tyrant should grow old and grizzled. Surely, had Stalin lived to reach a ripe old age, he might have turned into a pitiful shadow of his former dictatorial self, although this would not have detracted from his gigantic crimes against humanity. Similarly, the God of Pullman's fiction, about whom Metatron informs us that "his heart was fixed against [human beings], and he made me prophesy their doom" (399), deserves no pity either. On the contrary, his tottering condition in the end further dramatizes His transformation from an object of worship to an image of loathing.

Such a radical inversion of religious attitudes must surely have precedents in the history of heretical thought. Surprisingly, though, the outspoken antipathy against God has no well-established pedigree. Albert Camus called the attitude "metaphysical rebellion," and he defined it as "the movement by which man protests against his condition and against the whole of creation. It is metaphysical because it contests the ends of man and of creation" (23). This definition reveals Camus's rootedness in the philosophy of existentialism, and it limits the usefulness of his term. Indeed, his own existentialistic despair about the coldness and radical contingency of the universe seems miles away from the attitude of contemporary writers such as Hitchens and Pullman, who rail against God and religion in an altogether more detached, playful, and affirmative manner. Although Camus's notion of metaphysical rebellion is thus a dated one, the French philosopher did outline a seminal history of God-hatred in his great essay *The Rebel* (1951), and this achievement can serve as a point of departure for further inquiries into this hidden (or perhaps suppressed?) tradition of spiritual radicalism.

Moreover, Camus must be credited with clarifying the distinction between metaphysical rebellion and atheism: "The metaphysical rebel is therefore not definitely an atheist, as one might think him, but he is inevitably a blasphemer. Quite simply, he blasphemes primarily in the name of order, denouncing God as the father of death and as the supreme outrage. . . . And so the history of metaphysical rebellion cannot be confused with that of atheism" (24). It bears repeating that atheists cannot possibly feel hostile toward God, since one cannot hate that which one declares to be nonexistent. Yet, this distinction is so casually overlooked that Pullman proudly reveals himself to be an atheist while Peter Hitchens scornfully calls him the same. Both are wrong, of course, for the simple reason that Pullman creates a world that teems with gods and angels and that gives preeminence to an imaginative sphere called the Republic of Heaven, something no card-carrying atheist would care to do.[2]

Since the enemies of God cannot be atheists, and since metaphysical rebellion is such a dated concept (with agnosticism not even in the running as a candidate), a new concept has to be created to properly denote the attitude of God-hatred. Faced with the need for proper distinctions, Christopher Hitchens suggested the following solution: "I am not a religious believer. In order to be absolutely honest, I should not leave you with the impression that I am part of the generalized agnosticism of our culture. I am not even an atheist so much as I am an anti-theist; I not only maintain that all religions are versions of the same untruth, but I hold that the influence of churches, and the effect of religious belief, is positively harmful" (*Letters* 55). At first sight, "anti-theism" seems an appropriate term to capture the spiritual antagonism of those who have declared their enmity toward God. Nevertheless, the problem of conceptual imprecision remains. Robert Flint, a nineteenth-century theologian, devoted a book-length study to the theme of *Anti-Theistic Theories* (1880). Flint distinguished the term anti-theism from atheism as follows:

> Short of atheism there are anti-theistic theories. Polytheism is not atheism, for it does not deny that there is a Deity; but it is anti-theistic since it denies that there is only one. Pantheism is not atheism, for it admits that there is a God; but it is anti-theism, for it denies that God is a Being distinct from creation and possessed of such attributes as wisdom, and holiness, and love. Every theory which refuses to ascribe to God an attribute which is essential to a worthy conception of His character is anti-theistic. (2–3)

Thus, anti-theism refers to a bundle of dissenting religious ideas; it is an umbrella term applicable to all kinds of nontraditional, even highly affirmative, religious beliefs.

But Pullman's heresy is, as Alan Jacobs has rightly pointed out, based on a different premise: "Pullman's echoes of Lewis are thus revisionary gestures, revealing his hatred not only of Lewis but of the Christianity Lewis represents" (41). The operative word here is "hatred," and I suggest that Pullman's attitude can be identified as a species of "misotheism," based on the Greek root meaning of "misos" (hatred) and "theos" (divinity).[3] This word is not my own invention, since it figures in the *Oxford English Dictionary*, but it has virtually dropped out of usage since the end of the nineteenth century and therefore needs to be revived to fulfill its destined role in the nomenclature of religious heresies. Besides its conceptual precision and grammatical adaptability (it serves equally well as an identity marker [misotheist], and as an adjective [misotheistic]), the term serves as a point of departure for historicizing inquiries into this type of religious outlook.

Among the more famous representatives of this radical tradition is William Empson in his polemic book *Milton's God* (1965), which contains the memorable words "the Christian God the Father, the God of Tertullian, Augustine and Aquinas, is the wickedest thing yet invented by the black heart of man" (251). Then there is the spiritual anguish of Tennessee Williams's disillusioned priest, Reverend Shannon, in *The Night of the Iguana* (1961), who accuses "God of being a cruel, senile delinquent, blaming the world and brutally punishing all he created for his own faults in construction" (60). We further have the devastating denunciation of God in Elie Wiesel's play *The Trial of God* (1979), where Jahweh is put in the dock for His responsibility in the holocausts of history and where the devil masquerades as His only credible defender. It is in this context that Phillip Pullman's trilogy *His Dark Materials* appears as a continuation and an imaginative elaboration of an intellectual tradition whose philosophical roots lie in the works of Thomas Paine, Max Stirner, and Friedrich Nietzsche, and whose literary progenitors include Marquis de Sade and Lautréamont.

But while these God-haters exude unrestrained revulsion against the concept of deity, Pullman's misotheism comes with one specific qualification. Although his disdain for both "the Authority" and Metatron is strong, Pullman seems to be receptive to a different kind of deity, notably a female one. Toward the end of the trilogy, the angel Xaphania makes her appearance as an entirely benevolent, graceful, and wise deity worthy of religious reverence.[4] Thus, it is possible to identify Pullman's antireligious animus with a feminist rejection of patriarchal theological doctrines. In this sense, Pullman's project resembles that of Mary Daly, the feminist reform theologian whose book *Beyond God the Father* (1973) contains a sustained attack against "the God who is the Judge of 'sin,' who confirms the rightness of the rules and roles of the reigning system, maintaining false conscience and self-destructive guilt feelings" (31). Daly goes on to state that "it is the woman's movement which appears to play the key role in the overthrow of . . . oppressive elements in traditional theism" (18) and that "women's growth in self-reliance will deal the death blow to this as well as to the other demons dressed as Gods" (31). Taking into account that Pullman's heroine is a female prophetess, that his witches are powerful and dignified characters, and that the only positive god figure in the trilogy is Xaphania, we might well conclude that Pullman is leaning toward Mary Daly's feminist theology. While both Daly and Pullman advocate the overthrow of masculine gods, they acknowledge a form of spiritual transcendence that recognizes the value of female experience and therefore puts the female element back into grace. Indeed, when Xaphania identifies "grace" (*AS* 491) as the source of Lyra's prophetic powers, we hear echoes of the other meaning of grace, namely, feminine elegance. On the other hand, Xaphania reminds Lyra that even after the loss of her "involuntary" grace, she could regain the same state of bliss "after a lifetime of thought and effort" (491). This seems to suggest a feminine understanding of grace as fusing both sex and wisdom, something that is more wholesome and affirmative than the arbitrary operations of providence that were worked out in the masculine theology of St. Augustine.

There's an unmistakable didacticism involved in such revisions of religious thought. In his Carnegie Medal acceptance speech, Pullman emphasized that "all stories teach, whether the storyteller intends them to or not. They teach the world we create. They teach the morality we live by. They teach it much more effectively than moral precepts and instructions." As a testimony to the influence of literature on our moral and spiritual values, this statement reveals Pullman to be an inveterate novelist of ideas. Indeed, for writers such as Hitchens and Pullman, God no longer denotes a personified figure in need of iconoclastic destruction but rather a system of ideas, a social construct that has to be attacked from an ideological point of view. Hence, their misotheistic rebellion is really an attempt to dismantle a system of ideas that is premised upon the acceptance of theism.

Of course, the days are irrevocably past when a novelist of ideas, say H. G. Wells, would stir up public controversy, be boycotted by libraries, and preached against from the pulpit. We seem no longer obsessed with the notion that books can corrupt the minds of our youth, since television and the Internet are now in a much better position to perform that function. But the phenomenal success of *His Dark Materials* has to some degree revived the old question whether it is our obligation to shield children (and not just children) from the dissemination of "forbidden knowledge." Indeed, Pullman's trilogy abounds precisely in the kind of knowledge that Roger Shattuck would classify as "forbidden"—namely, attacks against established religious doctrine and subversions of God's wisdom. In his candidly titled book *Forbidden Knowledge* (1996), Shattuck writes that "the religions of the West (as well as most Eastern faiths) answer yes, there are things we should not, cannot, need not know. To probe brashly beyond what God has revealed to us and to explore final questions by reason alone will distract us from the responsibility of living our lives according to an established moral code" (305). This formulation merely serves to highlight the degree to which Pullman goes against such thinking. On the story level, his protagonists constantly strain against the bounds of the knowable, and on the ideological level, Pullman insists that the sacred is no excuse for the perpetuation of untruth. For even Shattuck would agree that certain kinds of knowledge are "forbidden" not because they are false but precisely because they are only too true. The inherent conservatism of Shattuck's project is revealed in his identification of the "lust" for forbidden knowledge with "a drive carrying a strong element of perverseness and a penchant for transgression" (69). By contrast with such piety, the debunking of religion can thus be linked to a progressive, secular, humanistic project.

But this leaves the question open whether Pullman's books are suitable for children. David Gooderham thinks they are not. His shrewd exercise in literary history titled "Fantasizing It As It Is" (2003) finds fault with the explicitness of Pullman's religious references. According to Gooderham, Pullman's theological specificity goes against the whole tradition of veiled religious analogies practiced by Kingsley, Tolkien, Lewis, and others: "The use of an ecclesiastical discourse . . . ties the reader too closely to the conventions of realism . . . and inhibits a free range of imaginative response" (159). Besides accusing Pullman of undermining the fantasy genre, Gooderham warns against exposing children to *His Dark Materials* because "the specific references to God in the texts and the clever representation of his demise serve only to produce a distracting buzz of partisanship and contention" (165), with readers' responses ranging "from the horrified, to the troubled, to the gleeful" (164). Gooderham's entire argument, well informed as it is, rests on such prescriptive formulations. But his reasoning is flawed. For one thing, if it were true that the use of realistic, technical discourses harmed fantasy books, then a large segment of science fiction could pack its bags. More to the point, however, I take exception with Gooderham's claim that Pullman's "explicit terminology invites at best a rational and critical consideration . . . and at worst a partisan response" (161). Ironically, that would be the case only with readers who are already partisan. The large majority of children, who are spared religious indoctrination at a young age, would see in Pullman's heresies just story elements, twists of the plot, surprises. Does this make of Pullman an author who is spreading "confusion, offense and . . . indoctrination" (165)? Nonsense. As for confusion, a dose of that is to be welcomed as a stimulant for budding intellects. As for offense, that depends on your ability to suspend disbelief. As for indoctrination, much greater harm is being done in that department by our mass media with their mind-numbing reality shows and manipulative commercial messages that turn children into full-fledged consumers. Within the larger picture of our contemporary culture, it would be wrongheaded in the extreme to seek (and find) indoctrination in one children's author's output of admittedly antireligious lore.

With all due respect for the didactic potential of books, one should beware of censorship and let common sense prevail. In the case of Pullman's trilogy, it is particularly important not to throw out the baby with the bathwater. Although religious parents may be distressed by the misotheistic undercurrent of *His Dark Materials*, there are significant gains to be reaped from letting our children indulge in this kind of fiction, since Pullman's message is also powerfully liberating and positive. What he places in the void created by his iconoclasm are important values that define modern liberal societies: gender equality (Lyra becomes the savior), tolerance of sexual orientation (there are homosexual angels), affirmation of sex (the salvation at the end of the book is keyed into sexual consummation), celebration of the life force (the daemons are a symbol of animal vitality), tolerance toward other races and ethnicities (the book's multicultural agenda is reinforced by its elaboration of multiple worlds), and anti-imperialism (one of the story's collective heroes, the *mulefa*, are threatened by foreign invaders), to name only some of the book's virtues. If God and His servants on earth stand in the way of fulfilling such liberal objectives, then it is legitimate that the system be overhauled and dismantled by the story's protagonists, no matter their age, race, or gender.

Notes

1. A case in point is Zora Neale Hurston's novel *Their Eyes Were Watching God*, which contains the following lightning bolt of a statement: "All gods who receive homage are cruel. All gods dispense suffering without reason. Otherwise they would not be worshipped. Through indiscriminate suffering men know fear and fear is the most divine emotion. It is the stones for altars and the beginning of wisdom. Half gods are worshipped in wine and flowers. Real gods require blood" (145). Though Hurston comes at this statement from the perspective of racial oppression, where the object of divine homage is equated with the white patriarchal power structure, the implications of her condemnation are highly unfavorable to the Christian conception of divinity. Yet, Dolan Hubbard's lengthy essay on the religious implications of *Their Eyes* doesn't even mention the passage. It is implausible that he overlooked it. More likely, he simply did not want to confront it, much less write about it in print. Instead, Hubbard remarks that "Janie's re-

sponse [to the flood] is a religious response born out of her having come to terms with the impenetrable majesty of the divine" (111). How can this statement be reconciled with Hurston's meditation on divine cruelty? Indeed, it would be more in keeping with the book's religious implications to argue that *Their Eyes* reveals a God who hides His face and rains down perdition on the hapless inhabitants of the earth, thereby ruining rather than reinforcing Janie's religious piety. Be that as it may, the open misotheism of Hurston's narrator has caused many critics to look the other way.

2. At a literary conference in 2000, Pullman reportedly stated the following: "The King is dead. That's to say I believe the King is dead. I'm an atheist. But we need Heaven nonetheless . . . we need a connection with the universe, we need all the things that the Kingdom of Heaven used to promise us but failed to deliver" (qtd. by Peter Hitchens).

3. I do not wish to associate the word "misotheism" with the suggestion of a condemnatory attitude. While its sister terms such as "misanthropy" and "misogyny" are loaded with negative connotations, the ideological overtones of "misotheism" depend entirely upon one's religious convictions. To me, the word connotes a heroic stance of humanistic affirmation and the courage to defy the powers that rule the universe.

4. When Balthamos talks about God's opposition to one "who came later and was wiser than he was, and she found out the truth, so he banished her" (32), he may well be referring to Xaphania.

Works Cited

Camus, Albert. *The Rebel.* Trans. Anthony Bower. New York: Vintage, 1991.

Daly, Mary. *Beyond God the Father: Toward a Philosophy of Women's Liberation.* Boston: Beacon, 1985.

Empson, William. *Milton's God.* London: Chatto and Windus, 1961.

Flint, Robert. *Anti-Theistic Theories.* Edinburgh: Blackwood, 1880.

Grenier, Cynthia. "Philip Pullman's Dark Materials." *Crisis* (October 2001). http://www.crisismagazine.com/october2001/feature4.htm.

Hitchens, Christopher. *Letters to a Young Contrarian.* Cambridge, MA: Basic, 2001.

Hitchens, Peter. "This Is the Most Dangerous Author in Britain." *The Mail on Sunday* January 27, 2002.

Hubbard, Dolan. "'. . . Ah said Ah'd save de text for you': Recontextualizing the Sermon to Tell (Her)story in Zora Neale Hurston's *Their Eyes Were Watching God.*" *Critical Essays on Zora Neale Hurston.* Ed. Gloria L. Cronin. New York: Hall, 1998.

Hurston, Zora Neale. *Their Eyes Were Watching God.* New York: HarperCollins, 1998.

Jacobs, Alan. "The Devil's Party: Philip Pullman's Bestselling Fantasy Series Retells the Story of Creation—with Satan as the Hero." *Weekly Standard* October 23, 2000, Books and Art section.

Maughan, Shannon. "Whose Dark Materials?: The Culmination of Philip Pullman's *His Dark Materials* Trilogy Raises Theological Questions." *Publishers Weekly* December 18, 2000: 25

Pullman, Philip. *The Amber Spyglass.* New York: Knopf, 2000.

———. "Carnegie Medal Acceptance Speech." http://www.randomhouse.com/features/pullman/philippullman/speech.html.

———. *The Golden Compass.* New York: Knopf, 1996.

———. *The Subtle Knife.* New York: Knopf, 1997.

Shattuck, Roger. *Forbidden Knowledge: From Prometheus to Pornography.* New York: St. Martin's, 1996.

Wartofsky, Alona. "The Last Word: Phillip Pullman's Trilogy for Young Adults Ends with God's Death and Remarkably Few Critics." *Washington Post* February 19, 2001.

Williams, Tennessee. *The Night of the Iguana.* New York: New Directions, 1962.

Winston, Kimberly. "Other Worlds, Suffused with Religion." *Publishers Weekly* April 16, 2001.

II

Rediscovering Faith through Science Fiction: Pullman's *His Dark Materials*

ANDREW LEET

In her review of Ursula K. Le Guin's most recent collection of science fiction short stories, Margaret Atwood writes: "some commentators have proposed 'science fiction' as the last fictional repository for theological speculation . . . [and that] within the frequently messy sandbox of sci-fi fantasy, some of the most accomplished and suggestive intellectual play of the last century has taken place" (23). Atwood's comments serve as a fitting introduction to Philip Pullman's *His Dark Materials* trilogy, which disrupts the placid waters of unquestioned religious belief in the same manner that other science fiction works—including Sheri S. Tepper's *Grass*, Keith Roberts's *Pavane*, James Blish's *A Case of Conscience*, and Mary Doria Russell's *The Sparrow* and *The Children of God*, to name just a few—have done. In these books, and especially in Pullman's trilogy, the realm of science fiction serves as fertile ground for "theological speculation" because "[it] asks the questions—where did we come from? Why are we here? Where do we go from here?—that religions exist to answer. . . . [Science fiction] cannot surrender that questioning for any revealed truths without losing its soul" (Gunn 382–84).

From a practical perspective, science fiction works as a genre because it differentiates itself from fiction through its use of what literary theorist Darko Suvin denotes as the novum. Literally identified as "(novelty, innovation) validated by cognitive logic" (63), Suvin notes that science fiction authors refuse to adopt the traditional art form of mimesis utilized by other fiction writers, preferring instead to create environments or situations that are novel or alien: "the essential tension of SF [science fiction] is one between the readers, representing a certain number of types of [Person] of our times, and the encompassing and at least equipollent Unknown or Other introduced by the novum" (64). Like other science fiction works that come before it, the *His Dark Materials* trilogy exemplifies Suvin's novum theory; even before beginning *The Golden Compass*, Pullman notes in the frontispiece that he will be creating a variety of worlds: "The first volume is set in a universe like ours, but different in many ways. The second volume is set partly in the universe we know. The third volume will move between the universes." The more deeply the reader delves into the trilogy, the more he distances himself from what is considered everyday, or normal, and the more he opens himself up to what Suvin describes as the "Unknown or Other." He may begin his reading journey thinking that he comprehends both himself and the world around him, but he will ultimately discover at the end of the trilogy that this understanding has been challenged by new ideas and new questions; he has, as Suvin argues, just discovered "the essential tension of SF."

Science fiction aficionado James Gunn suggests that "science-fiction stories deal with religion in three basic ways: as a social force, as truth under [the] test [of reality], and as transcendence . . . or experience beyond the world of sense" (384). Although most science fiction stories dealing with religion might satisfactorily use one—or even two—of these viewpoints, the sheer length of Pullman's trilogy allows him to successfully utilize all three perspectives, progressing from basic questioning of organized religion's hierarchical structures in *The Golden Compass* to more complex questioning of religious faith in *The Subtle Knife* and *The Amber Spyglass*. After reviewing both the general relationship between science fiction and religion and Pullman's candid assessment of his own religious beliefs, this essay will explore three of the trilogy's many theological themes. These themes include a study of the popular perceptions that characterize heaven and hell, the role of the soul—conceptualized as having the physical form of a daemon—and its significance as a marker of individuality and humanity, and finally, Pullman's depiction of the individual's faith journey and his or her quest to explore spiritual mysteries as constituting the basis of faith.

When comparing the *His Dark Materials* trilogy to other works of religious science fiction, it doesn't take long to discover that Pullman aligns himself with those science fiction authors who write against mere religiosity, or religion operating for its own sake. As far as these authors are concerned, "when religion turns into religiosity, insights into the fundamental nature of the cosmos become naïve oversimplifications of reality . . . human life and its meaning are devalued, and in their place various individuals and objects, rituals and traditions are invested with ultimate value" (Frisch and Martos 12). Pullman certainly doesn't disagree, for in an interview with a book reviewer from The (London) *Times* he states: "I am very suspicious of ceremony, hierarchy, ritual. . . . It represents the ossification of something that was once genuine" (Wagner).

Besides his suspicion of religiosity, Pullman is also concerned about a potential future scenario where organized religion may someday regain its former powerful standing as the unopposed moral regulator of society. As history suggests, such a prospect is frightening because religious organizations—especially large ones—have tended to resist change by cementing outdated hierarchical structures and regulations and preventing the questioning of anything labeled doctrine. Recall, for example, the Catholic Church's condemnation of Galileo's astronomical theories in seventeenth-century Italy and his house arrest, or the attempted suppression over a century ago of Darwin's evolutionary theories by Christian churches, which saw Darwinism as contradictory to the doctrine of divine creation; in these and numerous other cases, the church organization involved chose to undermine the individual's right to personal reflection and instead bolstered its own position by identifying itself as the final arbiter between humanity and God.

The situation Pullman creates in *His Dark Materials* shares some uncanny similarities to both of these historical examples. In Lyra's world, nothing escapes the scrutiny of the Church—"Ever since Pope John Calvin had moved the seat of the Papacy to Geneva and set up the Consistorial Court of Discipline, the Church's power over every aspect of life had been absolute" (*Golden Compass* [*GC*] 30)—and those who question the theological framework established by the religious hierarchy are readily dealt with: "[two] renegade theologians who postulated the existence of numerous other worlds like this one, neither heaven nor hell, but material and sinful . . . were silenced" (30). Because people are afraid of being accused as heretics and punished by inquisitors, including such low-level clerics as Fra Pavel, the decisions of the Church leadership are not questioned and their theocratic powers remain intact (*Amber Spyglass* [*AS*] 67). A Church in the formal sense of the word controls Lyra's world, but it is a church in name only, an empty shell run by "ancient and rheumy-eyed" men who are superstitious of, and hostile toward, everything outside of their sphere of control (69). Although possessing a form similar to that of Anglicanism or Catholicism, the Church that these men represent is actually non-Christian in nature, as there is no mention of a Christ figure or incarnation and there is no sense of the Holy Spirit at work.

Although Pullman may be critical of hierarchical religious organizations, this does not mean that religious values, or such moral virtues as prudence, fortitude, justice, and temperance—often placed in the care of such organizations—are absent from his trilogy. Quite the contrary, these virtues are very much exemplified by the actions of Lyra, her companions, and even the larger gyptian community. For example, compared to the Church's bureaucratic structure, where discussion and debate are the norm but little ever changes, John Faa prudently suggests at the first gyptian gathering in *The Golden Compass* that change requires movement: "Talk all we may, we won't change owt. We must act if we want to change things" (115). Even the expedition that the gyptians mount to rescue their children from the Gobblers is put together in a selfless manner, using family donations of gold and manpower; this rescue mission, which John Faa says will require fortitude, or "all the craft and courage we can muster," will be further guided by a sense of justice and compassion, since the "landloper kids" who have been kidnapped will also be rescued (115). This natural presence of virtue in the gyptian community is presented in stark contrast to the absence of similar virtues in those representing the Church, whether they are at the top of the religious hierarchy—like the hardened, fanatic Consistorial Court president Father MacPhail—or near the bottom, like Father Semyon Borisovitch. Concerning the case of the latter, the intemperate Father Borisovitch appears to be much more of a vodka-drinking boozer, with "fat, dirty fingers" and smelling of "stale sweat [with] . . . food stains on [his] cassock," than a spiritually minded priest (*AS* 100–01). His description and mannerisms reinforce an image that is less than flattering: he is neither an upstanding citizen of his community nor, to use a biblical metaphor, a shepherd actively keeping watch over his flock.

Pullman's keen religious distinction between those who merely preach moral virtues and those who actually practice them on a daily basis was not something that he discovered in a single evening while outlining the plot of *His Dark Materials;* rather, Pullman's understanding of theology can partially be attributed to the childhood time spent with his grandfather, who was a clergyman in the Church of England and deeply influenced his grandson's outlook on religion and life. Ironically, although Pullman continues to love "the language and atmosphere of the Bible and the prayer book" as taught to him by his grandfather, he no longer recognizes the language used in church—"It's sort of modern and it's flat and it's bureaucratic and it's derivative." As he continues to tell an interviewer: "Since growing up and since thinking about it, I've come to realize that the basis on which these [religious] belief systems were founded isn't there. I no longer believe in the God I used to believe in when I was a boy. But I do know the background very well, and I will never escape it" (Odean 52). Certain reviewers of Pullman's trilogy have argued that this self-description implies that he is an atheist, and while he does admittedly call himself one, he refuses to allow himself to be determined solely by the connotations of that single word, suggesting instead that he is a "Christian atheist . . . and very specifically, a 1662 Book of Common Prayer atheist. I can't escape [the religious] influences on my background, and I would not wish to" (52).

Critics might argue that there can be no such thing as a "Christian atheist," but Pullman defies this argumentation by separating the *formal practice* of religion from the *spirit* of religious faith itself. As he says above, although he no longer recognizes "the language used in church," he still does continue to love "the language and atmosphere of the Bible and the prayer book," suggesting that the value he places on the written word matches his religious values—ultimate interpretation, meaning, and experience should reside at the level of the individual, not at the larger organizational level. He might "no longer believe in the God [he] used to when [he] was a boy," but then, very few adults probably see God in the same way as when they were children either. Just as the young "barbarian" Lyra first assumes through "guesswork" that experimental theology "was concerned with magic, with the movement of the stars and planets, with tiny particles of matter," and just as she "couldn't conceive" what the Chaplain was doing when he looked up to the stars and spoke "loftily," so too do other individuals begin their faith journey in the same unquestioning manner—there may be little interest or understanding at first, but there will come a time when that inner stirring for something beyond themselves will arrive and challenge their perceptions of the human experience (*GC* 34).

Recalling Hamlet's statement that "There are more things in heaven and earth, Horatio, / Than are dreamt of in your philosophy" (Shakespeare 1.5.166), one realizes that organized religion has given little thought to the universe as a whole, choosing instead to focus its energies on earthly conditions and those limited human-oriented constructions of the afterlife, namely, heaven and hell. From a historical perspective, one could argue that organized religion attempts to reinforce the heaven and hell reward/punishment schemas in order to bolster its own importance in people's lives and establish itself as humanity's conscience. Recognizing the danger of such control, it is not surprising that Pullman and other science fiction authors have chosen to shake up this particular dichotomy.

As Pullman's trilogy implies, the fear of not following the rules of organized religion and being punished in hell or, in contrast, following the rules and being rewarded with eternal happiness in heaven, makes little sense in the grand scheme of things, for humanity cannot pierce that ultimate of mysteries: what lies beyond this world of the living. Heaven and hell and other dualistic black-and-white images work because they are more understandable to the human mind than the problematic middle-of-the-road gray, but as Pullman's description of the world of the dead in *The Amber Spyglass* suggests, the afterlife cannot be so neatly organized into such simple dichotomies: "The edges of things were losing their definition as well and becoming blurred . . . the color was slowly seeping out of the world. A dim green gray for the bright green of the trees and the grass, a dim sand gray for the vivid yellow of a field of corn, a dim blood gray for the red bricks of a neat farmhouse" (248). Without either color or clarity, the powerful visual images of the afterlife that have been so carefully crafted throughout the generations and reinforced by popular culture suddenly seem less clear-cut in Pullman's world.

Suggesting that the attributes of the afterlife sow more confusion and fear than provide clarity, and recognizing that the attributes of heaven and hell arise out of a later tradition that revolves around the theme of a "moral" death, Pullman instead adopts what Alan Bernstein describes as an earlier conception of death: "Written records expressed the first concept, 'neutral' death, in Mesopotamia in the middle of the third millennium B.C.E. That view, according to which the dead survive en masse in a pallid half-life without either reward or punishment, later informed classical antiquity through Persia" (3). Pullman's gray and unfocused afterlife closely adheres to the "pallid" realm described by Bernstein, even down to the large masses of dead: "Standing on the floor of this huge space were adults and children—ghost people—so many that Lyra couldn't guess their number. . . . No one was moving about, or running or playing" (*AS* 294–95). Not surprisingly for a person who values the concept of mystery, Pullman's afterlife doesn't fit into the usual dichotomies of heaven and hell, despite the attempts by the female martyr and male monk to verify their presence in one of those two places (320–21).

The debate concerning the afterlife is an interesting one, but it ultimately pales in comparison to Pullman's greatest achievement in *His Dark Materials*: the creation of the daemon as a visual reflection of the soul. Despite the term's close resemblance to the word "demon" and the connotation of evil spirits, *daemons* are different in that they instead represent a type of guardian, or inner spirit. According to one study of John Milton and angelology, the image of the daemon can be traced back to Plato's general theory of separable forms; later followers of this particular philosopher "identified souls, which in Plato's myths sometimes seemed indistinguishable from the beings he called genii or daemons, with the daemons of animistic religion, beings between gods and men, often conceived as human souls detached from bodies" (West 7–8). Although defining the role of the soul can be philosophically and theologically problematic, from the practical perspective of the author, asking questions about the soul serves a useful purpose: "the greatest human dramas naturally involve the salvation or loss of the soul. Where there is no belief in the soul, there is very little drama" (O'Connor 167). Pullman obviously subscribes to this same belief, for the animal daemons in his trilogy play a prominent role, closely mirroring the emotions and attitudes of the human person they are attached to. As an old seaman tells Lyra, when it comes right down to it, daemons are merely reflections of a person's true inner being: "[they let you know] what kind of person you are" (*GC* 167).

In its never-ending quest to control "every aspect of life," the wing of the Magisterium known as the General Oblation Board begins to study the core of life itself—that is, the soul, as represented by the daemons—by authorizing Lyra's estranged mother, Mrs. Coulter, to set up an experimental medical facility at Bolvangar. In a manner almost reminiscent of vivisection, experiments are done on kidnapped children and their daemons, experiments that literally end with daemons being cut away from their host in a process known as intercision. When Lyra discovers a child who has undergone the intercision process, her first reaction is one of fear and disgust: "A human being with no daemon was like someone without a face, or with their ribs laid open and their heart torn out; something unnatural and uncanny that belonged [elsewhere], not the waking world of sense" (*GC* 215). Strangely, both the scientists at Bolvangar and Mrs. Coulter don't see daemonless humans as unnatural; in fact, they actually believe that their experiments will lead to a greater good: "Perhaps if the daemon were separated from the body, we might never be subject to . . . original sin" (375). With these words, the real reason for the intercision process is finally revealed: take away original sin and all will be well again on a re-created earthly paradise, Eden II.

A utopian vision of a world without sin may be an appealing one, but as Pullman realizes and reaffirms throughout his trilogy, such a world would be both unnatural and ultimately disastrous from the perspective of free will. In his analysis of various Edens in science fiction, science fiction scholar Andrew Burgess argues that the philosopher Søren Kierkegaard recognizes an "anxiety . . . pervading even human innocence" and further suggests that "[e]ven some atheist existentialist thinkers point to this pervasive anxiety as the distinctive mark of human existence" (75–76). The suggestion that original sin is "the distinctive mark of human existence" may be horrifying to some, but it is one that makes sense. Without sin we would not be human and we would have nothing to strive for—ours would be an empty existence.

Such a statement is a difficult one to accept, because it runs counter to the long-held belief that sin is the negative aspect of ourselves, a darkness that must be held in check or denied with the same "brutal discipline" that Father MacPhail imposes on his body. Yet as the biblical author of I John notes,

> If we say, "We have no sin,"
> we are deceiving ourselves,
> and truth has no place in us . . .
> If we say, "We have never sinned,"
> we make him a liar, and his word has no place in us.
> (*New Jerusalem Bible* 1:8–10)

In essence, we need sin, for without it we cannot begin to experience grace.

Although his own background and familiarity with biblical passages and prayers gave him some insight into the nature and purpose of sin, Pullman doesn't fail to credit some of his thoughts in this area to that seventeenth-century author, John Milton, who, from a religious perspective, leaned toward Arminianism, or the belief that individuals have the freedom to choose whether they accept divine grace or not (Dale 84–85). As Pullman tells one interviewer, he finds it fascinating that "some of the materials [Milton] pictures God using to create the world are 'dark' ones" (Alderdice 119), and it is this fascination that ultimately inspired him to adopt the phrase "His dark materials" from Book II of *Paradise Lost* as the title of his trilogy. From a theological perspective, the passage that incorporates this phrase suggests that because He does not "ordain" otherwise, God purposefully allows elemental confusion and chaos to exist. If this is true, then the possibility that free will—that often-chaotic realm from which sin originates—is also allowed to exist by God cannot be denied.

If there is any confusion about Milton's message concerning free will, it is dispelled by the hopeful ending of *Paradise Lost*, where freedom of choice remains the penultimate thought:

> Some natural tears they dropped, but wiped them soon;
> The world was all before them, where to choose
> Their place of rest, and providence their guide;
> They hand in hand with wandering steps and slow,
> Through Eden took their solitary way.
> (XII: 645–50)

Like Milton, Pullman also recognizes the value of choice, and it is for this reason that he makes such a point of choice and free will toward the end of

The Golden Compass when he has Lord Asriel explain the living dead to Lyra: "The Africans have a way of making a slave called a *zombi*. It has no will of its own; it will work day and night without ever running away or complaining. It looks like a corpse. . . . It's a person without their daemon!" (375). Within the larger context of Pullman's trilogy, the General Oblation Board's intercision experiments pose a very real threat to humanity: removing original sin implies the removal of free will, which would thus mean the destruction of that which makes us human.

As Pullman challenges long-held perceptions concerning organized religion, the afterlife, original sin, and the role of the soul, it is not surprising that certain critics have reacted negatively to his trilogy; in fact, one reviewer of *The Amber Spyglass* even went so far as to title her piece "The Man Who Dared Make Religion the Villain" (Lyall). Another scholar has argued that "metaphorical adumbrations which promote thought, sensibility and the exercise of the imagination are fine, but [Pullman's] use of specific terminology and other accoutrements of theological discourse lay themselves open to the charges of confusion" (Gooderham 166). It is somewhat ironic that the large, complicated issues of *His Dark Materials* hotly debated by religious critics often cause the subtle, yet pervasive themes of faith and openness to mystery evinced by many of Pullman's characters to be pushed aside. However, perhaps this shouldn't come as such a surprise, since even the most seasoned scholar may find both of these areas of theology difficult to define and conceptualize. For example, when attempting to define faith, religious psychologist James Fowler states: "Faith is not always religious in its content or context" (4), while author Ken McLeod suggests in his book *Wake Up to Your Life* that "Faith is the willingness to open to the mystery of experience. It contrasts with belief, which is the attempt to interpret experience to conform with habituated patterns that are already in place, including those inherited from your culture and upbringing" (9). Theologian Paul Tillich adds yet another dimension to both definitions when he states that "Faith is the state of being ultimately concerned: the dynamics of faith are the dynamics of [a person's] ultimate concern" (1). Although these three definitions are helpful, they aren't necessarily easy to comprehend, and even Tillich is forced to conclude that "almost every word by which faith has been described . . . is open to new misinterpretations. This cannot be otherwise, since faith is not a phenomenon beside others, but the central phenomenon in [a person's] personal life, manifest and hidden at the same time. It is religious and transcends religion, it is universal and concrete, it is infinitely variable and always the same" (126). Because the term "faith" often connotes something externally prescribed and regulated, perhaps it would be more reflective of Pullman's philosophy to use the word "spirit" instead, which suggests internal direction. In Lyra's case, her "ultimate concern" or journey of the spirit is driven almost entirely by compassion and self-sacrifice; that she begins a quest to save Roger and numerous others without knowing if, how, or when she will reach a happy end only reaffirms the strength of this inner drive.

Despite this strength, it should be noted that Lyra's inner spirit does not operate entirely without guidance but in conjunction with what the British poet William Blake and his German contemporary Heinrich von Kleist would describe as innocence. When writing his trilogy, Pullman must have often reflected on the dual themes of innocence and experience that Blake and von Kleist examined, for both themes frequently reappear in the discussions related to Lyra, who, from a developmental perspective, is mentally moving beyond simple childlike innocence into the early stages of adolescent questioning. As the wise witch Serafina Pekkala notes, Lyra's journey from innocence to experience must be a personal one; with an implied moral for the reader, Lyra must be allowed to move intuitively, always keeping in touch with the compassionate center that serves as her spiritual guide, her ultimate concern.

Although Lyra's compassion earns her the friendship of various characters, she also keeps in touch with her center by following the guidance of the alethiometer, a truth measure that is reminiscent of so many other inventions seen in the science fiction genre. Because of its complexity, one may wonder how a twelve-year-old girl can use the alethiometer and do so with little guidance. The answer is simple: Lyra's youthful innocence and inexperience with life allow her to remain in tune with herself, or centered, without major questions or spiritual issues to distract her. The compassion and sacrifice she exemplifies throughout the trilogy define her—they are her truth. When Lyra suddenly loses her ability to decipher the alethiometer after kissing Will toward the end of *The Amber Spyglass*, the female angel Xaphania calms the panicked girl by offering her a message of hope: "You read it by grace . . . and you can regain it by work. . . . But your reading will be even better then, after a lifetime of thought and effort, because it will come from conscious understanding. Grace attained like that is deeper and fuller than grace that comes freely, and furthermore, once you've gained it, it will never leave you" (491). Xaphania's message confirms that Lyra has left the world of childhood innocence and entered the world of adult experience; her entrance into the turbulent, yet beautiful, emotional realm of love has changed her. She can no longer read the alethiometer because simple compassion no longer suffices as her center of truth. This does not mean that her center no longer exists. Rather, just as it happens to all adolescents, her center has moved due both to the chaotic push and pull of outside events and through her own realization that actions initiated by free will can have positive and negative consequences. If she chooses to rediscover her spiritual center and redefine her unique purpose in life, then she can do so in the same manner that all people do—through "a lifetime of thought and effort." Furthermore, just as she could only read the alethiometer "without fretting at it or pushing for an answer," so too must she continue to be open to the spirit within, regardless of what external sources—religious or otherwise—define as authentic truth or faith. Contrary to what certain critics may think of this, Pullman's theology remains true to contemporary theological teaching, for, as Pope John XXIII—one of the leaders in modern religious history least like Father MacPhail—affirmed in his 1959 encyclical *Ad Petri Cathedram* (On Truth, Unity and Peace, In a Spirit of Charity): "God gave each of us an intellect capable of attaining natural truth. If we adhere to this truth, we adhere to God Himself, the author of truth, the lawgiver and ruler of our lives. But if we reject this truth, whether out of foolishness, neglect, or malice, we turn our backs on the highest good itself and on the very norm for right living" (§ 7).

Associating Xaphania's statement with John XXIII's encyclical may be further problematic for Pullman's harshest critics, who accuse him of being not only vindictive toward religion—recall Mary Malone's comment to Lyra and Will that "the Christian religion is a very powerful and convincing mistake" (*AS* 441)—but a God-killer as well. What is not realized, however, is that these accusations are based on faulty analyses of textual evidence, evidence that actually reaffirms both a point in religious history and the theological concept of mystery.

Regarding the first accusation against religion, Mary Malone's statement concerning Christianity at first seems irrefutable. However, a close reading of the next six pages after this statement suggest that it comes more from a personal reflection about her former identity as a nun than anything else. As Mary seems to admit, her "innocent . . . good little girl . . . [calling to] the spiritual life" was not a true vocation, for it did not originate out of a desire to serve others but out of a desire to be both "holy *and* . . . clever" (441). Following the Christian concept of holiness that was ingrained into her in church really seemed to mean following the rules and thinking "whatever the Church taught [her] to think"—neither of which allowed her real freedom of thought or emotional interaction with others. Because she could not naturally progress from innocence to experience—that is, through sin or through love—that which was truly human within her could not fully develop (441). Furthermore, if looking toward heaven and being Christian means that she must somehow separate herself from the rest of humanity in order to be "saved," then the endeavor is not worth it, for as Pullman reminds us: "Here is where we are and now is where we live" (Kellaway). In contrast to what C. S. Lewis seems to suggest in his Narnia series, which Pullman sees as "life-denying rather than life-affirming," our duty should be to the present time and those around us, not to an image of a potentially rewarding afterlife (Wagner).

The second accusation that Pullman is a God-killer is a complete misreading, for in a critical portion of text early in *The Amber Spyglass*, the angel Balthamos very clearly tells Will that the figure who calls himself God is *not* God: "The Authority, God, the Creator, the Lord, Yahweh, El, Adonai, the King, the Father, the Almighty—those were all names he gave himself. He was never the creator. He was an angel like ourselves—the first angel, true, the most powerful. . . . He told those who came after him that he had created them, but it was a lie. One of those who came later was wiser than he was, and she found out the truth, so he banished her" (31–32). The male angel that Pullman visually creates is only a godlike representation of what mankind has designed for its own purposes and needs, not an actual image, as God is a mystery—in theological terms, defined as something that is beyond normal human understanding. That this is merely a human construct of God can be further supported by the final sentence of the paragraph ending with "so he banished her," which perhaps is the mythologist/storyteller in Pullman recollecting the historical point at which a male form of religious monotheism at last usurped Western society's previous acceptance of pagan gods and goddesses. Religious scholar Karen Armstrong further reinforces such a historical moment when she states: "Even though monotheists would insist that their God transcended gender, he would remain essentially male. . . . In part, this was due to his origins as a tribal god of war. Yet his battle with the goddesses reflects a less positive characteristic of the Axial Age, which generally saw a decline in the status of women and the female" (50). Recognizing that Pullman wants to challenge his readers' traditional conceptions of organized religion as a male-dominated community, it is probably no coincidence that the primary theological "movers" in his trilogy are of the female gender.

The second piece of evidence supposedly supporting God's "death" comes from Lyra and Will, who come upon the crashed crystal litter that contains the aged figure of God, that is, the Authority: "Only a few moments later he had vanished completely, and their last impression was of those eyes, blinking in wonder, and a sigh of the most profound and exhausted relief. Then he was gone, a mystery dissolving in mystery" (*AS* 410–11). Two items are worth observing here. The first is that the Authority sighs with "the most profound and exhausted relief," indicating that he was ready to die long ago but had been prevented from doing so by Metatron and those who needed him to serve as a figurehead for their own "religious" policies. From a theological perspective, this quotation further intimates that an old-fashioned, rigid image of God fostered by an uncompromising religious organizational structure is both abnormal and unnatural. The second item worth noting is Pullman's use of the word "mystery," which is almost certainly not a random word choice. Because God is not fully knowable, the rigid religious structures and belief systems that are constructed around His divinity by various peoples are limited and cannot be otherwise if one is to fully respect the essence of mystery, which allows for questioning, probing, and seeking—all the things that Lyra is doing at the end of *The Golden Compass:* "She was aware of how small they were, she and her daemon, in comparison with the majesty and vastness of the universe; and of how little they knew, in comparison with the profound mysteries above them" (398).

The belief systems and concepts that Pullman tackles in his trilogy—from questioning the role of organized religion and popular perceptions of heaven and hell to examining the critical importance of the soul as a specific marker of individuality and humanity—are difficult to process with just a single reading; they deserve further introspection and additional discussion. Using Darko Suvin's theory of the novum as a basis for categorization, it can't be denied that Pullman's trilogy provides the necessary space required for that "essential tension of SF" between the reader and the "Unknown or Other" to operate. Writing from within the fold of the science fiction genre, Pullman's questioning of that which is often unquestioned in the realms of organized religion and faith development is neither unnatural nor meant to be corruptive. As another science fiction author states in the reader's guide included in her book, it is important to recognize "that you can't know the answer to questions of faith but that the questions are worth asking and worth thinking about deeply" (Russell, n.p.). I think Philip Pullman would agree without hesitation.

Works Cited

Alderdice, Kit. "PW Talks with Philip Pullman." *Publishers Weekly* September 25, 2000: 119.

Armstrong, Karen. *A History of God: The 4,000-Year Quest of Judaism, Christianity, and Islam.* New York: Ballantine, 1993.

Atwood, Margaret. "The Queen of Quinkdom." Rev. of *The Birthday of the World and Other Stories,* by Ursula K. Le Guin. *New York Review of Books* September 26, 2002: 23–25.

Bernstein, Alan E. *The Formation of Hell: Death and Retribution in the Ancient and Early Christian Worlds.* Ithaca: Cornell UP, 1993.

Burgess, Andrew. "The Concept of Eden." *The Transcendent Adventure: Studies of Religion in Science Fiction/Fantasy.* Ed. Robert Reilly. Westport, CT: Greenwood, 1985. 73–81.

Dale, James. "Arminianism." *A Milton Encyclopedia.* Ed. William B. Hunter, Jr. 9 vols. Lewisburg, PA: Bucknell UP, 1978.

Fowler, James W. *Stages of Faith: The Psychology of Human Development and the Quest for Meaning.* San Francisco: Harper, 1981.

Frisch, Adam J., and Joseph Martos. "Religious Imagination and Imagined Religion." *The Transcendent Adventure: Studies of Religion in Science Fiction/Fantasy.* Ed. Robert Reilly. Westport, CT: Greenwood, 1985. 11–26.

Gooderham, David. "Fantasizing It As It Is: Religious Language in Philip Pullman's Trilogy, *His Dark Materials.*" *Children's Literature* 31 (2003): 155–75. http://muse.jhu.edu/demo/childrens_literature/v031/31.1gooderham.html.

Gunn, James E. "Religion." *The New Encyclopedia of Science Fiction.* Ed. James E. Gunn. New York: Viking Penguin, 1988.

Kellaway, Kate. "A Wizard with Worlds." *Observer* October 22, 2000. http://www.guardian.co.uk/print/0,3858,4079774-99943,00.html.

Lyall, Sarah. "The Man Who Dared Make Religion the Villain; In British Author's Trilogy, Great Adventures Aren't Pegged to the Great Beyond." *New York Times* November 7, 2000, late ed.: E1.

McLeod, Ken. *Wake Up to Your Life.* New York: Harper, 2001.

Milton, John. *Paradise Lost.* Ed. Alastair Fowler. 2nd ed. New York: Longman, 1998.

The New Jerusalem Bible. Ed. Henry Wansbrough. New York: Doubleday, 1985.

O'Connor, Flannery. *Mystery and Manners.* Ed. Sally and Robert Fitzgerald. New York: Noonday, 1992.

Odean, Kathleen. "The Story Master." *School Library Journal* October 4, 2000: 52–54. http://www.schoollibraryjournal.com.

Pope John XXIII. *Ad Petri Cathedram* January 29, 1959. http://www.vatican.va/holy_father/john_xxiii/encyclicals.

Pullman, Philip. *The Amber Spyglass.* New York: Knopf, 2000.

———. *The Golden Compass.* New York: Knopf, 1996.

Russell, Mary Doria. *The Sparrow.* New York: Ballantine, 1996.

Shakespeare, William. *Hamlet.* Ed. Sylvan Barnet. New York: Signet-Penguin, 1987.

Suvin, Darko. *Metamorphoses of Science Fiction: On the Poetics and History of a Literary Genre.* New Haven: Yale UP, 1979.

Tillich, Paul. *Dynamics of Faith.* New York: Harper, 1951.

Wagner, Erica. "Divinely Inspired." Rev. of *The Amber Spyglass,* by Philip Pullman. *The Times* (London) October 18, 2000: Times 2, 12. http://www.newsint-archive.co.uk.

West, Robert H. *Milton and the Angels.* Athens: U of Georgia P, 1955.

12

Circumventing the Grand Narrative:
Dust as an Alternative Theological Vision in Pullman's
His Dark Materials

ANNE-MARIE BIRD

Building on an English tradition of religious dissent, Philip Pullman's *His Dark Materials* trilogy envisages a world in which God is thought to be redundant and traditional Christianity deemed dangerously repressive—merely "a very powerful and convincing mistake" (*Amber Spyglass* [*AS*] 464). This appears to echo modernity's challenge to religion and traditional authority that led some of the foremost nineteenth-century thinkers to declare their independence from God—that if God was not yet dead, it was the duty of rational emancipated human beings to kill him. Nietzsche, for example, regarded the God of Christianity as "a crime against life" (*Antichrist* 163), Marx considered religion to be "the sigh of the oppressed creature . . . the *opium* of the people, which made this suffering bearable" (qtd. in Pelikan 80), while Freud (56) believed that religion belonged to the infancy of the human race—that it was a necessary stage in the transition from childhood to maturity, but now should be left behind and science, the new *logos,* could take its place.

Indeed, key representatives of modernity have some resonance with the trilogy's rebellious forces lined up against the Kingdom of Heaven, led by Lord Asriel. Asriel represents the new enlightened man, he is an intellectual and a pioneer; in fact, he appears to be "Mr. Modernity" himself, who, rather than being an upholder of tradition, believes that enlightenment can be achieved only by means of humanity's own exertions. Like Nietzsche's Übermensch with his tightrope (*Zarathustra* 39–53), Asriel too walks a bridge between the worlds, proclaiming the imminent death of God—an obvious metaphor of humanity in the process of transformation, "going across" from the current stage of human consciousness to a more advanced stage: "we've gone beyond being *allowed,* as if we were children. I've made it possible for anyone to cross, if they wish. . . . This will mean the end of the Church . . . the end of all those centuries of darkness!" (*Northern Lights* [*NL*] 394). Also, like Nietzsche, Pullman clearly believes in the realties of the world we live in rather than those situated in a world beyond. Thus, in the final volume of the trilogy, the Kingdom of Heaven is overthrown and re-placed by the "Republic of Heaven," which he sees as being in all of us, in the here and now, "because for us there is no elsewhere" (*AS* 382).

However, Pullman's status as a representative of modernity is question-able, since modernity is often seen as responsible for a general disenchant-ment with the world—a calculating rationalism that invades all areas of life—whereas Pullman believes not only in the realities of the here and now but also in the joy and enchantment of everyday life. In fact, his Republic is a world open to wonder, to the nonrational, such as the supernatural, and indeed, all forms of "Otherness" that had, on the whole, been rejected by modernity. For some thinkers, this is a postmodern conception; one that re-jects not only the grand narrative of religion, with its talk of a better life beyond, but the whole project of modernity as well. Drawing on theories of postmodernism and poststructuralism—in particular, Derrida's theory of Deconstruction—this essay will explore Pullman's attempt to construct an alternative theological vision that is particularly attuned to the secular humanistic climate of the twenty-first century.

Creating a Weave of Differences

Central to Pullman's alternative vision is his rich and paradoxical concept of Dust. To the God of Genesis, Dust contains humankind's origins and is lit-erally the substance that marks its demise: "for dust thou *art,* and unto dust shalt thou return" (Genesis 3:19). Unsurprisingly, the Church depicted in the trilogy views Dust as "physical proof that something happened when in-nocence changed into experience" (*NL* 373), therefore emphasizing not only its "earthiness" or sinfulness but also foregrounding the consequences of human physicality: T. S. Eliot's "I will show you fear in a handful of dust" (64) encapsulating the Church's response to the biblical connection between sexual awakening and the expulsion of "man" from Eden. Pullman, however, uses the concept of Dust in order to disturb traditional Christian hierarchies (Bird 112)—namely, the value-laden binaries of innocence-experience, good-evil, and spirit-matter that lie at the core of the Fall myth. Thus, al-though Dust is "earthy" and, hence, is associated with matter, by envisaging it as "the energy that links body and daemon" (*NL* 375), Pullman connects it with consciousness or spirit, thereby emphasizing that neither term in the spirit-matter binary is hierarchically superior or capable of existing independently of the other term.

In essence, this seems related to Derrida's original conception of "deconstruction"—the notion that each term inevitably bears the "trace . . . of other elements in the system" (*Positions* 26). However, Pullman's deconstructive strategy involves more than merely demonstrating that the negative term is precisely the very condition of the positive term; it entails the creation of something that defies binary logic—that is, a concept that includes both the physical and the metaphysical, and yet somehow also goes beyond their scope. Hence, Dust is transformed from a conventional metaphor for human physicality/mortality into an ambiguous, almost mystical presence in which everything coexists. In the first text, Dust is described as "a new kind of elementary particle" (*NL* 370), as "the physical evidence for original sin" (371), and is experienced by Lyra as "dark intentions, like the forms of thoughts not yet born" (390). In the second text, Dust is the "dark matter" that comprises the bulk of the universe, "Shadows," "shadow particles," "particles of consciousness" (*Subtle Knife* [*SK*] 90–92), and hosts of "rebel angels" (260). In the final book, Dust is thought to confer "memory and wakefulness"(*AS* 263), "happiness and life and hope" (384), and "thought, imagination, feeling" (476). Moreover, "the first angel . . . the most powerful . . . was formed of Dust" (33).

The development of Dust into "a weave of differences" (Derrida, *Margins of Philosophy* 12), in which the meaning of each component is a function of its contrasts with other components, could be interpreted in various ways. On one level, it could be considered as an extremely unsophisticated narrative device—an ad hoc solution to the fundamental problem confronting the trilogy, namely, that we find it easier to think in terms of either body or mind. Consequently, we think by ignoring, or by attending to one term of the binary and neglecting the other. Hence, the inevitability of our tendency to privilege one term over the other. In the narrative, Dust, operating almost as a *deus ex machina*—the literal realization of Lord Asriel's statement that "Dust will change everything" (*NL* 394)—offers Pullman a means of fusing together and thus equalizing everything in an attempt to replace our "either/or" way of thinking with the notion of "and" or "both."

For example, Dust is described as a simple substance—an "elementary particle"—so called, as Lord Asriel tells Lyra, "because you can't break them down any further: there's nothing inside them but themselves" (*NL* 370). This appears to be contradictory, since the profuse and diverse concepts contained in Dust would make it more of a compound substance. Describ-

ing it as an elementary particle, however, constitutes a rejection of the idea
of division and separation as a means of making sense of the world. This,
in effect, represents a rejection of one of the central ideologies underpin-
ning Western modernity—that is, the desire to describe, categorize, and finally to segregate all that is ordered and rational from all that is chaotic or
"other." The idea, in Pullman's scheme, is that each elementary particle consists of, or reflects different aspects of one and the same substance. In this
sense, the texts reflect Spinoza's monistic doctrine that there exists one and
only one substance (qtd. in Cooper 289): that is to say, the spiritual and the
physical are simply two aspects of a single substance; we cannot see both at
once, or it is difficult to do so. For instance, in the second text, the angels
are described as "not beings of flesh like us, they're beings of spirit" (*SK*
143). Yet, in the same text, in an overt attempt to disturb the spirit-matter
binary, the angels claim: "From what we are, spirit; from what we do, matter. Matter and spirit are one" (260)—an incongruous statement made possible only if we envisage everything as a part of a single whole.

The Quest for an Absolute Foundation

When considered this way, the trilogy appears to be about something else
that in effect pushes other more prominent themes, such as the story of
humanity's coming of age, to one side. Thus, an alternative reading of Pullman's narrative and its desire for one elemental—an absolute universal substance—is that it reveals the longing for a central point of reference; a
"center" that would not only eradicate conceptual opposites but one that
is also capable of anchoring "meaning" and fixing "truth": what Derrida
describes as the misguided yet "irrepressible desire" for a "transcendental
signified" (*Of Grammatology* 49). God is just one of the names that the West
has ascribed to its need for a transcendental signified. In Pullman's work,
the suggestion is that Dust functions as a replacement for the redundant
God, who, even before he is eradicated in the final volume of the trilogy,
is described as having "withdrawn" (*AS* 344): as having "gathered [the
clouds] around him more and more thickly" (34). In other words, he is the
remote God whom Blake describes as dwelling in some "distant deeps or
skies" ("The Tyger" 36).

Thus, posited as the central presence in the trilogy, Dust is the *logos* or
"Total Being," the ultimate cause or "ground . . . from which beings as such
are what they are . . . [and] can be known, handled and worked upon" (Heidegger 374). In other words, Dust is a point of origin, a First Cause—a
"presence" responsible for whatever else is "present"—in much the same

way as the Christian God, or Spinoza's Substance is. This is made explicit
in the final volume of the trilogy when the angel Balthamos explains to Will
that Dust preceded God: "The first angels condensed out of Dust, and the
Authority was the first of all. He told those who came after him that he had
created them, but it was a lie" (*AS* 33). Furthermore, under the term "dark
matter," Dust is the cosmic material from which the universe is composed,
and it is thought that "*sraf* [the *mulefa* word for Dust] came from the stars"
(289). Therefore, Dust and the universe appear to be interchangeable in that
there is no distinction between the "source" and the "product." The view
echoes Spinoza's pantheistic view that absolutely everything is in the single
substance that he refers to as "God or Nature," or *deus sive natura* (qtd. in
Cooper 269). Thus, Pullman's conception of Dust is very like what Derrida terms "full presence, the reassuring foundation" (*Writing and Difference*
292), and the search for this universal substance—the desire experienced by
most of the protagonists in the trilogy "to go to the source of Dust itself"
(*NL* 376)—can be read as a logocentric quest.

    This interpretation raises several issues. As the central metaphor in the
trilogy, aiming to unite what is divided in terms of thought, language, and
culture, Dust has a tremendous amount of meaning thrust upon it. This
provides great potential for a strong counter-reading, in which the trilogy
undermines itself because it contains traces of other positions exactly opposite to those it aims to uphold. On the one hand, Pullman's dissent is
comparable to Western modernity's radical shift of consciousness (brought
about by humanity's increased knowledge, power, and control over the natural world), which made it difficult to believe in any kind of transcendent
being or world. And following on from this was the humanist project to
erect a different structure in its place—a new system of belief that would
provide individuals with a "true" explanation of things. On the other hand,
Pullman's narrative is ostensibly concerned with the necessity of humanity's
rebellion against oppressive, totalizing metanarratives (those "interpretations of the past" that Lyotard refers to as "master" or "grand narratives,"
xxiv), as epitomized in the trilogy by the Church's rigid hierarchical ideology in which truth is a univocal concept. In this sense, the trilogy reflects
the postmodern antipathy toward modernity—the notion that "the grand
narrative has lost its credibility, regardless of what mode of unification it
uses, regardless of whether it is a speculative narrative or a narrative of
emancipation" (Lyotard 37).

    For example, in terms of the plot, Pullman's trilogy is an indictment of
the whole Enlightenment vision in that it rejects the notion of systems that
have one prevailing objective viewpoint—systems such as those that under-

pin modernity and that Lyotard refers to as "terroristic" (63). In the total-itarian theocracy depicted in the trilogy, "Brytain" is ruled by the Church, whose rigid doctrines are fused with economic, political, military, and educational institutions; in effect, the Church has control "over every aspect of life" (*NL* 31). Indeed, one of the Church's departments, the "Ministry of Theology" (147), has obvious parallels with George Orwell's "Ministry of Truth," whose slogan is "ignorance is strength" (7). Likewise, the Church does not want people to grow up, but to keep them in an infantile ignorance. And as the Master of Jordan College notes, the Church possesses the absolute power to impose intellectual conformity: "Barnard and Stokes were . . . *renegade* theologians who postulated the existence of numerous other worlds like this one, neither heaven nor hell, but material and sinful. The Holy Church naturally disapproved of this abominable heresy, and Barnard and Stokes were silenced" (*NL* 31–32). Furthermore, "the most active and the most feared of all the Church's bodies" is the "Consistorial Court of Discipline" (31), which, like an Orwellian "Big Brother" (5) watches over all human activity, rigorously monitoring and systematizing knowledge to the extent that it "can't allow any other interpretation than the authorized one" (*NL* 275): "Every philosophical research establishment . . . had to include on its staff a representative of the Magisterium, to act as a censor and suppress the news of any heretical discoveries" (*SK* 130).

Similarly, if viewed through the character of Lord Asriel, the narrative is a rejection of totalizing explanations that, in their exclusivity, completely suppress intellectual free agency. For instance, Lord Asriel tells Lyra about other universes and the Church's refusal to accept their existence: "the first theologians [to] prove it mathematically were excommunicated" (*NL* 376). Lord Asriel challenges the foundations of traditional Christianity, condemning the "slave morality" endorsed by religious establishments in his direct attack on the Church: its political power, suppression of free exercise of reason, and all its theological dogma. As Thorold, Lord Asriel's manservant, says: "Lord Asriel has never found hisself at ease in the doctrines of the Church . . . I've seen a spasm of disgust cross his face when they talk of the sacraments, and atonement, and redemption, and suchlike" (*SK* 47).

The condemnation of a system that rules out all forms of "otherness" is made even more explicit when the witch Ruta Skadi says: "He [Lord Asriel] told me of . . . hideous cruelties dealt out in the Authority's name— of how they capture witches, in some worlds, and burn them alive" (*SK* 283). The trilogy, therefore, appears to be simultaneously pulling in two directions as, while striving for the communion of everything in Dust, it demonstrates the hazards of such a system, going to considerable lengths to persuade us that totalizing discourses can be sustained only by the evils of repressing or excluding what does not fit.

Possibility Collapses

Consequently, the creation of an authorizing presence, capable of organizing reality and fixing meaning, is highly problematic in that such a system requires the silencing or negation of those different or opposite meanings it is situated against: what Derrida describes as "The subordination of the trace to the full presence summed up in the logos" (*Of Grammatology* 71). In short, such a system would inevitably evolve into a totalitarian one. In placing Dust at the center, Pullman appears to have created a system that renders all phenomena subject to one explanatory discourse; a replacement grand narrative: in fact, Dust as "truth" (indeed, Lyra's alethiometer, from the Greek *aletheia*, is described as a "truth-measure" [*NL* 126]).

The subordination of the "trace," or negation of alternatives, is described in Lord Asriel's account of what happens when a coin is tossed. He tells Lyra that everything occurs "as a result of possibility": that a coin

> can come down heads or tails, and we don't know before it lands which way it's going to fall. If it comes down heads, that means that the possibility of it coming down tails has collapsed. Until that moment the two possibilities were equal.
>
> But on another world, it does come down tails. And when that happens, the two worlds split apart . . . these possibility collapses happen at the level of elementary particles . . . one moment several things are possible, the next moment only one happens, and the rest don't exist." (*NL* 377)

What Lord Asriel's explanation implies is that when Dust is specifically referred to as Dust, it is a comprehensive term in that all meanings are equal and, therefore, possible. When Dust is referred to by other descriptions, such as dark matter, for example, all other options are silenced, or cease to exist, leaving only the one meaning in place. These "possibility collapses" are in direct contrast to the way in which Dust generally operates in the texts as a means of disturbing the hierarchical nature of binary opposites. Thus, the meaning of Dust and its exact function becomes "undecidable." To borrow one of Derrida's terms, this is one of the "symptomatic" points that he refers to as the "aporia" (Kamuf xi), and can be used to describe where Pullman's trilogy appears to undermine its own basic presupposition.

This could be considered in various ways. For instance, if we read Dust as simply the creation of another grand narrative, it could be argued that Pullman, like Blake, merely believes in the free and active life of the creative imagination, particularly the Blakean notion: "I must Create a System or be enslav'd by another Man's" ("Jerusalem" 203). Alternatively, perhaps the construction of a replacement grand narrative suggests that Pullman recognizes, more so than Lyotard, that there is a deep-seated human need to seek recourse and solace in some kind of system—a "higher" authority that will eliminate uncertainty and take command of humanity's destiny. Undoubtedly, the trilogy suggests that without such a system in place, the individual is adrift amid a confusing babble of narratives. This is particularly evident in the final volume when Mary Malone explains to Lyra and Will how she felt when she was a nun: "I knew what I *should* think: it was whatever the Church taught me to think" (*AS* 470). Moreover, when God and the Church were central to her life, she experienced "the sense of being connected to the whole of the universe" (471), whereas, in the absence of this grand narrative, the conviction "that everything was connected to everything else by threads of meaning" vanishes: "it was impossible to find a connection, because there was no God" (473). In this reading, then, rather than endorsing modernity's view that the absence of God constitutes a positive liberation of humanity, it appears to be an absence that leaves a spiritual void similar to the "God-shaped hole in the human consciousness" that Sartre (523) refers to. Mary's new focus of meaning with which to fill this void is clearly related to Dust, and more significantly, with "the struggle to keep the Shadow-particles in this universe" (*AS* 476).

The Free Play of Meaning

However, as an all-encompassing system, Dust does not accomplish its apparent purpose. Despite Pullman's attempt to posit it as a central unifying presence, it is unable to avoid the problem of binary opposites completely, serving, in part, to emphasize the difference between such conceptual opposites as matter and spirit.

Indeed, as Derrida (*Of Grammatology* 71) notes, the desire for a "center" generates further oppositions. Dust, therefore, *is* a confusing babble of narratives in that its inherent qualities are subject to infinite and radical displacement as one property is continually exchanged for another. For example, in the first text, Dust shifts from its purely physical associations (original sin, sexual awareness) toward a metaphor for the interface between daemon and body that enables them to operate jointly. In the second and third texts, Dust oscillates between literal meanings (Dust as the dark matter of the universe) and metaphorical ones (Dust as symbolic of pure spirit itself: particles of consciousness, rebel angels, God, self-awareness and wisdom). The frequent substitution of one concept for another—from one end of the spectrum to the other, and between the literal and the metaphorical—introduces a distracting additional problem to the ontological issues already inherent in Dust, since it blocks our efforts to establish an integrated symbolic interpretation of it.

It is not, then, simply that there are too many meanings in Dust, but that the "free play" (Derrida, *Writing and Difference* 289) among the various elements in the system results in meaning continually proliferating and dividing, forming plural and provisional subdivisions. Hence, the is/isn't tension found within a metaphor—that which creates meaning—breaks down. Thus, rather than deconstructing the hierarchical nature of binary opposites, Dust deconstructs itself and must keep on doing so. This harmonizes with Derrida's view that deconstruction is an interminable activity, for "the hierarchy of dual oppositions always reestablishes itself" (*Positions* 42). Consequently, the reader is forced to enter into an endless play of contradictions and multiple meanings as regards the precise nature and function of Dust.

And yet, conversely, inasmuch as Dust is characterized by a high degree of uncertainty, it frequently manages to evade the issue of difference altogether, since the suppressed term always returns to "haunt" the text. According to deconstructionist theory, this is due to the unavoidable play of "traces"—an inevitable effect of "the strange 'being' of the sign: half of it always 'not there' and the other half always 'not that.' The structure of the sign is determined by the trace or track of that other which is forever absent" (Spivak xvii). In this sense, then, there can be no center that "arrests and grounds the play of substitutions" (Derrida, *Writing and Difference* 289), and thus, it could be argued that Pullman's conception of Dust expresses Derrida's position on "the limit of totalisation": "Totalisation is sometimes defined as *useless,* and sometimes as *impossible.* . . . If totalisation no longer has any meaning, it is not because the infiniteness of a field cannot be covered by a finite glance or a finite discourse, but because the nature of the field—that is, language and a finite language—excludes totalisation" (*Writing and Difference* 289).

Conclusion

Consequently, given the radical instability of Dust, building an alternative theological vision with Dust at its center enables Pullman to avoid constructing a new grand narrative. Indeed, the very term "Dust" is an extremely apposite one, as not only does its intrinsic amorphousness allow for great adaptability, but the very vagueness of the term suggests that, as opposed to the notion of a solid fixed foundation, what the trilogy actually presents is a shifting field of relations in which there is no secure and stable point. For this reason, Dust can never be the final explanation. In the words of William Butler Yeats, "Things fall apart; the centre cannot hold" (99).

This is not to suggest that the alternative theological vision depicted in the trilogy is necessarily a postmodern conception, characterized by pluralism and provisional meanings. While there are myriad diverse things that make up Pullman's universe, the trilogy is not about pluralism, as this system would require more than one ultimate principle. Rather, through its insistence that it is both desirable and in fact possible to incorporate everything within one foundational substance, the trilogy seeks to reject both dualistic and pluralistic interpretations of the world, while simultaneously, and paradoxically, demonstrating that there are many different and perhaps incommensurable kinds of things that constitute a world, none of which is deemed more fundamental than any of the others.

Therefore, while Pullman has undeniably created a "system" of sorts, given the immense potential for the free play of meaning, Dust is evidently a system characterized by contingency and uncertainty. Thus, any anxiety as to whether the system purports to represent universal "truth" is averted. In this way, Pullman circumvents the grand narrative, creating instead an open, more egalitarian vision in which Dust functions as a new focus for people's spirituality, without which, according to Pullman's trilogy, humanity not only lacks purpose or meaning, but equally as important, a sense of wonder and mystery.

Works Cited

Bird, Anne-Marie. "'Without Contraries Is No Progression': Dust as an All-Inclusive, Multifunctional Metaphor in Philip Pullman's *His Dark Materials.*" *Children's Literature in Education* 32.2 (2001): 111–23.

Blake, William. "The Tyger." *William Blake: Selected Poetry.* Ed. H. Stevenson. Harmondsworth: Penguin, 1988.

———. "Jerusalem." *William Blake: Selected Poetry.* Ed. H. Stevenson. Harmondsworth: Penguin, 1988.

Cooper, David E. *World Philosophies: An Historical Introduction.* Oxford: Blackwell, 1996.

Derrida, Jacques. *Of Grammatology.* Trans. Gayatri Chakravorty Spivak. Baltimore: Johns Hopkins UP, 1976.

———. *Margins of Philosophy.* Trans. Alan Bass. Chicago: U of Chicago P, 1982.

———. *Positions.* Trans. Alan Bass. Chicago: U of Chicago P, 1981.

———. *Writing and Difference.* Trans. Alan Bass. London: Routledge, 1978.

Eliot, T. S. "The Burial of the Dead." *The Waste Land. Collected Poems: 1909–1962.* London: Faber and Faber, 1963.

Freud, Sigmund. *The Future of an Illusion. The Standard Edition of the Complete Psychological Works.* Trans. James Strachey. Vol. 21. London: Hogarth, 1953–74.

Heidegger, Martin. *Basic Writings.* Trans. D. F. Krell. London: Routledge and Kegan Paul, 1978.

Kamuf, Peggy, ed. *A Derrida Reader: Between the Blinds.* New York: Columbia UP, 1991.

Lyotard, Jean-François. *The Postmodern Condition: A Report on Knowledge.* Trans. G. Bennington and B. Massumi. Manchester: Manchester UP, 1984.

Nietzsche, Friedrich. *Thus Spoke Zarathustra: A Book for Everyone and No One.* Trans. R. J. Hollingdale. London: Penguin, 1961.

———. *The Antichrist in* The Twilight of the Gods *and* The Antichrist. Trans. R. J. Hollingdale. London: Penguin, 1968.

Orwell, George. *Nineteen Eighty-Four.* Harmondsworth: Penguin, 1949.

Pelikan, Jaroslav, ed. "Contribution to the Critique of Hegel's 'Philosophy of the Right.'" *The World Treasury of Modern Religious Thought.* London: Time Warner, 1990.

Pullman, Philip. *The Amber Spyglass.* London: Scholastic, 2000.

———. *Northern Lights.* London: Scholastic, 1995.

———. *The Subtle Knife.* London: Scholastic, 1997.

Sartre, Jean-Paul. *Being and Nothingness: An Essay on Phenomenological Ontology.* Trans. H. Barnes. London: Methuen, 1957.

Spivak, Gayatri Chakravorty. Translator's preface to *Of Grammatology.* Baltimore: Johns Hopkins UP, 1976.

Yeats, William Butler. "The Second Coming." *W. B. Yeats: Selected Poetry.* Ed. A. Norman Jeffares. Macmillan: London, 1962.

13

Unexpected Allies?
Pullman and the Feminist Theologians

PAT PINSENT

The extreme hostility with which the views expressed in Philip Pull-man's *His Dark Materials* trilogy (1995–2000) have been greeted by many Christians, notably Evangelicals and right-wing Roman Catholics, has not, however, characterized the reaction of all serious thinkers about religion. While admitting that the books are intended as "a direct attack on organised religion," distinguished children's writer Gillian Cross, herself a Christian, in a recent article (*Books for Keeps* 11) says: "When it [*His Dark Materials*] is most truly a story, it is close to the central insights of Christianity." Like Cross, and unlike the fundamentalists, many Christian readers of *His Dark Materials* who are familiar with feminist theology have felt comfortable with much of the message of Pullman's saga. As I hope to demonstrate, many of the challenges that Pullman poses to established religion have already, quite independently, been set by feminist theologians.[1]

In her introduction to *Feminist Theology: A Reader*, Ann Loades para-phrases theologian Gerda Lerner: "Where the male has been thought to represent the *whole* of humanity, the half has been mistaken for the whole. . . . As long as men believe that their experiences, viewpoint, and ideas represent all of human experience and all of human thought, abstract definitions and description of the real will alike be inaccurate. What she [Lerner] calls this 'androcentric fallacy' has been built into all the mental constructs of western civilization" (Loades, 1–2). Loades goes on to a definition: "Feminist theologians want to eliminate the androcentric fallacy, and rely on themselves for understanding the God they have found to be theirs, though mediated to them by a religious tradition which causes them profound problems as one powerful form of mediating that fallacy" (1–2). As Mary Malone states:[2] "The task of rereading the Scriptures through the eyes of women is an essential task for today's Church" (18). This rereading, particularly in areas such as the nature of God and the Church, the interpretation of the Fall narratives in Genesis, and expectations about the afterlife, has in many instances resulted in perceptions not dissimilar to those imaginatively represented in Pullman's novels. Additionally his representation of Lyra as the most significant character in the establishment of the "Republic of Heaven" is consonant with the renewed understanding of the female role in a religious context, which is central to feminist theologians' readings of both biblical texts and the history of the Christian Church.

I should like to emphasize that in no way am I suggesting that Pullman has been influenced by feminist theology. Rather, my claim is that when people think deeply about traditional religious ideas and are prepared to reassess and reinterpret the Bible and tradition without taking as axiomatic the meanings usually read into them, there may be a surprising degree of kinship between their conclusions.[3]

Images of God

A major area of disagreement between Pullman and most religious writers might be expected to lie in the area of portrayal of the divine. Pullman describes himself as finding belief in "a personal God and a Saviour . . . impossible,"[4] while the majority of feminist theologians would appear to accept the objective existence of some form of deity. The situation is not, however, quite so simple, for the kind of image of God that Pullman seeks to destroy is one that is equally uncongenial to many Christians, especially those of a feminist persuasion. Particularly in *The Amber Spyglass* [*AS*], the "Authority" is portrayed as abrogating to himself titles to which he has no claim: "The Authority, God, the Creator, the Lord, Yahweh, El, Adonai, the King, the Father, the Almighty—those were all names he gave himself" (33). Portrayal of the pathetic decline into nothingness of this figure is how Pullman deals with the (presumably gentle and gradual) death of belief in an omnipotent and omniscient deity: "Demented and powerless, the aged being could only weep and mumble . . . he was as light as paper . . . in the open air there was nothing to stop the wind from damaging him, and to their dismay his form began to loosen and dissolve. . . . Then he was gone: a mystery dissolving in mystery" (431–32). Carefully chosen words, notably "paper" and "mystery," draw the alert reader's attention to how what is in effect "Godness" has become the province of sterile conjecture rather than of living belief. As Pullman observed in an interview (Billen 15): "The idea that there is a personal God . . . is dead. Intellectually the life's gone out of it. It's hollow . . . and empty. God is dead. That's what I'm killing with the death of my God in this."

There is considerable similarity in the way such titles excite the concern of feminist theologians. In her search for "Models of God," Sallie McFague first looks at "the tradition's monarchical mythology for imaging God's relationship to the world. The classical picture, an imaginatively powerful one, employs royalist, triumphalist metaphors, depicting God as king, lord and patriarch who rules with the world and human beings, usually with benevolence." She claims that this understanding is not helpful today, and suggests in its place the image of "the world as God's body," which is more consonant with fulfillment for all of creation. She explains that this comparison, like the others she applies, such as God as mother, lover, or friend, is not intended to be taken literally; all are, rather, intended to express "some significant aspects of the God-world relationship in our time. . . . A heuristic theology plays with ideas in order to find out . . . [and] suggest[s] metaphors that create a shock of recognition" (62–63).

Brian Wren, one of an increasing minority of male writers on the periphery of feminist writing, creates a fascinating imaginative scenario featuring Art-Xela, a researcher from Roq:un, a distant planet, who is investigating the way God is addressed in Christian hymns on earth. The researcher concludes that "the dominant metaphor system is KINGAFAP—the King-G-d-Almighty-Father-Protector" (119). These titles recall those quoted above from Pullman in his mythologizing of the attribution of titles to the Authority and form a cluster similar to those McFague depicts as inappropriate in the modern world. The expiration of the Authority is a direct parallel, not necessarily to "the death of God," but to the realization by contemporary theologians that the well-established metaphors have in many cases served their turn and new ones need to be created.

As far as both Pullman and the feminist writers are concerned, these new metaphors can be sought in two main areas—in matter itself and in the spirit of Wisdom. Pullman's metaphoric use of "Dust" implies, as Anne-Marie Bird (114) suggests: "every elementary particle of Dust contains the entire universe." As suggested by Gooderham (166), Pullman's use of the Dust metaphor recalls the work of process theologians, a school that has been influential on feminist theology (cf. Ruether, *Gaia and God* 247).

Feminist theology also makes much of the figure of Wisdom, personified as female, as an alternative, Bible-based image of God. Rosemary Ruether claims that such female imagery for an aspect of the godhead (perhaps most appropriately related to the Holy Spirit), far from being a deviation of heretical Christianity, displays "an earlier Christianity, which used such female imagery, gradually being marginalized by a victorious Greco-Roman Christianity that repressed it" (*Sexism and God-Talk* 59). Elisabeth Moltmann-Wendel also emphasizes the importance of this figure in the Hebrew tradition, observing that "no ideas of retribution or reward are associated with her" (*Land* 96). Elisabeth Fiorenza shows how the images of God in the parables of Jesus and his insistence on the equality at his table of "tax collectors, prostitutes and sinners" relate to the Sophia tradition: "Divine Sophia is Israel's God in the language and *Gestalt* of the goddess. Sophia is called sister, wife, mother, beloved, and teacher. . . . She seeks people, finds them on the road, invites them to dinner. 'She is but one but can do everything, herself unchanging. She makes all things new' (*Wis* 7:27). . . . Goddess-language is employed to speak about the *one* God of Israel whose gracious goodness is divine Sophia" (132). Fiorenza (130–33) quotes several texts about Sophia, divine wisdom, from the book of *Enoch*,[5] in an attempt to establish the qualities of this figure.

Sophia is most nearly paralleled in Pullman's books by the angelic figure Xaphania, though she is clearly far from omnipotent. She both rebels against the folly of the Authority (*AS* 219–20) and shows the compassion and wisdom characteristic of the biblical Sophia. The character Mary Malone recounts how Xaphania has "always tried to open minds . . . for most of the time wisdom has had to work in secret" (506), while the protagonists are moved by Xaphania's presence: "Her expression was austere and compassionate, and both Lyra and Will felt as if she knew them to their hearts" (519). Pullman may not be reinstating a deity, but he is certainly making use of the Wisdom tradition.

Treatments of the Genesis Story of the Fall

Unlike traditional Christian theology, Pullman's trilogy presents the story of the Fall not as a disaster but as a coming of age for the human race, with his main protagonist, Lyra, becoming the new Eve. However, his positive interpretation of the myth is foreshadowed by several feminist interpreters of scripture. Ruether (*Gaia and God* 144) provides a lengthy discussion of the anthropological studies of Near Eastern religion, which serves to locate the Fall within the cultural practices of its period and thus to account for the negative readings. Other feminist scholars have been more interested in reinterpreting the story as it appears in the Hebrew Bible. Notable among these is Anne Primavesi's rereading of Genesis in her search for an ecological basis for theology. She is concerned with how Christianity has all too often been seen as providing a justification for human subjugation of the natural world, and observes: "The basic assumption on which the others [interpretations] depend is that this [the Genesis story] is a story of sin, of the fall of humankind through Eve's initiative. Her punishment, to bear children in pain, is judged as a more severe punishment than man's struggles with the soil. Therefore her sin is assumed to be greater than man's" (210). Primavesi goes on:

> It is Eve in the Genesis narrative who perceives the desirability of procuring wisdom, in dialogue with the wisest of animals, the serpent. It found in the woman that intense thirst for knowledge that the simple pleasures of picking flowers and talking with Adam did not satisfy. Its wisdom is recommended to us by Jesus (*Matt.* 10:16) Such attention to the text should make us wary when it is assumed that God did not want the woman and man to know good from evil. What a very infantile stupid pair they would have remained! (226)

Primavesi claims that this rereading leads to "uncommon perceptions" about humanity: humans are seen as being required to serve the earth, women are not set as inferior to men, and the serpent, as a representative of the animal world, is seen as "a symbol of wisdom" when it exposes for humans "the problem of keeping rules of conduct, imposed norms of behavior" (232). Any readjustment in the view of God that this rereading of the story implies should, she suggests, remind us about the anthropomorphic nature of the tale.

If the Fall is regarded by many feminist scholars not as an evil deed that demands a redemptive act, but rather as an opening up of the human race to knowledge, much of the abundance of Christian theology devoted to theories of atonement becomes irrelevant. This lack of interest parallels the absence of any need for a redeemer, or indeed an explicit Christ figure, in Pullman's rewriting of this material, though in her centrality and behavior Lyra comes closest to this.[6] If the Fall is not seen as a disaster but as a necessary stage in human evolution, the whole notion of sin in general, and original sin in particular, comes to be seen in a different way, as a means to enlightenment and self-knowledge rather than as a major offense against God. In the fourteenth century, the mystic Dame Julian of Norwich gave perhaps the most significant expression to the view that the Fall and subsequent sin were not totally to be deplored, in her comforting words: "Sin is behovely. . . . All shall be well and all manner of thing shall be well."[7] Sin has its place within the divine scheme of things, and even "original sin" is not totally to be deplored.

Beliefs about the Afterlife and Their Consequences

Fundamental to Pullman's position throughout *His Dark Materials* is the conviction that there is no eternity in heaven to be looked toward as a reward for denying oneself in this world and hoping to be happy in the next. In the world of the dead, a young woman who died as a martyr puts into words what Pullman views as the Church's creation of an illusion in order to keep people obedient to its rules:

> When we were alive, they told us that when we died we'd go to heaven. And they said that heaven was a place of joy and glory and we would spend eternity in the company of saints and angels praising the Almighty in a state of bliss. . . . That's what led some of us to give our lives, and others to spend years in solitary prayer, while all the joy of life was going to waste around us. (*AS* 336)

Instead of the traditional view of heaven, Pullman's mythology involves the imprisonment of the dead in an underworld, much like the classical Hades. The incident in *The Amber Spyglass* involving their release from this non-place also recalls the "harrowing of hell," a key scene of the medieval Mystery plays, in which Christ, between his death and his resurrection, was able to release from limbo the souls of those who had died before his coming. In an inevitably Christlike parallel, Lyra releases the dead from this deadly place, not so that they can go to heaven but rather to allow them to be dissolved into the elements of their being. Nearer the end of the book, Lyra expresses her own hopes related to the dissolution of her own being, but with a more personal slant:

> I'll be looking for you, Will, every moment, every single moment. And when we do find each other again we'll cling together so tight that nothing and no one'll ever tear us apart. Every atom of me and every atom of you. . . . We'll live in birds and flowers and dragonflies and pine trees and in clouds and in those little specks of light you see floating in sunbeams. And when they use our atoms to make new lives, they won't just be able to take *one*, they'll have to take two, one of you and one of me, we'll be joined so tight. (526)

While the use of natural imagery in this passage seems justified by the facts of physical existence, the romantic hope that Lyra expresses to Will about their future union may be seen as her own—or, since he offers no corrective to it, Pullman's own—creation of a kind of myth of faithful love enduring forever, contrary to the harsh impersonal reality of indiscriminate final oblivion.[8]

Among some feminist theologians, notably Daphne Hampson, Rosemary Ruether, and Elizabeth Stuart, a similar thrust against belief in personal immortality is to be discerned. As Ruether observes: "Although hope for life after death remains a residual idea in modern Christianity, the focus of redemptive hope shifts to . . . a hope for a this-worldly transformation of unjust relationships that would bring about a time of justice and peace within history" (*Women and Redemption* 273–74). Elizabeth Stuart highlights how the "hope in life after death has been used by Christianity to encourage people into passively accepting situations of oppression in the present" (42). Daphne Hampson, an influential feminist theological writer, quotes Charlotte Perkins Gilman, who distinguishes between "death-based" religion, for which the main question is "What is going to happen to me after I am dead?" and birth-based religion, which asks: "What must be done for the child who is born?" (qtd. in Hampson 142). Hampson quotes research to suggest that the hope of personal immortality is less important to females than to males; despite being male, Pullman seems to be more aligned with the "birth-based" than the "death-based" position in his vision of the behavior needed to establish the "Republic of Heaven" on this earth. The discourse between Lyra and Pantalaimon at the end of *The Amber Spyglass* confirms the importance to Pullman of this kind of hope for the future; Lyra recalls how Will's parting words had given a rule for life: "He meant the Kingdom was over, the Kingdom of Heaven, it was all finished. We shouldn't live as if it mattered more than this life in this world, because where we are is always the most important place. . . . We have to be all those difficult things like cheerful and kind and curious and brave and patient, and we've got to study and think and work hard, all of us, in all our different worlds, and then we'll build . . . the Republic of Heaven" (548). As Gooderham points out, this list of virtues "is so entirely uncontentious that no doubt secular humanists, liberal humanists and Christian humanists can all be comfortable with it" (173).

The Critique of the Christian Church

Throughout the *His Dark Materials* trilogy, Pullman subjects, by analogy, the Christian Church in this world to a savage attack for its sterile adherence to a code of rules, its proffering of the hope of an illusory heaven, and indeed, its cruelty and unscrupulousness. In an interview, he said that his portrayal comes from the record of the Inquisition, persecuting heretics and torturing Jews, from the Protestants burning the Catholics . . . the insensate pursuit of innocent and crazy old women, and from the Puritans in America burning and hanging the witches (Spanner 22). While it might be expected that those with a stronger link to Christianity than an unbeliever such as Pullman would see the Church in a more positive light, this is not generally the case among feminist theologians. Although it is sometimes possible to draw a distinction between those, like Hampson, who see themselves as out-side the official structures of Christianity, and those who endeavor to achieve reform from within, like Ruether, Stuart, and Moltmann-Wendel, there is little if any difference in the degree of hostility expressed toward what is seen as the patriarchal structure of the Church as it is today. Fiorenza devotes much attention to the development of patriarchalization of Christian ministry, and in her briefer compass, Malone proposes that this situation derived from "the gospel vision of equality running up against a patriarchal structure [in both Jewish and Hellenistic tradition] which was all-pervasive." The result of this process Malone regards as being the situation that: "There is a place for women—at the bottom of a God-ordered hierarchy" (107–09). She goes on to demonstrate the consequences of this situation, in terms of the association of sin with the body, and the projection of the causes for sin (especially in the area of sexuality) on to women. The result of patriarchy was the establishment of a hierarchical model of Church government, which in itself has led to a lack of flexibil-ity (cf. Isherwood and McEwan 86) and an agreement as to the impossibil-ity of changing perceived ideas—an attitude fatal to much scientific inquiry in the past. It is not difficult to identify the male-dominated Church as per-ceived by Christian feminists with Pullman's Magisterium.

Female Spirituality

A large part of feminist theological writing has been devoted to the theme of women's spirituality. Because women's part in the development of the Christian Church has so often been ignored in history, feminist scholars such as Fiorenza (1983) and Moltmann-Wendel (1982) have looked par-ticularly closely at women in the Bible and in the unseen areas of Christian tradition. Much work too has been done on the role of women mystics in expressing the prophetic voice all too often silenced in the official Church (e.g., Frances Beer, 1992, and the many books that focus on outstanding fig-ures such as Julian of Norwich and Hildegard of Bingen). Thus, to be able to identify Lyra in the *His Dark Materials* chronicles as a female character who could be described as embodying the essence of spirituality suggests an almost prophetic role for its author—using the word with its primary meaning of someone whose vision interprets the present (like William Blake) rather than someone who attempts to predict the future.

The word "spirituality" is much used, and also much misused. Older, traditional definitions tended to focus on explicitly religious activities, such as saying prayers, attending religious services, and receiving the sacraments, but contemporary thinkers have been broader in their definitions. David Hay and Rebecca Nye, in their investigation of the spirituality of children, found that the people whom they asked to define this quality emphasized elements such as "love, inspiration, wholeness, depth, mystery and personal devotions like prayer and meditation." They found a substantial degree of agreement with the perception that "Each of us has the potential to be much more deeply aware both of ourselves and of our intimate relationship with everything that is not ourselves. This holistic notion of spirituality is probably widely acceptable" (Hay and Nye 6–8). Ursula King, while admitting the difficulty of defining this quality, suggests that

> Spirituality . . . has to do with an age-old human quest to seek fulfill-
> ment, liberation and pointers towards transcendence amidst the welter
> of human experience. . . . [It] must not be understood as something
> apart from or as something added on to life. Rather it is something
> which permeates all human activities and experiences rather [than]
> being additional to them. Spirituality can be described as a process of
> transformation and growth, an organic and dynamic part of human
> development, of both individual and society. (5)

This sense of feeling connected to other living beings, and indeed to nature itself, sometimes involving a degree of awe and a recognition of some form of presence, is by no means exclusive to those who believe in God or organized religion; in fact, it is often expressed by people who feel alienated from religious bodies as such. It has much similarity with the way Lyra expresses her feelings of connectedness with nature in her promise to the dead, whom she releases from their confinement in a dark and lifeless world: "When you go out of here, all the particles that make you up will loosen and float apart, just like your daemons did. . . . But your daemons en't just *nothing* now; they've gone into the air and the wind and the trees and the earth and all the living things. They'll never vanish. They're just part of everything. And that's exactly what'll happen to you . . . you'll be out in the open, part of everything alive again" (*AS* 335). Pullman's use of imagery here, as in Lyra's impassioned outburst to Will near the end of the book (quoted earlier), emphasizes a degree of attachment to the natural order that is an essential part of the view of spirituality put forward by many religious writers, explicitly feminist and otherwise. What Lyra says here about the nature of the afterlife may or may not reflect Pullman's own ideas, but it has many analogies in the beliefs of non-Christian religions, notably Buddhism.

Lyra's development throughout the saga relates to her growth into her role as the new Eve,[9] who will negate the evil effects of the rule of the Magisterium and is most strongly linked with her search for truth. This is most evident in her instinctual understanding of how to interpret the alethiometer, which, as its derivation from the Greek word for "truth" implies, is always accurate in its fidelity to the nature of things and to the future. Lyra's loss of her innate understanding of the meanings of the alethiometer when she becomes an adolescent recalls the claim of Hay and Nye that the natural spirituality of childhood is all too often destroyed by the sophistication demanded by the adult world (21–24). Lyra still, however, craves to be able to read the alethiometer and is prepared to "learn consciously what [she] could once do by intuition" (*AS* 545). As Xaphania has already explained to her, in the past "you read it by grace . . . and you can regain it by work . . . but your reading will be even better then, after a lifetime of thought and effort, because it will come from conscious understanding. Grace attained like that is deeper and fuller than grace that comes freely, and furthermore, once you've gained it, it will never leave you" (520). Pullman's endorsement of what might be described as mature spirituality is powerful.

Lyra's attachment to the deeper levels of truth may seem paradoxical in one who is never reluctant to tell a lie when necessary (the similarity of her name to the word "liar" has frequently been observed by readers), but it could be claimed that her lies in fact arise out of a deeper understanding of truth than that possessed by her opponents. She tells the Oxford Scholars: "I know I haven't always told the truth, and I could only *survive* in some places by telling lies and making up stories . . . but my true story's too important for me to tell you if you're only going to believe half of it" (542). Being truthful seems to be portrayed by Pullman as one of the most important, perhaps indeed the supreme, human quality; his opposition to what he sees as the falsehood propounded by the churches provides the motivation for much of his writing. Fidelity to what is judged to be the truth has always been admitted, even by the Catholic Church, as a quality that supersedes adherence to a religious body against conscience (even though everyone has a duty to ensure that their conscience is well formed). The mystic and scholar Simone Weil, whose writings have been very positively received by the Christians, whose ranks she could never quite bring herself to join, would have approved Pullman's stance; she claimed: "Christ likes us to prefer truth to him because, before being Christ, he is truth" (36).

An important element in Lyra's search for truth, as in her personal development, is her continual dialogue with her daemon, Pantalaimon,[10] especially at the end of the trilogy when she is no longer able to talk to Will, and her daemon reminds her of his parting words about building "the Republic of Heaven" (*AS* 548, quoted above). Pullman's imaginative creation of the daemon, a kind of externalized personal spirit, is an aspect that adds greatly to the appeal of *His Dark Materials*, and the fact that the daemon is usually of opposite sex to that of its owner inevitably recalls Jung's concepts of the anima and the animus. Though Jung's sometimes unrealistic idealization of the feminine has meant that his theories are not accepted uncritically by feminists, the emphasis he gives to the spiritual has made him more congenial than Freud.[11] As King remarks: "The contemporary world is suffering an immense spiritual hunger. In Carl Jung's words people are 'in search of a soul,' in search of something that will give them wholeness, a sense of meaning and a purpose which can direct their thoughts and actions" (36).

Conclusion

Altogether, readers who are responsive to the themes of feminist theology and spirituality are likely to have felt that in many ways Pullman is a kindred spirit, if only he could be brought to realize that the debunking of religion he has undertaken should ideally be part of a positive process—not just to establish the somewhat debatable "Republic of Heaven" but also to revalue the more profound spiritual insights that already are latent within religious and spiritual sources. In this process the feminist theologians could be seen as allies. Although the language, admitting the presence in creation of a God very different from "the Authority" might be alien to him, surely Pullman might be prepared to endorse Mary Grey's hope for the future:

> In celebrating Wisdom's feast we can allow ourselves to be shaken at the very foundations . . . and speak truth from the heart. . . . The deepest insight of theology is always the simplest. God's is the initiative in grace. Faith in creation *is* faith in redemption. God is giving birth to the redeemed city, redeeming time and space and broken-heartedness. God is promising flourishing to all earth creatures: "your bodies shall flourish like grass." Is this enough to keep us hoping, keep us dreaming, outrageously, for a future for this earth, a cosmic integrity, a future that God offers to all the children of Sophia-Spirit? (95ff.)

Notes

I would like to express my thanks to two University of Surrey Roehampton students, Katie Posey and Helen Swinyard—whose MA dissertations, respectively on spirituality and children's literature and on Philip Pullman and religion, I recently supervised—for stimulating my interest in this topic.

1. I am not suggesting that Gillian Cross is herself a feminist theologian; I have no knowledge of the extent of her familiarity with the writers I refer to in this essay.
2. I refer to the feminist theologian by this name, not Philip Pullman's character, presumably coincidentally so named!
3. In choosing feminist theological texts for comparison, I have tended to select what may be described as the "classics" of the discipline, bearing in mind that readers may be unfamiliar with the writers cited.
4. Personal communication between author and Philip Pullman, March 3, 2000.
5. This creates an interesting link with a source much used by the Gnostics, who also figure among Pullman's intertextual references.
6. In a television interview on the *South Bank Show* (March 9, 2003), Pullman explained that Jesus was part of his schema for *His Dark Materials,* without actually being present in the book. In an earlier interview, reported by H. Spanner in *Third Way* (2002, 22–26), he described Jesus as a "moral genius" ignored by the churches.
7. Quoted from Shewing XIII of *Revelations of Divine Love,* in Frances Beer, *Women and Mystical Experience in the Middle Ages* (Woodbridge, Suffolk, UK: Boydell, 1992), 145.
8. To me, this recalls the failure of death to divide the romantic lovers of Emily Bronte's *Wuthering Heights,* or siblings Tom and Maggie Tulliver at the end of George Eliot's *The Mill on the Floss.*
9. The title "the new Eve" is traditionally applied to Mary, the Mother of Jesus, who by agreeing at the Annunciation to her role in bringing the redeemer into the world is even seen as a kind of co-redemptrix. Since Pullman admits to having been influenced by everything he has read, it would not be surprising if his choice of a female character to perform Lyra's role was affected by knowledge of the high regard in which Christians have held Mary.
10. Nicholas Tucker, in *Darkness Visible: Inside the World of Philip Pullman* (Cambridge: Wizard, 2003), says that the name Pantalaimon means "all merciful" (141).
11. Feminists find it difficult to forgive Freud for attributing "penis envy" to all females!

Works Cited

Beer, Frances. *Women and Mystical Experience in the Middle Ages.* Suffolk, UK: Boydell, 1992.

Billen, Andrew. "A Senile God? Who Would Adam and Eve It?" *The Times* (London) January 21, 2003: T2, 14–15.

Bird, Anne-Marie. "'Without Contraries Is No Progression': Dust as an All-inclusive, Multifunctional Metaphor in Philip Pullman's *His Dark Materials.*" *Children's Literature in Education* 32.2 (2001): 111–23.

Cross, Gillian. "Whose Dark Materials?" *Books for Keeps* May 2003: 10–11.

Fiorenza, Elisabeth S. *In Memory of Her.* London: SCM, 1983.

Gooderham, David. "Fantasizing It As It Is: Religious Language in Philip Pullman's Trilogy, *His Dark Materials.*" *Children's Literature* 31 (2003): 155–75.

Grey, Mary. *The Outrageous Pursuit of Hope: Prophetic Dreams for the 21st Century.* London: Darton, Longman & Todd, 2000.

Hampson, Daphne. *Theology and Feminism.* Oxford: Blackwell, 1990.

Hay, David, and Rebecca Nye. *The Spirit of the Child.* London: HarperCollins, 1998.

Isherwood, Lisa, and Dorothea McEwan. *Introducing Feminist Theology.* Sheffield: Sheffield Academic Press, 1993.

King, Ursula. *Women and Spirituality: Voices of Protest and Promise.* Basingstoke: Macmillan, 1989.

Loades, Ann. *Feminist Theology: A Reader.* London: SPCK; Louisville, KY: Westminster/John Knox, 1990.

McFague, Sallie. *Models of God: Theology for an Ecological, Nuclear Age.* London: SCM, 1987.

Malone, Mary T. *Women Christian: New Vision.* Dubuque, IA: Wm. C. Brown, 1985.

Moltmann-Wendel, Elisabeth. *The Women around Jesus.* Trans. J. Bowden. London: SCM, 1982.

———. *A Land Flowing with Milk and Honey.* Trans. J. Bowden. London: SCM, 1986.

Primavesi, Anne. *From Apocalypse to Genesis: Ecology, Feminism, and Christianity.* Tunbridge Wells: Burns and Oates, 1991.

Pullman, Philip. *Northern Lights.* London: Scholastic, 1995.

———. *The Subtle Knife.* London: Scholastic, 1997.

———. *The Amber Spyglass.* London: Scholastic, 2000.

Ranke-Heinemann, Uta. *Eunuchs for the Kingdom of Heaven: Women, Sexuality, and the Catholic Church.* Trans. P. Heinegg. Harmondsworth: Penguin, 1991.

Ruether, Rosemary R. *Sexism and God-Talk.* 1983. London: SCM, 1992.

———. *Gaia and God: An Ecofeminist Theology of Earth Healing.* London: SCM, 1992.

———. *Women and Redemption: A Theological History.* London: SCM, 1998.

Schneiders, Sandra M. *Beyond Patching; Faith and Feminism in the Catholic Church.* Mahwah, NJ: Paulist, 1991.

Spanner, Huw. "Heat and Dust." *Third Way* April 2002: 22–26.

Stuart, Elizabeth. *Spitting at Dragons: Towards a Feminist Theology of Sainthood.* London: Mowbray, 1996.

Weil, Simone. *Waiting on God.* Trans. E. Crawford. 1951. London: Collins, 1959.

Wren, Brian. *What Language Shall I Borrow: God-Talk in Worship: A Male Response to Feminist Theology.* London: SCM, 1989.

14

"Eve, Again! Mother Eve!":
Pullman's Eve Variations

MARY HARRIS RUSSELL

What seemed attractively preeminent to many readers of Pullman's *His Dark Materials* trilogy, especially in the first two volumes, was that Lyra Belacqua was a vibrant young girl-becoming-woman who apparently avoided the fate of far too many women in high fantasy, of being drafted into subaltern service to the patriarchy.[1] *The Amber Spyglass*, however, in both its foregrounding of the Edenic myth and its treatment of the Authority, suggests that an exploration of religious interpretive traditions might be in order. It is Lyra's religious pedigree that most distinguishes her from other heroines of high fantasy and helps us see the necessary role her character plays in the trilogy's plotted rising against the Kingdom of Heaven. Pullman's narrative is, after all, about a revolution, a change of power on the same ground. If we see Lyra as Eve—the most contested "ground," if you will, in the Edenic myth—then we can better understand why two major, diversely received plot events occur as they do in *The Amber Spyglass:* the sexual knowing that takes place between Will and Lyra and the disintegration of the Authority. When the new Eve is ready for the new creation, built on truth, the old Authority, built on a lie, must vanish. Their portraits are inextricably linked.

In exploring the religious backgrounds, this essay will not claim particular source relationships. Pullman has acknowledged a familiarity with the broad outlines of Gnostic thought (Cooper 355), and critics analyzing his work take it as a given (Bird 112; Lenz 161; Wood 257). Certainly both Blake and the German Romantics whom Pullman knows so well were familiar with these traditions. This is, however, a study not of sources but of sympathies. Pullman fits comfortably into the position of a Gnostic outsider, interrogating authority, and he has chosen to retell a myth where this outsider point of view will make for the most dramatic reversals.[2] Throughout the writing and publication of the trilogy, in interviews (Parsons and Nicholson 129), talks, and journalistic and electronic material, Pullman has trumpeted his intention to retell the story of Adam and Eve, "probably the best known biblical complex of boundary and transgression" (Stephens and McCallum 36). Any retelling of the myth of the Fall will have larger ideological consequences certainly, and these will affix themselves particularly to the central female figure. Stephens and McCallum make this clear in *Retelling Stories:* "[T]he myth of the Fall has had two primary ideological functions. First, it constructs an authority paradigm, that is a paradigm for a hierarchical relation between individuals and God. . . . Second, the Fall sets up a gender paradigm" (37). Pullman's trilogy, in its reshaping of both Eve and Authority, plots a direct link between endings on one level and beginnings on another.

After a look at some alternative Eves that precede what we consider the mainstream Eve of Christianity, we will consider Pullman's most interesting Eve variations—Marisa Coulter, Mary Malone, and Lyra herself.

Anyone's Eve, of course, is an interpretive event, since Genesis 1:3 is a text so filled with contradictions—the two different creation narratives, the mysterious interdiction, and the ambiguities of who is responsible for what. Especially in the early decades of Christianity, at a period of time when neither the Hebrew nor the Christian canons were fixed, there was considerable literary activity, in authoring and preserving a wide variety of texts about the events of the Creation and Fall (Charlesworth II xxi–xxiv). Neither Christian writers nor the authors of rabbinic Judaism of roughly the same time offer conformity to any one version of the Edenic events. "The situation of early Christianity was simply much more fluid—indeed, confused—than has been acknowledged" (Philips 160). What eventually became non-canonical, non-Scriptural writings for both the Christian and Hebrew communities flourished in this period. *Jubilees* (Charlesworth II) and *The Life of Adam and Eve* (Charlesworth II) are examples, as well as the various Enochic texts (Charlesworth I). The Enochic texts, for example, which date from several centuries B.C.E., stand outside the Hebrew canon but have maintained a presence, carried forward into early Christian interpretations, with their tales of the Watchers, the *bene elim,* and of fallen angels as a source of evil. The term "Gnostics" usually refers to a dissident group of early Christian believers. Just as the Enochic writers set themselves apart from the temple priesthood, so the dissident writers we now characterize as Gnostic—from the first through the third century C.E. and known to us now largely through the texts designated as the Nag Hammadi Library (Robinson)—insisted on a private, different knowledge that explains the way the world is, spoken in resistance to orthodoxy and any acceptance of universal beliefs. Not all Gnostic texts agree, but they can frequently be seen seeking a different explanation for the events in Eden. As Elaine Pagels explains in *Adam, Eve, and the Serpent:* "Some of these followers of Jesus, often called gnostics, read the story of Adam and Eve in ways that dismayed and outraged orthodox Christians. For gnostic Christians declare that the story, taken literally, made no sense; thus they themselves set out to read it symbolically, often allegorically. The most radical gnostics turned the story upside down and told it, in effect, from the serpent's point of view" (xxiv). Within these variations, the Lord of Creation is often viewed as tyrannical, and the serpent and/or Eve's rebellion against him is seen as reasonable (Evans 60). In traditions from both Christian and Jewish non-Scriptural writings, we can assemble a definition of this alternative Eve—she is mother of us all, sometimes linked to knowledgeable serpents, but above all an insistent seeker of knowledge. As John Phillips explains, there are various explanations for the connections made here. "The Mother Goddess of ancient Near Eastern religions, by whatever name she was called, was honored and worshipped with the title, 'the Mother of all the Living'" (3). The connection of Eve with the serpent "may have begun with "the relationship whether in derivation or in sound between *hawwah* (mother of all Living) and Aramaic and Arabic words for snake" (Phillips 41). A resisting and wise serpent often is affiliated with Sophia (a female divine principle), or Wisdom, who is seen as creating a helper for Adam. In one version, Sophia sends Zoë (literally life), her daughter, who is also called Eve, as an instructor or adviser for Adam. When Adam rises up from a sleep, he sees her and tells her, "You will be called the mother of the living" (Pagels, *Gnostic Gospels* 30). Another linking of Eve's name, *hawwah*, may be to the "Aramaic *hawa,* 'to instruct'" (Phillips 165), which makes Eve a seeker of knowledge, because that is what advisers need. While Eve's knowledge seeking is eventually conflated with Hesiod's negative vision of Pandora in the works of Origen and Tertullian and bolstered by the pseudo-Pauline epistles, these early Christian and Hebrew traditions valued an Eve who, "mother of us all" in some way, sought knowledge like the serpent. For a period of time from roughly the second century B.C.E., in the early Enochic texts through the third and even fourth century C.E., interpretations of Eve's identity abounded, and it is not until the fourth century at least that they become more regularized and Eve's quest for knowledge becomes only and always what is summed up in Ruth Bottigheimer's quotation from an early Genevan Bible: "Desire to know hath wrought our woe" (199).

For all of Pullman's Eves, knowledge is an approved goal. Marisa Coulter and Mary Malone, associated with knowing and capable of a resisting outsider stance, each provide Lyra, albeit in different ways, a surrounding context for her journey to self-knowledge.[3] Marisa embodies qualities of both Eve and Lilith, the apocryphal first woman created for Adam, and hence the first alternative Eve. Lilith chose to leave Adam's domination. Like Marisa, like Eve, Lilith is "the prototypical *femme fatale*" (Phillips 51), over the top in "unfettered female sexuality, assertiveness and independence" (39). Marisa Coulter occasions adulation (one might even say particularly from her creator, Pullman) even at her nastiest. Imperfect as she is, she has a role to play in bringing Lyra to her most important moment, and hence she glitters before us, only ever so slowly changing into the sacrificing mother she finally becomes. Like Lilith, Marisa Coulter is sexual, assertive, and independent, not one to sit quietly in anyone's garden.

Before meeting Marisa Coulter, Lyra has never seen knowledge and beauty combined. She is mesmerized: "That was it; nothing and no one else existed now for Lyra. She gazed at Mrs. Coulter with awe, and listened rapt and silent to her tales of igloo building, of seal hunting, of negotiating with the Lapland witches" (*Amber Spyglass* [*AS*] 68). Like an infant in the primal dyad, Lyra has bonded with this seeker of knowledge. Within Mrs. Coulter's flower-wallpapered London apartment, a sort of *House and Garden* Eden, Coulter's reptilian identity becomes clearer, because she has the knowledge Gnostic serpents have. She "knew everyone who was important in London" and appears to Lyra to know everything—which animal livers are edible, which bad, how to eat asparagus, plus geography, mathematics, and "lipstick, powder and scent" (83). Initially, however, the knowledgeable Coulter does not seem to even qualify as "mother of one," let alone "of us all": "[S]he thought it best to hide you away and give out that you'd died," explains John Faa, in telling Lyra the story of her mother, "a clever woman. A Scholar even" (122). It's finally her latent motherhood, however, which, quite slowly, over two volumes, redirects Marisa Coulter from pursuing a completely independent path toward power and ego satisfaction and turning instead toward supporting Lyra. One of its earlier manifestations is seen when she first sees Lyra in the intercisor machine at Bolvangar: "Lyra saw her totter and clutch at a bench; her face, so beautiful and composed, grew in a moment haggard and horror struck" (278). We have already been told that she seems to almost enjoy previous demonstrations of the intercisor; the only difference here is that her own motherhood is evoked when she sees her child.

Appearing in *The Subtle Knife* less frequently, Marisa Coulter still resembles both Lilith and Eve. She seeks knowledge and wields it politically. She remains smart, very smart. And yet her moral nature is still deeply flawed, as is clear in the scene where she directs the torture and herself breaks a witch's finger. She overwhelms Will, who sees her for the first time, because her voice is "intoxicating" (198), and she is "lovely in the moonlight" (204). Always strategic, she controls Specters in a way Carlo cannot understand, and, though she eventually poisons Carlo, she is careful to do so only after gaining knowledge she seeks from him, as she is careful to obtain Lena Feldt's knowledge of Lyra's true name before consigning Feldt to the Specters.

When Feldt cries, "Eve! Mother of all! Eve, again! Mother Eve!" (314), however, another turning point occurs in Marisa Coulter's development, as she feels an allegiance to a motivation outside herself: "And she breathed a great sigh, as if the purpose of her life was clear to her at last. . . . 'As before, so again. And Lyra is Eve. And this time she will not fall. I'll see to that'" (314). Pullman signals the significance of this episode by reminding us—through Will's eyes—that Coulter does not take the alethiometer. She is thus renouncing the quest for knowledge and, slowly, the quest for maternal identity emerges as the center of her actions.

At first, in *The Amber Spyglass,* readers distrust Marisa Coulter. She is identified with knowledge—knowing a bit of the language of mountain tribes—and she is still vicious, slapping Lyra when she refuses to drink the drugged potion. When Will confronts her, she is formidable in both her assured, calm sexuality and in her knowledgeable cunning. Yet, at the moment when Will and Lyra do leave the cave, and Coulter is still suffering from the poison inflicted by the Gallivespian, her face is described as "a mask of tragic passion," and she cries out to Lyra, "you're tearing my heart" (160). She grieves for the defeat, yes, but she also grieves for the loss of Lyra. In her subsequent appearances, she is apparently speaking the truth about her conversion to motherhood: "I have been the worst mother in the world . . . [until] I remembered that I was a mother and Lyra was . . . *my* child. . . . Oh, I felt such a love, such a tenderness" (204, 206).

Readers share the trepidations of Lord Asriel's council about Coulter's truth or loyalty, and we see that even Asriel distrusts her and sets her up to get away with only an early version of the intention craft. But it is not long before she and Asriel decide together that they will give their lives to save Lyra.[4] Significantly, when Coulter is seducing Metatron, so as to lead him to his demise, it is her motherhood she lies about, because she knows she must lie about the most important part of her life in order to be believed. As Asriel and Marisa Coulter pull Metatron downward into the abyss, Asriel's last words are for her—"*Marisa! Marisa!*" (409). Pullman's last specific reference to Mrs. Coulter is, however, not expressed in dialogue addressed to her personal, sexual self, but in a phrase descriptive of her mothering function that now dominates all she does: she is only and essentially "Lyra's mother" (409).

Lyra's first model is the proto-Eve/Lilith/Marisa. Her second model is Mary Malone, whose very name evokes the tradition of Christ's mother, Mary, as the second Eve, even though the Consistorial Court wants to label her a tempter. Pullman jumps between times and distorts orthodoxy's sequencing. The Lyra, the new Eve, is able to learn from both the first Eve and the second Eve. If Marisa *becomes* the mother of us all, Mary Malone is more clearly the serpent mother, the initiator into knowledge—rational knowledge and sensual knowledge. Malone's academic college world is familiar to Lyra, but Malone's task with Lyra (in a sort of reverse Annunciation) is to teach her the unfamiliar truth, that there are many different ways of naming the objects of knowledge—both inside and outside the college walls—and that the different names are less important than the realities behind the names. Precise synonymy among Dust, the Shadows in the computer, Rusakov Particles, or *sraf* is no longer important. With Malone's help, Lyra (and readers) learn that it doesn't matter whether the way of knowing is the alethiometer or the I Ching, or the amber spyglass.

Mary Malone thrives in her journey to a world where everything is new and must be learned. When she first starts living in the land of the *mulefa,* for example, "In the next few days, she learned so much that she felt like a child again, bewildered by school" (123). Mary is the first character who with her own knowledge, and patience, actually fabricates the title object—the amber spyglass—and gains enough understanding of what is happening with the *sraf* that she can then understand what worries the *mulefa* and what needs doing. She also functions (as discussed elsewhere in this volume) as sexual educator for Lyra and Will, the only adult who describes to them the world of sense pleasures. Only in that world can Lyra approach her adulthood, and only as an adult can she make her free choice.

If Lyra were not to be Eve, then Mary's achievement as either Sophia or the second Eve would have been all that was needed to save the world from losing its consciousness. But Lyra is the only one who's going to be able to make the most important decision. It's not going to be a choice of motherhood (as in Marisa's case), and it's not going to be a choice of an epistemology or technology (as in Mary's case). Marisa Coulter is instrumental; Mary Malone is instrumental. Both eventually vanish, leaving Lyra the only Eve on the garden bench. That this was her destination has been clear from her first appearance as an impulsive and curious child. While foreshadowed by aspects of both Marisa and Mary, Lyra alone is Eve as knowledge seeker, maker of important decisions. From the beginning, Lyra is in pursuit of knowledge: "Everyone knows they get up to something secret. They have a ritual or something. And I just wanted to know what it was" (4). The interdictions she is not afraid to challenge here are against children and against females, but she's not afraid of crossing boundaries even when she's not sure of an interdiction: "She had the feeling that being on the roof was forbidden, though no one had actually said so" (38). Initially, the knowledge Lyra desires is largely experiential—going on the roof, going into the crypts, "what did wine taste like?" (47), stealing the gyptians' boat to have a victory. As the novel progresses, however, the child once thought "not spiritually promising" (51) develops a hunger for more abstract, conceptual knowledge: "She would have listened eagerly now to anyone who could tell her about Dust. She was to hear a great deal more about it in the months to come, and eventually she would know more about Dust than anyone in the world" (39).

The move into Mrs. Coulter's London provides her with more new knowledge, again at first of the experiential variety (new clothes, new scents, a garden, so to speak, of flowered wallpaper). The satisfactions of this are very brief. Put off by the attempts of Mrs. Coulter and her daemon to take the truth meter from her, she becomes rebellious: "Because Lyra was feeling rebellious and uneasy, she didn't answer this patronizing question with the truth, or with one of her usual flights of fancy. Instead she said, 'I'm learning about Rusakov Particles, and about the Oblation Board'" (93). Now she begins to learn about the political consequences of knowledge, for now she becomes dangerous and is pursued when she flees. She discriminates various kinds of knowing, recognizing that the alethiometer "knew things like an intelligent being" (147). She explains to Coram how she listens to the voices, in a way that describes it almost like a classroom or tutorial situation: "It's almost like talking to someone, only you can't quite hear them, and you feel kind of stupid because they're cleverer than you, only they don't get cross or anything. . . . And they know such a lot, Farder Coram! As if they knew everything, almost!" (150). When ignorance is mentioned in conjunction with Lyra, it is only about not knowing her destiny, and not about being ignorant of cognitive material. And, now, she begins to be aggressive, and logically contending. When Mrs. Coulter, at Bolvangar, tries to argue that "Dust is something bad, something wrong, something evil and wicked," Lyra dissents, replying, "If he's [Asriel] got Dust and you've got Dust and the Master of Jordan and every other grownup's got Dust, it must be all right" (283).

Moving into *The Subtle Knife*, we are increasingly told that others view Lyra as knowledgeable. About Lyra's work with the alethiometer, Fra Pavel says to Mrs. Coulter, "She is like no human Scholar I can imagine" (35). Lyra is now able to reveal to Mary Malone her desire for knowledge: "'And I got to find out about Dust,' Lyra explained. 'Because the Church people in my world, right, they're frightened of Dust because they think it's original sin'" (85). Even in the face of very different methodologies, such as computer or the narratives of paleontology, Lyra is beginning to accumulate knowledge just as Stanislaus Grumman had, broadly acquisitive yet evaluative. By the end of *The Subtle Knife*, she knows how much there is to know and how to function in relationship to it, by maintaining a state of negative capability. In *The Amber Spyglass* she will show that she can learn as she goes, in her journey to the underworld.

Lyra must learn to ask questions, to accept new information, even as it reshapes her knowledge of her own self, as she experiences separation from her daemon, for instance, and begins to experience her sensual nature.[5] Finally, when she is ready to participate in the events that will lead to the reversal of Dust's departure from the universe, it is knowledge that signals Lyra's readiness: "and she smiled at him, a smile of such sweet knowledge and joy that his senses felt confused" (439). Her quest for knowledge has taken her across many borders, most interdicted by someone in authority: into the Retiring Room, across the sky bridge to a new universe, and, in the last stage of knowledge gathering, to a recognition of her own developing sexuality. As Mary Malone speaks of her own awakening to passion, "Lyra felt something strange happen to her body. She felt as if she had been handed the key to a great house she hadn't known was there, a house that was somehow inside her, and as she turned the key, she felt other doors opening deep in the darkness and lights coming on" (444). The "knowing" that occurs between Lyra and Will in *The Amber Spyglass* crowns Lyra's Eve-like knowledge quest. The exact time of that knowing is arguable. Many readers find the moment here: "and she lifted the fruit gently to his mouth. She could see from his eyes that he knew at once what she meant, and that he was too joyful to speak" (465). When they return home from this moment, the flow of Dust does reverse and "these children-no-longer-children, saturated with love, were the cause of it all" (470). Note, however, that their daemons have still not "settled," and until they do, the young people cannot make an adult decision about their future. On the next day, Will and Lyra went out by themselves again, looking "as if some happy accident had robbed them of their wits" (481). The happy accident, the moment of *felix culpa*, is approaching, but still remains in the "as if" zone.

Their daemons then appear to them, still shifting, and convey the difficult choice that lies ahead; the two young people move through stages of anger and pain and grief. And then, only then, the daemons settle. Described in the language of knowing, their union becomes complete: "Knowing exactly what he was doing and exactly what it would mean, he moved his hand from Lyra's wrist and stroked the red-gold fur of her daemon. Lyra gasped . . . and as her fingers tightened in the fur, she knew that Will was feeling exactly what she was" (498). Lyra the curious child has become Lyra the knowing woman.[6]

Marisa/Lilith/the mother of all; Mary Malone, the second Eve and Wisdom figure; Lyra the knowledge-seeking woman: how does this sequence of Eve figures relate to what Pullman wants to do with the Authority in this story? To summarize, within the trilogy there are diverse explanations for the Authority. The Church version identifies him with the Creator. Baruch and Balthamos convey other pictures, of a "first angel" who "told those who came after him that he had created them, but it was a lie" (31). Now said to be "contemplating deeper mysteries" (60) but actually under the control of his Regent, Metatron, the Authority is one who appears to pursue knowledge and be the source of it, yet is revealed as a deliberate liar or a consciously maintained sham, whose name has been evoked to establish the most arbitrary of boundaries. Lyra, the new Eve, is breaking through his boundaries. Freeing the dead, she breaks out of an enclosed territory instead of being expelled from one, as was the traditional Eve.

She does not, however, break out for purposes of deicide. It is important to note that this new Eve's arrival *signals* the end of the Authority's reign but does not actually cause it. The Authority is shown as falling victim to his own age and his own predilection for deceit. When first seen, by Marisa Coulter, "she had the impression of terrifying decrepitude, of a face sunken in wrinkles, of trembling hands, and of a mumbling mouth and rheumy eyes" (396). His demeanor and physical movements are those one sees at the deathbed of a very elderly individual. Will and Lyra come upon him only because they "stumbled right into the middle of the troop." Stumbled—not planned. After the cliff-ghasts are repelled at the cost of Tialys's life, Lyra's reaction to the Authority is empathy, couched in terms of mothering: "Oh, Will, he's still alive! But—the poor thing" (410). The Authority is now only "the aged being" who "could only weep and mumble in fear and pain and misery . . . uttering a wordless groaning whimper that went on and on, and grinding his teeth, and compulsively plucking at himself with his free hand" (410). He isn't destroyed; he vanishes: "Then he was gone: a mystery dissolving in mystery" (411).

This is not murder but a transition, between deceit seen as "aged" and true knowledge embodied as "youth." Only the newest Eve, nurturing mother of us all, seeker of knowledge and truth, can provide the youth that displaces age. The Authority is a being whose end of time has come. In contrast to Lyra, who seeks knowledge, and eventually gets it and moves from telling lies to telling the truth, the Authority persisted in a lie and never moved to truth, sought deception because he wanted power, and now, finally, loses it. Our new common life, in Pullman's *His Dark Materials* trilogy, begins in a garden and must, therefore, begin with Lyra, mother of us all, the new Eve.

Notes

1. Peter Hunt, in his introduction to *Alternative Worlds in Fantasy Fiction*, notes the problem: "There is, however, one area of formulaic writing that is increasingly difficult to justify: the treatment of gender" (3). He notes Pullman's work among fantasists who have tried to move the genre into new gender areas.

2. Pullman's description of his place in such a tradition emphasizes its dissenting position. "I'm in a line with the English dissenters" (Cooper 355). In that interview he distinguishes himself from the Platonic dualism at the base of Gnosticism: "My myth is almost the reverse." Pullman cannot resist reversing, it seems, even when he's reversing revisers.

3. While Ma Costa plays an important nurturing role for Lyra (and did so also in her infancy), Pullman casts her more as an earth mother and less as a seeker of knowledge. Her character and actions are homage to ancient protective guardians of the young, but she is not seen as striving, aggressive, and ambitious in any way.

4. Perhaps because Pullman has spent so much time with Marisa Coulter/ Eve/Lilith, her conversion to totally support Lyra's cause comes as less of a surprise than Asriel's does. Asriel has been playing chiefly the role of commander in chief, and as such we have not been privy to his emotional life. Hence, for many readers it is too quick a change from the Asriel who arranges Roger's death to the Asriel who is proud and protective of his daughter.

5. This is similar to Mary Jo Kietzman's characterization of Milton's Eve: "Eve turns her experience into stories and offers them as subjects for conversation and interpretation while remaining open to making his [Adam's] point of view a part of her self—a self continually under construction" (57).

6. Millicent Lenz notes that Xaphania, who conveys knowledge to Lyra and Will and is sorrowful with them over their parting, "may owe something to the Gnostic belief in the 'divine Mother,' or 'Wisdom' (Greek Sophia)" (148). I have not included Xaphania in the catalog of Eves, because her angelic nature makes her less clearly a formative influence for Lyra than are Marisa Coulter and Mary Malone.

Works Cited

Bottigheimer, Ruth. *The Bible for Children: From the Age of Gutenberg to the Present.* New Haven: Yale UP, 1996.

Charlesworth, James H. *The Old Testament Pseudepigrapha,* I (New York: Doubleday, 1983) and II (New York: Anchor/Doubleday, 1985).

Cooper, Ilene. Interview. *Booklist* October 1, 2000: 354–55.

Evans, J. M. *Paradise Lost and the Genesis Tradition.* Oxford: Clarendon, 1968.

Hunt, Peter. Introduction to *Alternative Worlds in Fantasy Fiction.* By Peter Hunt and Millicent Lenz. London: Continuum, 2001. 1–41.

Kietzman, Mary Ann. "The Fall Into Conversation with Eve: Discursive Difference in *Paradise Lost.*" *Criticism: A Quarterly for Literature and the Arts* 39 (1997): 55–88.

Lenz, Millicent. "Philip Pullman." *Alternative Worlds in Fantasy Fiction.* By Peter Hunt and Millicent Lenz. London: Continuum, 2001. 122–69.

Pagels, Elaine. *Adam, Eve, and the Serpent.* New York: Vintage/Random House, 1989.

———. *The Gnostic Gospels.* New York: Vintage/Random House, 1989.

Parsons, W., and C. Nicholson. "Talking to Philip Pullman: An Interview." *Lion and the Unicorn* January 1999: 116–34.

Phillips, John A. *Eve: The History of an Idea.* New York: Harper and Row, 1984.

Pullman, Philip. *The Amber Spyglass.* New York: Knopf, 2000.

———. *The Golden Compass.* New York: Knopf, 1996.

———. *The Subtle Knife.* New York: Knopf, 1997.

Robinson, James M., gen. ed. *The Nag Hammadi Library in English.* 3rd ed. revised. San Francisco: HarperCollins, 1988.

Stephens, John, and Robyn McCallum. *Retelling Stories, Framing Culture: Traditional Story and Metanarratives in Children's Literature.* New York: Garland, 1998.

PHILIP PULLMAN: A BIOGRAPHICAL NOTE

Philip (Nicholas) Pullman was born in Norwich, Norfolk, England, on October 19, 1946. He was brought up in Rhodesia (now Zimbabwe), Australia, London, and Wales. His father was an airman. As a child, his imagination was shaped by stories told to him by his grandfather (an Anglican clergyman), as well as through omnivorous reading and listening to radio serials (e.g., "Superman"). Philip was educated at Oxford University, earning his BA in 1968 and, in 1973, a degree in English. He married Judith Speller (a hypnotherapist) on August 15, 1970, and they have two children, James and Thomas. Before becoming a full-time writer, from 1972 to 1988 he worked as a teacher for the Oxfordshire Education Authority in Oxford, England. During this time, he honed his dramatic talents, writing a number of plays for his students and narrating for them his favorite stories, including the Greek myths and Homer's *Odyssey*. He continued to do part-time lecturing at Westminster College, Oxford, as a senior lecturer in English, where his responsibilities included a course in storytelling for young teachers.

An active public speaker and lecturer, he describes himself as "left" in his politics, in a long tradition of dissenters. His avocational interests include music and drawing; a skilled artist, he created the illustrations for his trilogy, *His Dark Materials* (*Northern Lights*/*The Golden Compass*, *The Subtle Knife*, and *The Amber Spyglass*). He is the author of many highly acclaimed, award-winning books for young readers, from contemporary fiction to Victorian thrillers. In May 2003 *His Dark Materials* was voted one of the nation's twenty-one best-loved novels by the British public as part of the BBC's "The Big Read." Pullman was named a Commander of the Order of the British Empire in December 2003. In March 2005 he was the winner of the prestigious Astrid Lindgren Memorial Award for children's literature. *His Dark Materials* was presented at the National Theatre in an adaptation by Nicholas Wright. (New Line Cinema plans a film version, with Tom Stoppard to write the screenplay.) His exceptionally inventive novels, plays, and picture books appeal to readers of all ages.

WORKS BY PHILIP PULLMAN

Books for Young Readers

Ancient Civilizations. Illustrated by Gary Long. Exeter: Wheaton, 1978.

Using the Oxford English Dictionary: A Book of Exercises and Games. Illustrated by Ivan Ripley. Oxford: Oxford UP, 1979.

Count Karlstein, or the Ride of the Demon Huntsman. London: Chatto and Windus, 1982.

How to Be Cool. London: Heinemann, 1987.

Spring-Heeled Jack: A Story of Bravery and Evil. Illustrated by David Moslyn. London: Doubleday, 1989; New York: Knopf, 2002. Graphic novel version. Illustrated by Patrice Aggs, London: Doubleday, 1991. New edition, with a new introduction, London: Doubleday, 2002.

The New Cut Gang: Thunderbolt's Waxwork. Illustrated by Mark Thomas. London: Viking, 1994.

The Wonderful World of Aladdin and the Enchanted Lamp. Illustrated by David Wyatt. London: Scholastic, 1995.

Clockwork; or All Wound Up. Illustrated by Peter Bailey. London: Doubleday, 1996; New York: Scholastic, 1998. Illustrated by Leonid Gore.

Detective Stories (Editor and Introduction). Illustrated by Nick Hardcastle. London: Kingfisher, 1998.

The Gas-Fitters' Ball. Illustrated by Mark Thomas. London: Penguin Puffin, 1995, 1998.

Mossycoat. Illustrated by Peter Bailey. London: Scholastic, 1998.

I Was a Rat; or, The Scarlet Slippers. London: Doubleday, 1999. New York: Yearling, 2002.

Puss in Boots. Illustrated by Ian Beck. London: Doubleday, 2000; New York: Knopf, 2001.

The Firework Maker's Daughter. Illustrated by Nick Harris. London: Doubleday, 1995; New York: Scholastic, 2001.

Lyra's Oxford. Oxford: David Fickling, 2003; New York: Knopf, 2003.

Books for Young Adults:

The Broken Bridge. London: Macmillan, 1990; New York: Knopf, 1992.

The White Mercedes. New York: Random House, 1988. Published as *The Butterfly Tattoo,* London: Pan Macmillan, 1992; New York: Knopf, 1993.

Sally Lockhart Series for Young Adults

The Ruby in the Smoke. Oxford: Oxford UP, 1985; New York: Knopf, 1987. Selected for Best Books for Young Adults listing, *School Library Journal,* 1987.

The Shadow in the Plate. Oxford: Oxford UP, 1987. Published as *Shadow in the North,* New York: Knopf, 1988. Best Books for Young Adults listing, American Library Association, 1988. Edgar Allan Poe Award nomination, Mystery Writers of America. Children's Book Award for Older Readers from International Reading Association, 1988.

The Tiger in the Well. London: Penguin, 1991; London: Scholastic, 1999; New York: Knopf, 1990.

The Tin Princess. London: Puffin, 1994; New York: Knopf, 1994.

His Dark Materials Fantasy Trilogy for Young Adults

Northern Lights. London: Scholastic, 1995. Published in the United States as *The Golden Compass,* New York: Knopf, 1996. Audio Cassette Unabridged, Listening Library, 1999. Carnegie Medal, Guardian Children's Fiction Award, and the Publishing News British Children's Book of the Year Award, all 1996. *Booklist's* Top of the List in youth fiction, 1996.

The Subtle Knife. London: Scholastic; New York: Knopf, 1997. Audio Cassette Unabridged, Listening Library, 2000.

The Amber Spyglass. London: Scholastic; New York: Knopf, 2000. May Hill Arbuthnot Honor Lecture Award, 2001, for *His Dark Materials* trilogy. Whitbread Awards in both children's and adult categories, 2002. Audio Cassette Unabridged, Listening Library, 2001.

Books for Adults

The Haunted Storm. London: NEL, 1972.

Galatea. London: Gollancz, 1978; New York: Dutton, 1979.

Plays

Sherlock Holmes and the Adventure of the Sumatran Devil, produced at Polka Children's Theatre, Wimbledon, England, 1984, published as *Sherlock Holmes and the Limehouse Horror.* Cheltenham, Gloucester: Nelson Thornes, 1992.

The Three Musketeers (adaptation of the novel by Alexandre Dumas), produced at Polka Children's Theatre, Wimbledon, 1985.

Frankenstein (adaptation of the novel by Mary Shelley), produced at Polka Children's Theatre, Wimbledon, 1987. Oxford: Oxford UP, 1990.

Media Adaptations

How to Be Cool. Adapted and broadcast by Granada TV as a television show, 1988.

His Dark Materials. Based on the novels of Philip Pullman, adapted by Nicholas Wright. London, National Theatre, 2004.

FURTHER READING

Brantley, Ben. "The National's Dark Machinery." *New York Times* January 25, 2004, sec. 2: 1, 33.

"Bridge to the Stars" http://www.bridgetothestars.net/index.php?p=InterviewsMai.

Butler, Robert. *The Art of Darkness: Staging the Philip Pullman Trilogy.* London: Oberon/National Theatre, 2003. http://www.nationaltheatre.org.uk/bookshop.

Gamble, Nikki, Pat Pinsent, and Kimberley Reynolds. "*His Dark Materials* Workpack." Ed. Kimberley Reynolds and Emma Thirlwell. Design by Alexis Bailey and Patrick Eley. London: National Theatre Education, 2004. Available under "Learning" and "Workpacks" at http://www.nationalthreatre.org.uk/.

Gribbin, John, and Mary Gribbin. *The Science of* His Dark Materials. London: Hodder, 2003.

Von Kleist, Heinrich. "On the Marionette Theatre." Trans. Idris Parry. In Nicholas Tucker, *Darkness Visible: Inside the World of Philip Pullman.* Cambridge: Wizard, 2003. 197–207. The Idris Parry translation may also be found in *Essays on Dolls,* London: Penguin/Syrens, 1994.

Lenz, Millicent. "Story as a Bridge to Transformation: The Way Beyond Death in Philip Pullman's *The Amber Spyglass.*" *Children's Literature in Education* 34.1 (2003): 47–55.

Lyall, Sarah. "Staging the Next Fantasy Blockbuster." *New York Times* January 25, 2004, sec. 2: 1, 5.

Mosier, Alicia. "Philip Pullman's Secular Faith." United Press International story, December 4, 2002. http://www.upi.com/print.cfm?StoryID=20021125-035640-9181r.

Nikolajeva, Maria. "Children's Adult, Human . . . ?" In *Transcending Boundaries: Writing for a Dual Audience of Children and Adults.* New York: Garland, 1999. 63–80.

Pullman, Philip. "An Introduction to . . . Philip Pullman." In *Talking Books: Children's Authors Talk About the Craft, Creativity and Process of Writing.* London: Routledge, 1999. 178–95.

———. "Invisible Pictures." *Signal* 60 (September 1989): 160–86.

———. "Myths, Folktales, and Fiction." *Signal Journal* (NCTE) Fall/Winter 1998: 15–18.

———. "Picture Stories and Graphic Novels." In *Children's Book Publishing since 1945.* Ed. Kimberley Reynolds and Nicholas Tucker. Aldershot: Scholar, 1998. 110–32.

Random House Teacher's Guides for *The Golden Compass, The Subtle Knife,* and *The Amber Spyglass.* http://www.randomhouse.com/highschool/guides.

Squires, Claire. *Philip Pullman's 'His Dark Materials' Trilogy: A Reader's Guide.* London: Continuum, 2003.

Townsend, John Rowe. "Paradise Reshaped." *Horn Book* July/August 2002: 415–21.

Tucker, Nicholas. *Darkness Visible: Inside the World of Philip Pullman.* Cambridge: Wizard, 2003.

Wagner, Erica. "Divinely Inspired." *Times* [London] October 18, 2000.

Walsh, Clare. "From 'Capping' to Intercision: Metaphors/Metonyms of Mind Control in the Young Adult Fiction of John Christopher and Philip Pullman." *Language and Literature* 12.3 (2003): 233–51.

Warner, Marina. "Epilogue." In *Fantastic Metamorphoses, Other Worlds: Ways of Telling the Self.* Oxford: Oxford UP, 2002. 207–12.

Welch, Frances. "Jesus Was Like the Buddha and Galileo." Interview with Pullman. *Sunday Telegraph* (November 19, 2000): 4.

"Why the Plot Will Always Matter: Carnegie and Greenaway Medals." *Library Association Record* 98 (August 1996): 414–15. (Quotes from Pullman's Carnegie Medal Acceptance Speech.)

Wood, Naomi. "Paradise Lost and Found: Obedience, Disobedience, and Storytelling in C. S. Lewis and Philip Pullman." *Children's Literature in Education* 32.4 (2001): 237–59.

Articles in Reference Books

Authors and Artists for Young Adults. Vol. 15. Detroit: Gale, 1995.

Beacham's Guide to Literature for Young Adults. Vol. 8. Osprey, FL: Beacham, 1994. 3917–23, 3985–92.

Children's Literature Review. Vol. 20. Detroit: Gale, 1990.

Contemporary Authors. Vol. 50. Ed. Pamela S. Dear. Detroit: Gale, 1996. 365–67.

Something about the Author Autobiography Series. Ed. Anne Commire. Vol. 65. Detroit: Gale, 1994. 170–71.

Speaking for Ourselves, Too: More Autobiographical Sketches by Notable Authors of Books for Young Adults. Ed. Donald Gallo. Urbana, IL: National Council of Teachers of English, 1993. 162–63.

St. James Guide to Young Adult Writers. 2nd ed. Detroit: St. James, 1999.

Twentieth-Century Young Adult Writers. Ed. Laura Standley Berger. Detroit: St. James, 1994. 543–44.

Writers for Young Adults, Supplement I. Ed. Ted Hipple. New York: Charles Scribner's Sons, 2000.

CONTRIBUTORS

Millicent Lenz was professor emerita and adjunct research associate at the University at Albany, State University of New York. She held advanced degrees in library science (MA) and in English (MA and PhD). In her career of over thirty-five years of college and university teaching, she taught a wide variety of courses in American, English, and world literature, finally specializing in literature for children and young adults. Her publications include *Nuclear Literature for Youth: The Quest for a Life-Affirming Ethic* (1990) and, with Peter Hunt, *Alternative Worlds in Fantasy Fiction* (2001). She has contributed essays to *ChLA Quarterly, Children's Literature in Education,* and *The Lion and the Unicorn.* Her professional associations included the Children's Literature Association, the American Library Association, the Modern Language Association, and the International Research Society for Children's Literature. Dr. Lenz passed away on June 10, 2004.

Anne-Marie Bird is a part-time lecturer and research student at Bolton Institute in northwest England. Her research interests include postmodern theory, particularly in relation to contemporary fiction written for adolescents, with specific emphasis on texts by Melvin Burgess, Aidan Chambers, and Philip Pullman. Her recent publications include articles on Roald Dahl's *The Witches* and on Philip Pullman's *His Dark Materials* trilogy.

Burton Hatlen is professor of English at the University of Maine, where he also serves as director of the National Poetry Foundation. From 1982 to 2001 he edited *Sagetrieb: A Journal Devoted to Scholarship on Poetry After Modernism*. He has published a book of his own poetry, *I Wanted To Tell You*, and he has published many articles on Shakespeare, Renaissance poetry, modernist and postmodernist poetry, literary theory, and modern fantasy (especially the writings of Stephen King, a former student of his) in such journals as *College English, English Literary Renaissance, Contemporary Literature, Twentieth-Century Literature, American Poetry Review*, and *Paideuma*.

Maude Hines is assistant professor of English at Portland State University, where she teaches and conducts research in African American literature, children's literature, and cultural studies. Her essays have appeared in *The Lion and the Unicorn* and *Body Politics and the Fictional Double*.

Lisa Hopkins is professor of English at Sheffield Hallam University. Her most recent publications include *Writing Renaissance Queens: Texts by and about Elizabeth I and Mary, Queen of Scots* (University of Delaware Press, 2002) and *The Female Hero in English Renaissance Tragedy* (Palgrave, 2002). Her book *Giants of the Past: Literature and Evolution* is forthcoming from Bucknell University Press.

Shelley King is associate professor of English at Queen's University in Kingston, Ontario. Her research focuses on nineteenth-century British literature, especially Romantic women writers and children's literature. She is coeditor with John B. Pierce of Amelia Opie's *Adeline Mowbray* (Oxford World's Classics, 1999) and *The Father and Daughter with Dangers of Coquetry* (Broadview Literary Texts, 2003), and they are currently working on *Correspondence of Richardson's Final Years*, volume 12 in *The Cambridge Edition of the Correspondence of Samuel Richardson*.

Andrew Leet recently completed a master's degree in English at the University of St. Thomas in St. Paul, Minnesota. This is his first published essay as an independent scholar. He enjoys exploring the relationships between religion and science fiction and also has an interest in nineteenth- and twentieth-century American Catholic history.

Margaret Mackey teaches at the School of Library and Information Studies at the University of Alberta. She is the North American editor of *Children's Literature in Education* and has published widely in the area of young people's reading and media use. Her 1999 *Signal* article, "Playing in the Phase Space: Contemporary Forms of Fictional Pleasure," discusses Philip Pullman's approach to writing. Her most recent book is *Literacies across Media: Playing the Text,* published by RoutledgeFalmer in 2002.

Susan Matthews is senior lecturer in English literature at the University of Surrey Roehampton. She has published work on Blake, women's writing, and gender in the Romantic period, including *"Jerusalem* and Nationalism," in *Beyond Romanticism: New Approaches to Texts and Contexts, 1780–1832,* edited by Stephen Copley and John Whale (Routledge, 1992). Her most recent work on Blake, "Blake, Hayley, and the History of Sexuality," is forthcoming in *Blake, Nation, and Empire,* edited by Stephen Copley and David Worrall (Palgrave Macmillan). She is working on a book-length study of the female body as image in the Romantic period, tentatively titled *Pregnancy, Print, Production.*

Pat Pinsent was for many years a principal lecturer in English at the University of Surrey Roehampton, where she is now senior research fellow. She specializes in children's literature and seventeenth-century English literature and has a particular interest in theology. Her publications include seven books plus numerous journal articles and essays. She edits two journals, *IB-BYLink* and *Network,* and is a frequent contributor to conferences, largely on children's literature. She retired in 1998 but continues to participate in the Distance Learning mode of the MA in children's literature at University of Surrey Roehampton.

Mary Harris Russell is professor of English at Indiana University Northwest and the weekly reviewer of children's books for the *Chicago Tribune.* She has published on medieval works of spiritual advice, the Surgeon General's 1981 National Mailing on AIDS, book reviewing, gender in children's fantasies, and Philip Pullman—most recently, "Ethical Plots, Ethical Endings in Philip Pullman's *His Dark Materials," Foundations* (Summer 2003). Her earlier publications bear the last name "Veeder."

Bernard Schweizer is assistant professor of English at Long Island University, Brooklyn. He has authored two monographs: *Radicals on the Road: The Politics of English Travel Writing in the 1930s* (UP of Virginia, 2001) and *Rebecca West: Heroism, Rebellion, and the Female Epic* (Greenwood, 2002). He has edited Rebecca West's previously unpublished work *Survivors in Mexico* (Yale UP, 2003) and is currently editing a collection on Rebecca West as well as an anthology of essays on the female epic.

Carole Scott is professor of English at San Diego State University and a board member of its new Center for the Study of Children's Literature. She is on the board of the Children's Literature Association and the Nordic Children's Literature Network and has served on that of the International Research Society for Children's Literature. She has coauthored *How Picture-books Work* (Garland, 2001) and has published articles and essays on children's literature in a wide range of books and journals.

Lauren Shohet is associate professor of English at Villanova University. The recipient of fellowships and awards from the NEH, the Folger Library, the Huntington Library, and the Shakespeare Associate of America, she has published articles on early modern poetry and drama in *Milton Studies, Shakespeare Survey,* and the *Journal of Early Modern Cultural Studies,* among other venues. She is completing a monograph about the emergence of public culture and seventeenth-century English masque and is working on a book-length study of *His Dark Materials.*

Karen Patricia Smith is a professor at the Queens College Graduate School of Library and Information Studies in Flushing, New York, where she teaches courses in children's and young adult literature. She is the author of *The Fabulous Realm: A Literary Historical Approach to British Fantasy, 1780–1990* (Scarecrow, 1993) and "Forgiveness in Katherine Paterson's *Jacob Have I Loved* and *Preacher's Boy*" in *Bridges for the Young: The Fiction of Katherine Paterson,* edited by M. Sarah Smedman and Joel D. Chaston (Children's Literature Association and Scarecrow Press, 2003). She is also the editor of and a contributor to *African American Voices in Young Adult Literature: Tradition, Transition, Transformation* (Scarecrow, 1994) and *Library Trends* issues "Multicultural Children's Literature in the United States" (Winter 1993) and "Imagination and Scholarship: The Contributions of Women to American Youth Services and Literature" (Spring 1996).

INDEX

Abrams, M. H., 7
acquired grace, 121–22
Adam, 5, 6
Aeschylus: *Agamemnon*, 10
affect linking, 21, 58, 61, 62–64, 66
afterlife, beliefs about in *His Dark Materials*, 204–5
alethiometer: always accurate to nature of things and future, 208; effect of and innocence and experience on reading, 22, 103, 131, 183–84; experience takes away ability to read by intuition, 22; as a figure for engaging Renaissance traditions, 23; interpretation involves holding multiple levels of meaning in tension, 111; need for receptive mode of consciousness to read, 7; operates like Spencerian allegory, 34n2; paralleled by Mary Malone's computer, 99; reading of as complex interpretive act, 26, 107, 108; relation to canonicity, 19; three wheels, 50; two ways of understanding mysteries of, 73
Alger, Horatio, 39
Alice in Wonderland, 138
allegory: four levels of, 23, 34n2, 35n5; in *The Golden Compass*, 112–18
alternative worlds, 5–6, 83, 139–43
Althusser, Louis, 37
amber spyglass: double lens of perception, 30–31; metaphor for layering of textured narratives, 19
The Amber Spyglass (Pullman): abuses of

sexuality, 129; acquired grace, 121–22; consequences of creating portals, 145; contrasts with Miltonic tradition of Fall, 19; decline of God into nothingness, 88, 200; emphasis on Will's desire to be undetermined, 27; epigraphs, 133; foregrounding of Edenic myth, 212–21; harpies, 147–48; idea that one must be in awakened state to be truly alive, 2–3; imprisonment of dead in underworld, 204; journey to Hades, 144–45; knowing between Lyra and Will, 219–20; *mulefa*, 146–47; negative reviews of, 161–62; occurrence of third defining action of characters, 53–54; parental intervention to keep child from knowledge, 126–27; path from innocence through experience to higher innocence, 103; task of constructing the Republic, 12; tripling pattern, 50–51; undermining of God's claim to have created the universe, 165; Whitbread Prize, 1, 162
androcentric fallacy, 199
angelology, 179
anti-theism, 167
apocalyptic allegory, 23
Arminianism, 180
Armstrong, Karen, 185
Asriel, Lord. *See* Lord Asriel (character)
atheism, 166–67
Atwood, Margaret, 174

Loades, Ann: *Feminist Theology: A Reader*, 199

"logocentric quest," 157

Lord Asriel (character): Byronic role, 87–88; challenges foundation of traditional Christianity, 193; complexity, 54; insurrection against heaven, 164; meaning suggested by name, 111; as new enlightened man, 188–89; self-serving intention, 8

Lord of the Flies (Golding), 128

The Lord of the Rings (Tolkien): dualism, 79; most characters inherently good or evil, 80; revival of, 160; theological underpinnings, 76–77; token woman warrior, 91n3

Luria, Isaac, 11, 13n4

Luther, Martin, 106, 122n1

Lyall, Sarah, 116

Lyotard, Jean-François, 192, 193, 195

Lyra Belacqua (character): awareness of body, 132; both intuitive child reader and theological scholar-exegete, 112, 121; as essence of spirituality, 206, 207–9; as lyric/narrative/art, 25–26; natural superiority, 40–41; as new Eve, 83, 96–97, 116, 202, 208, 212, 217–18; nominal associations, 111–12; reading of alethiometer, 26, 109; relation to authority, 40; renegotiation of terms of death, 27–28; sympathetic imagination, 7

Macbeth (Shakespeare), 147

MacDonald, George: belief in deferred fulfillment of textual understanding, 109–11; *Curdie and the Goblin*, 49; "The Fantastic Imagination," 110, 118, 122n3; *The Princess and Curdie*, 74, 138; *The Princess and the Goblin*, 74, 110, 138, 144; youth not a barrier to complex text, 73

Mackey, Margaret, 12, 14n7, 21

Makarios, Tony, 115

Makdisi, Saree, 130

Malone, Mary. *See* Mary Malone

Manichaeism, 77

Marvell, Andrew, 104n2

Marx, Karl, 188

Mary, Mother of Jesus, 210n9

Mary Malone (character): absence of God as spiritual void, 195; awareness of body, 132; as a caregiver, 147; computer, 100; Dark Matter Research Unit, 99; explication of St. Paul, 20; on good and evil, 98; methods of entry into fantastic lands, 141–43; as second Eve, 217–21; as "serpent mother," 159, 217; statement concerning Christianity, 184; on women's rereading of scriptures, 199

Matthews, Susan, 73

Maughan, Shannon, 161

Mauss, Marcel: *A General Theory of Magic*, 150

McFague, Sallie, 158, 201

McLeod, Ken: *Wake Up to Your Life*, 182

Melville, Herman, 86

metaphysical rebellion, and atheism, 166

Milton, John: argument of Christians and anti-Christians over, 71; Blake on, 86, 95–96; lean toward Arminianism, 180. *See also Paradise Lost* (Milton)

Minnis, A. J., 114

misotheism, 156, 167–68, 172n3

modernity: challenge to religion and traditional authority, 188; desire to segregate ordered and rational from chaotic, 191; radical shift of consciousness, 192

Moltmann-Wendel, Elisabeth, 158, 202, 206

moral allegory, 23

Mrs. Coulter: as both Eve and Lilith, 215–17; complexity, 11, 54, 79–80, 91; experimental medical

Mrs. Coulter (*continued*)
  facility, 180; and intercision,
  42–43; as Lilith, 159; meaning suggested by name, 111; reptilian identity, 215; socially constructed femininity that is alluring yet
  destructive, 131–32
mulefa: compared to Swift's Houyhnhnms, 146–47; discovery of
  consciousness of self, 96; history of
  awareness, 100; ideally adapted ecological synergies, 31; interdependence, 30, 102; narrative art, 31–32;
  origin myth, 31; visibility of universal consciousness to, 31–32; world
  of compared to California, 75, 128
Myers, Mitzi, 122n8
myth: gives rise to high fantasy, 137; role
  of for children, 136–37

Nag Hammadi Library, 213
narrative allegory, 23
negative capability, 6, 13n4, 109
Nicholas of Lyra: central position in
  history of textual exegesis, 108,
  112–13; debt owed by Luther to,
  106, 122n1; defense of ability of
  lay reader to interpret Scripture,
  116–17; "duplex sensus litteralis,"
  117–18; four levels of textual
  meaning, 114; *Literal Postill on the
  Whole Bible,* 113, 114, 122n5
Nietzsche, Friedrich, 88, 157, 168, 188
North, 21, 43, 58–66
Northern Lights (Pullman). *See The Golden
  Compass* (Pullman)
Norton, Mary: *The Magic Bed-Knob; or
  How to Become a Witch in Ten Easy
  Lessons,* 144
novum theory, 174–75, 186
Nye, Rebecca, 207, 208

original sin, 120, 164, 180
Orpheic journey, 144

Orwell, George, 193
Other, primary status in theodicy, 87

Pagels, Elaine: *Adam, Eve, and the Serpent,*
  213
Paine, Thomas, 168
Pandora, 214
Pantalaimon (character), 40, 121, 130,
  208, 210n10
Paradise Lost (Milton): Blake's rereading
  of, 71, 76; "dust," 100; elevation of
  mutual erotic love, 33; Eve, 90,
  221n5; "His dark materials," 180;
  human separation from divine as
  price of fall, 28–29; melding of
  classical and Judeo-Christian traditions, 101; nature of Fall, 28–29,
  89–90; notion that work distinguishes humans from animals,
  22–23; orthodox reading of,
  84–86; Pullman's debt to, 71,
  83–84, 86–91, 95; redress of
  human incompleteness, 32–33;
  Satan's role, 26–27, 35n10; sense of
  debased church, 97; theologically
  hierarchical power structures, 98
patriarchy, resulted in establishment of
  hierarchical model of Church governance, 206
Paul, Saint, 113
Pêcheux, Michel, 37
Phillips, John, 214
"phrase space," 14n7
Pinsent, Pat, 12, 158
Plato, 179
Plotz, Judith, 12
postmodernism, 157, 192
poststructuralism, 157
Primavesi, Anne, 158, 202–3
process theologians, 201
Prometheus, 5
Pullman, Philip: ability of children to
  elucidate his narrative, 111, 125; on
  absence of God, 10–11; admiration